Puritan Influences
in American Literature

Puritan Influences in American Literature

Edited by
Emory Elliott

ILLINOIS STUDIES IN
LANGUAGE AND LITERATURE

65

UNIVERSITY OF ILLINOIS PRESS
Urbana   Chicago   London

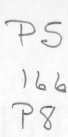

3/1980
Am. Lit.

©1979 by the Board of Trustees of the University of Illinois
Manufactured in the United States of America

Library of Congress Cataloging in Publication Data

Main entry under title:

Puritan influences in American literature.

   (Illinois studies in language and literature; 65)
     1. American literature—History and criticism— Addresses, essays, lectures.
2. Puritans—United States—Addresses, essays, lectures. 3. National characteristics,
American, in literature—Addresses, essays, lectures. I. Elliott, Emory, 1942- II. Series.
PS166.P8   810'.9'3   79-12270
ISBN 0-252-00733-6

Contents

FOR
EDWARD H. DAVIDSON

Preface

Those of us in early American studies have found that a strong sense of community among scholars in this field engenders cooperation and exchange which reinforce our individual labors. In this spirit the contributors to this volume are joined in our dedication to the greater understanding of American literature and culture. In addition, we are brought together because we have all had the good fortune to have been inspired in our commitment to scholarship by a remarkable teacher and scholar, Edward H. Davidson. Each of us whose essays are included here has reaped the rewards of Ed Davidson's instruction and guidance, most as doctoral candidates at the University of Illinois, one, William L. Howarth, as a student in his undergraduate classes at Illinois, and another, Nina Baym, as a Ph.D. candidate at Harvard University while Ed Davidson was teaching there.

Through his exciting ideas and by the excellence of his teaching and scholarship, Edward Davidson has had a powerful influence upon those of us who have been his students as well as upon the advancement of American literary studies. His authoritative study *Hawthorne's Last Phase* (New Haven: Yale University Press, 1949; rpt. Hamden, Conn.: Archon Books, 1967) and his definitive edition of Hawthorne's *Dr. Grimshawe's Secret* (Cambridge: Harvard University Press, 1954) are lasting contributions to Hawthorne scholarship, which will be in his debt again for his present work on the *Centenary Edition of the Works of Nathaniel Hawthorne*. His sensitive and insightful *Poe: A Critical Study* (Cambridge: Harvard University Press, 1957) stands as a major interpretation of Poe's poetry, and his valuable edition of Poe's *Selected Writings* (Boston: Houghton Mifflin, 1956) remains in wide usage. His interest in colonial American writing, long evident in his memorable undergraduate classes and graduate seminars, bore fruit in scholarship with *Jonathan Edwards: The Narrative of a Puritan Mind* (Boston: Houghton Mifflin, 1966), a provocative analysis of Edward's intellectual development which has added significantly to our understanding of this great artist-theologian and has moved others toward a reexamination of Edwards' thought.

Through his lively classroom teaching and his judicious and painstaking dissertation direction, Edward Davidson generates in his students a respect for the life of the mind in America and an appreciation of the interaction of human history and intellectual achievements. Although he strongly encourages his students to follow their individual ideas to their own conclusions, his critical principles, which stress the study of literature in the context of the history of ideas, have become the foundation of a literary criticism informed by historical knowledge that characterizes the methods of the essays presented here in his honor. In his rigorous dissertation supervision he insists upon clarity of thought and expression to such a degree that many of us have confessed to having learned finally how to write as we heeded his patient and detailed corrections and suggestions. The high standards he set will remain the ideal against which we shall always measure our efforts.

Because he is also a warm and accessible teacher who provides opportunities for a personal as well as a professional relationship to flourish, many of his former students continue to receive stimulation from his delightful correspondence. His open enthusiasm about the continuing work of his former students has led to many contacts among us as well, so that there is among his graduates a bond of mutuality which has fostered its own intellectual rewards and has made the preparation of this volume a rare pleasure.

I wish to thank the contributors for their diligence, patience, and enthusiastic encouragement. We all owe a special thanks to Allan Holaday and the editorial board of the Illinois Studies in Language and Literature and to Sacvan Bercovitch, E. N. Feltskog, Joseph T. Flibbert, Richard M. Ludwig, and Mason I. Lowance for their support. I am grateful also to Richard Wentworth of the University of Illinois Press for his continued guidance, to the Committee for Research in the Humanities at Princeton University for financial assistance for typing the manuscript, to Mrs. Helen Wright, who typed the final draft, to Francisco Rivero for research assistance, and to my wife, Georgia, whose various forms of aid are inadequately summarized as editorial assistance. My own contribution to this volume was made possible by a fellowship from the John Simon Guggenheim Foundation. Finally, I speak for all of us involved in this project in offering this book as a small token of the gratitude we feel to Edward H. Davidson.

Introduction

In 1928 Kenneth Murdock took a bold and controversial position in his essay entitled "The Puritan Tradition" when he asserted that scholars had not yet even begun to understand the complexities of the Puritan mind and the impact of Puritan thought and writing upon American literature and culture. The problem, he said, was that everyone from historians to journalists wrote authoritatively about the Puritans, but few had read the early literature: "Before the Puritan tradition can be intelligently written of, before the history of colonial literature or of American literature in general can be written as they deserve to be, Puritan books must be read." In the belief that fresh insights into the Puritan tradition would place the established literary landmarks in a new light, he predicted that "the patriotic writers of the Revolution, Emerson, Melville, Hawthorne, and Longfellow, Whitman and Emily Dickinson— even familiar names may take on new meanings," so that we "may evoke from the best thumbed of our books flashes of significance hitherto unseen." Murdock took up that challenge himself and was joined a decade later by his Harvard colleague Perry Miller in what became a remarkable reassessment of the Puritan mind.

Miller taught a generation of colonial historians to struggle tenaciously with the subtleties of seventeenth-century theology and to appreciate the rich cultural and intellectual life of the early settlements in New England. The very energy of his prose style and force of his ideas drew to his field some of the best young minds in American studies, so that by the time of Miller's death in 1963 Edmund S. Morgan could declare: "The historiography of early New England has reached in the past forty years a level of sophistication unmatched in the study of any other part of American history. . . . It could in fact be argued that we already know more about the Puritans than sane men should want to know." And yet the volume of scholarship in Puritan studies in the last fifteen years has exceeded that of the previous forty.

Especially for students of literature who came trained in the methods of explication and analysis developed by the New Criticism, the most intriguing questions which Miller's work raised, but did not answer, concern the nature of the Puritan aesthetic and the role of the imagination in Puritan literature. Miller destroyed the tired notion that the "plain style" was indeed plain, and in his famous introduction to his edition of Jonathan Edwards' *Images or Shadows of Divine Things,* he suggested that there was at work in Edwards' handling of what moderns call symbolism an entirely different mode of literary understanding, rooted in ancient biblical hermeneutics.

Thus, before one could speak intelligently of Puritan writing, it was evident that the Puritan books must be read again, this time with a mastery of the intricate relationships between biblical types and antitypes, between timeless sacred history and the unfolding present, between the signs of Divine Providence in nature and the mind of the perceiver. For the reader who could read the Puritan books as Edwards read them, there awaited the rich and rewarding experience of an imaginative and aesthetic vision which was Puritanism's most important legacy for American literature. Only when that high level of Puritan scholarship had been attained could critics of nineteenth-century American literature discover in the works of the great writers of the American Renaissance the complicated ways in which those masters had captured, exploited, and sometimes parodied what they received from the full imaginative wealth of the Puritan tradition. To properly assay the impact of colonial Puritanism upon the development of American literature is the task set before the present generation of students, and it is the purpose of this volume to make a contribution to that reassessment.

What the essays presented here and the work of others in this field are beginning to reveal is that when the entire system of thought and life which was New England Puritanism is fully comprehended, its pervasive presence in American literature and culture becomes apparent. Not merely a negative element in our intellectual tradition against which enlightened humanists have had to rebel, Puritanism contained the seeds of political and social ideals, structures of thought and language, and literary themes which inspired both the content and the forms of much American

writing from 1700 to the present. While not denying the importance of other influences, such as the classical tradition, Enlightenment thought, and German idealism, recent American criticism
had attempted to reestablish the balance between the contribution
of those forces to our intellectual and literary history and that of
the Puritan heritage.

In addition to the desire to understand the early culture better
for its own sake in order that we may have a fuller knowledge of
our past, this reevaluation has arisen out of the sense that without
knowing as much about the Puritan heritage as our great writers
have known and felt, we have been missing some of the richness
of our major literary texts. Certain elements of these works which
may seem obscure or puzzling are often illuminated when viewed
in the context of the Puritan backgrounds: the conversion experience of Isabel Archer to the religion of Gilbert Osmond in *The
Portrait of a Lady;* the comically twisted Calvinist theology of
many of Faulkner's characters, such as Anse Bundren in *As I Lay
Dying,* who offers thanksgiving to God for the terrible trials rained
upon him because they signify the Father's continuing attention;
and the haunting alternations between millennial optimism and
cosmic despair in Melville's works, self-parodied in the unfinished
pamphlet of Plotinus Plinlimmon in *Pierre,* where the Puritan
obsession with the relationship between sacred and temporal history is the foundation for the mysterious "horologicals and
chronometricals." The themes, imagery, and very structure of the
Puritan jeremiad persist in the works of writers as diverse as Mark
Twain, Henry Adams, and F. Scott Fitzgerald and as seemingly
anti-Puritan as Ernest Hemingway, Norman Mailer, and James
Baldwin.

The most exciting body of ideas to emerge from a deeper
understanding of the Puritans has resulted from a careful analysis
of how the New England colonists conceived of what we have
come to call the "American dream." As it was expounded by nineteenth-century political orators and later absorbed into the folk
knowledge of the twentieth century, the notion of America's
promise presents a contradiction: it seemed at once to guarantee
social equality for all and to offer every individual the opportunity
to achieve personal success surpassing his fellows. As it was elabor-
ated in Puritan writings, the American dream is part of a more

complex teleological framework that allowed for the later simplified political and economic interpretations but also supplied a
myriad of other interrelated meanings.

For the Puritans the establishment of the New England colony
was a sign that the world had entered into the last phase of history
and that the people of New England were fulfilling the biblical
prophecy by establishing the New Jerusalem. Their dream of
America was the establishment of a perfecting society which
would come to coincide with the invisible Church of God's chosen
on earth, and thus prepare the way for the Second Coming of
Christ. This conception of America caused the Puritan leaders
and ministers to interpret actual everyday occurrences as specifically connected to events in the Scriptures. Thus, every success
or failure in this divine corporate enterprise had profound meaning
beyond itself, and the strivings of each member of the elect
Church-Nation might have special cosmic significance.

As a result, the relationships between the individual saint and
the community, between the individual and the events of American
and biblical history, and between the individual and God constituted public as well as private issues. If the individual fell, the
community might follow him into apostasy and destruction; if
the corporate ship broke up in rough seas, each soul aboard would
perish. At times it seemed that the pressure of this divinely imposed
errand, which crushed the spirit of some individuals, might finally
crumble the emerging society, as changing fortunes would cause
the people to shift in mood from exuberant self-assurance to self-
castigating guilt. Ultimately, the community managed to survive
by transforming these tensions into a rhetoric of decay and
recommitment which released the guilt over failures and reasserted
the glorious future. Inherited by the pamphleteers of the American
Revolution and the historians of Jacksonian America, this intricate
social and verbal pattern, essentially biblical and theological in
origin, became the foundation for ways of thinking and feeling
in America which are still with us today. The particular elements
of the grand dream of America have thereby survived, not as a
unified whole as in the Puritan vision, but in fragments—in the
beliefs of political groups or of individuals. Such characters of our
later literature as Captain Ahab, Hank Morgan, or Jay Gatsby
reflect the persistence of certain ideas and impulses which are
rooted in American Puritanism.

The other key subject in Puritan studies which has begun to inform readings of later American literature is an appreciation of the allegorical or, more accurately, typological habit of mind of the Puritan writers. Critics had long looked upon the biblical allusions and references in Puritan writing as necessary religious encumbrances which distracted readers from what otherwise may have been a more natural human expression in a poem of Bradstreet or a prose passage of John Cotton. Scholars have now come to see that for the Puritans the biblical reference was the very jewel of their literature. A multifaceted verbal diamond which reflected various colors of meaning, the biblical reference stirred the imagination to discover its many complex associations.

For example, in calling Governor William Phips a "second Joshua" in his biography of Phips in the *Magnalia Christi Americana,* Cotton Mather evokes several associations: New England as the New Jerusalem, the enemies of Phips's people as the inhabitants of a New Babylon, the victory of Phips as a sign of the salvation of Christ since Joshua was a type of Christ, and the qualities of leadership and courage typified in Phips which would sustain God's chosen until Christ's impending return. The alert Puritan reader would also be quick to notice that the association of Phips and Joshua also reminds the reader of the dark ages of disobedience and disaster which followed the death of Joshua when the people fell into apostasy. Careful explications of Puritan texts have led to a new respect for the intricate workings of the Puritan imagination and fuller understanding of the continuity between Puritan typology and literary symbolism.

These two features—a better historical understanding of the Puritan vision which fostered so many persistent American themes and a more accurate evaluation of the Puritan literary aesthetic—suggest the advances in our methods of historical-literary analysis which have accompanied the renewed interest in the continuity between the Puritan and later American culture. For historians the Puritan society has often served as a test-tube culture for employing new methodologies. During the last decade the practitioners of quantitative investigation and psycho-history have produced fruitful studies of the Puritan communities. At the same time students of American literature have also been in the process of developing new critical methods to combine the techniques of formalist analysis perfected by the New Critics with sophisticated historical awareness, and, fittingly, they have begun their reexamination of American writing with the Puritans. The essays in this volume display not only a common interest in questions about the relationship of the Puritans to later American literature, but they also demonstrate the fusion of close reading and historical understanding which has characterized the reevaluation of our Puritan literary heritage.

In the opening essay of the collection, Glade Hunsaker examines the contrasting views of the calling of the writer held by the great English Puritan John Milton and the American writer-reformer Roger Williams. Their respective emphases upon certain aspects of Puritan theology led Milton and Williams to different conclusions about the role of the gifted writer in the community. Milton's resistance to the doctrine of predestination and his Arminianism provided grounds for his faith in the corrective power of the poet, while Williams' doctrinal interpretations prevented him from sharing Milton's high regard for the writer's calling. The general acceptance of Williams' attitude among American Puritans became one of the special burdens which those with literary talent in America have had to bear.

Two Puritan poets who understood that tension between the impulse to write and a belief that poetry may be little more than a private indulgence were Anne Bradstreet and Edward Taylor. In close examination of Bradstreet's important, but often slighted, longer poetry, Emily Stipes Watts shows the poet struggling toward a belief in the unity of man, God, and nature within the Puritan world view. While Bradstreet believed in the unity of God's design which Edward Taylor celebrated so exuberantly in his poetry, she recognized that unaided human reason might find only confusion and dualism in God's universe—the very dualism in the Puritan system which led to some of the contradictions which persist in American thought and literature. Watts finds in Bradstreet's long poems expressions of the kind of "profound uncertainty and intellectual insecurity" which the poet could resolve in her Puritan acceptance of divine sovereignty but which would torment later thinkers and writers.

In his analysis of Edward Taylor's controversial *God's Determinations,* William Scheick probes the nature of Taylor's literary aesthetic. Scheick shows that the fundamental biblical dichotomy between Christ and Satan provided the underlying structure of the poem, which Taylor embellished with the central image of the jaw-bone, where the Christian wrestles. As Scheick explains, for Taylor the notion that reality consists of a dichotomy between good and evil is a fallacy contrived by Satan, for the demon's very existence depends upon man's delusion that there can be a tempting alter-native to Christ. Taylor symbolizes the divine unity of all things as the vortex of the jawbone image toward which the saved Christian gravitates. The true saint knows that "temporal dichotomies dissolve into the unity of God." Taylor's poem could serve as the Puritan minister's answer to the doubts of Anne Bradstreet, and the difference between the intellectual positions of these two poets prefigures the contrast in the nineteenth century between Emerson's vision of transcendental unity and Melville's metaphys-ical doubt.

The shift of ideas in America from Puritanism to transcenden-talism has often appeared in textbooks and anthologies as a soar-ing leap of over one hundred years, during which time European Enlightenment philosophies emaciated Protestant theology and the influence of romanticism finally provided a foundation for the beginning of an American literature. From this standpoint the figure of Jonathan Edwards appears as the brilliant but beleaguered intellectual giant straining to accommodate Puritan theology to a society too intellectually advanced to need it. In his examination of Edwards, Michael Colacurcio provides a reevaluation of Edwards' idealism which places him at the center of the transition of ideas in American culture in the eighteenth century. Colacurcio's illum-inating explications of individual writings bring new clarity to our understanding of Edwards' most complex ideas and suggest that it is the persistence of his philosophical idealism in America that provided a key link between the Puritanism of seventeenth-century America and the thought and art of the American roman-tics.

While Colacurcio's focus is on the history of ideas, my own essay attempts to trace connections between Puritan and late eighteenth-century American thought and writing at the level of popular attitudes and political ideology. The orators and pamphle-teers of the Revolution employed the Puritan notions of public and private interest and exploited the established metaphors and biblical types of the Puritan sermon in their efforts to arouse the emotions of the people toward the cause of reform. Appealing to the religious emotionalism of the common people, the colonial leaders and their spokesmen created a powerful political rhetoric which generated evangelical fervor. Through their language they strengthened the popular movement to expel the malignant foreign influences in God's America and helped to justify the Revolution as a form of moral and spiritual purgation.

As the first five essays presented here examine various aspects of the Puritan mind and art which persisted into the period of the Revolution, the last four essays place the writing of five major nineteenth-century writers in the context of Puritan influences. In her essay on the problem of the artistic imagination and the moral man in Hawthorne's works, Claudia Johnson shows how Hawthorne interpreted the life of the individual and of the artist in terms which reflect the pattern of the Puritan conversion experience. In passing through the ritual of conversion, the Puritan saint moved from the unregeneracy of spiritual childhood through the dark night of the soul, when he became fully aware of his total corruption, to the light of new life, when he could reenter the world as a mature and confident member of the community. Johnson argues that Hawthorne frequently depicted the adjustment of the ordinary person to society as resulting from a similar social and psychological passage. In the early Hawthorne, though, the artist does not complete the rite of adjustment. Caught at that point in the process in which he is most deeply affected by his own and mankind's enormity, the artist observes his society from a perspective that is both tortured and childlike. Were he to mature, the artist would leave his art and join the society as an ordinary citizen, husband, and father. Johnson argues that Hawthorne's view of the role of the artist shifted from his early Puritanical position that the artist's imagination is somehow evil and must exist in a passive state apart from society toward the reconciliation of his artistic and moral impulses in his later writing, particularly *The Marble Faun*.

Just as the Puritans were careful observers of the details of nature as they searched for signs of Divine Providence, the transcendentalists read the book of nature as revealing divine truth. For the Puritan it was the minister with his profound learning and sober judgment who was privileged to interpret God's message, but for the nineteenth-century romantics it was the gifted poet whose insight and sensitivity qualified him as spiritual interpreter. William Howarth's analysis of Thoreau's use of the town of Concord as a microcosm in his *Journal* reveals Thoreau's nagging desire for universal unity which so troubled his Puritan ancestors. Just as the Puritans scrutinized the Scriptures to discover correspondences between the biblical Zion and New England in order to confirm the unity of the divine plan, Thoreau searched his Concord and the map of the world in order to bring together modern and ancient history, one place and all places into the single symbol of "Concord," an expression of sacred human unity. With the confidence of Edward Taylor's faithful Christian who moves steadily toward the vortex of the Divine Oneness, Thoreau insisted that seeming philosophical dichotomies and the proliferation of objects of human desire were the result of harmful illusions which blind man to the simple truths of life and nature. His *Journal* is a sermon on the enduring doctrines of self-sacrifice, austerity, and faith.

In his study of Melville's *Clarel,* Bernard Rosenthal demonstrates how Melville exploited the biblical typology so central to Puritan thought for his own ironic purposes as he presents a quest in which his pilgrim, Clarel, finds in place of the Promised Land only a dusty wilderness of broken dreams. Melville turns the figure of the Wandering Jew into a type of the universal man who must return eternally to the next Jerusalem, as America had once promised to be, where he repeatedly discovers only ruins in place of a society of sane values. Reversing the biblical promise and the Puritan promise of America, Melville has his descendent of the New England Puritans abandon the failed errand, deny the salvation of Christ, and depart with his Jewish wife and daughter to seek the truth in the Old Jerusalem, where the biblical covenant ends in self-mockery and death. Yet, according to Rosenthal, for Clarel, and for Melville too, there is no basis for genuine faith, but the very existence of the human race is grounds for the conviction that man's search for truth must continue.

In her essay on the poetry of Emily Dickinson, Nina Baym examines the poet's use of the childlike *persona* as a fitting mask for expressing the forbidden truth that the authority which rules the universe may have sinister intentions. Neither a reflection of her own personality nor an articulation of a psychological reaction to her human father, Dickinson's childlike speaker is an effective device for projecting a sense of metaphysical bafflement in the face of a seeming absence of divine, universal unity. Unlike Anne Bradstreet, who finally resolved her debts, Dickinson, like Melville, could not be satisfied with the answers provided by the Calvinism she inherited. Baym shows how Dickinson explored, and sometimes ironically twisted, the traditional Puritan imagery. In the Puritan sermon Christ was often represented as the Redeemer/Bridegroom who embraces and comforts the fainting soul and protects her from the wrath of the Father, but Dickinson protested that by creating such an image Christian writers had substituted an empty idea for genuine life-giving human love. Ultimately, though, Dickinson seems unable to escape the hold of her Puritan roots, for she resigns her childlike speaker to dependence upon the authority of the father and acceptance of the capriciousness of the male lover. Her *persona* thereby stands as a symbol of the place of women in a patriarchal American society and the insecure position of all humans in an inexplicable universe.

The essays presented in this volume certainly do not pretend to examine every facet of American Puritanism, nor do they attempt to show the presence of Puritan influences and ideas in the entire canon of American literature. To the list of nineteenth-century American writers represented here, many more names could be added, as well as those of writers of our own century. It is not the purpose of this collection to conclude the study of Puritanism and American literature but to contribute to the beginning of that labor. Though they employ widely diverse methods in their examinations, the contributors to this collection are dedicated to the advancement of the understanding of American literary history, and they recognize, as Kenneth Murdock did in 1928, that "if literary history is to be written as it should be, those who write it must look in literature for traces of the Puritan turn of mind which in other fields left so bold a mark."

EMORY ELLIOTT

Puritan Influences
in American Literature

ONE

Roger Williams and John Milton: The Calling of the Puritan Writer

O. GLADE HUNSAKER

The major prose contributions of both Roger Williams and John Milton were dedicated to the vital religious and political issues which sorely divided the English people during the struggle of 1640–60. During these latest years of the English Renaissance and Reformation, which supposedly saw a hastening of the transition of the medieval world to that of the modern, the critical questions concerning the nature and function of the one right religion and the one right government seemed as unanswered as they had been during the earliest years of the sixteenth century. Williams and Milton contributed their ideas to the dilemma because each of them perceived a critically important relationship between civil and religious liberty and the divine plan of regeneration; the tyrannical abuse of this relationship was to them a matter of urgent concern. But even their seemingly parallel positions toward freedom lacked the elements of concord essential to a satisfactory solution, for Williams approached each aspect of the controversy with his uniquely tempered ideas of Calvinistic election while Milton approached the same issues with his ideas of Arminian reparation.

Of the broad and unsolved questions of church and state, which were the major concern of Williams and Milton and which illuminated the major philosophical difference between them, there is one important issue which has special bearing upon the relationship between Puritanism and literature in the seventeenth century and upon those later American writers who were inheritors of the Puritan tradition. As men of literary talent who often employed their writing skills to the service of religious and political issues, Milton and Williams were especially concerned with the question of the role of the writer in their societies. They believed that those

properly called by God to be writers shared the gifts of the ancient
prophets themselves. They would serve as interpreters of the
divine message for the less insightful and the inarticulate. In
approaching the question of the proper function of the gifted
writer in a Christian world, both Williams and Milton moved logically through a series of crucial questions beginning with the
challenge of interpreting the divine messages offered to man by
the Book of Nature.

As they studied the Book of Nature in seeking the truths of
Divine Providence, both writers were led to the following questions: Was there a relationship between the adversities of nature
and the moral and spiritual development of man, or were such
hardships nothing more than a proper setting for man's depraved
condition? Were men to find within the pages of the Book of
Nature the signs of their predetermined election, or were they
rather to observe in its hierarchical structure a pattern for a curriculum of study essential to their regeneration? Was the "chain
of being" concept sufficient justification for the supremacy of
kings and archbishops, or was the spiritual aristocracy of the
regenerate saints the proper authority in matters of church and
state?

The second issue confronting both writers was the problem
of justifying individual interpretations of scripture against widely
divergent views imposed by others. Did the holy scripture really
offer a pattern which could effect a regeneration of man's nature
if devotedly followed? In this setting, was Christ really man's
exemplar, or was the scripture little more than a past record of
God's relationships with his chosen few? Was the holy scripture
a handbook for civil magistrates to follow in casting the wicked
out of Israel, or were all such scriptural citations nothing more
than Old Testament physical types of New Testament spiritual
antitypes which were to come?

The final question they had to consider was the role of the
"called" writer in relationship to God and his people. This moves
from the relative security of interpreting God's infallible word to
the insecurity of establishing relationships with a wider range of
conflicting views, all purporting to have been divinely urged. Was
the chosen writer a modern-day exemplar called to set forth the
plan of reparation, or was he called to make a plea for all to search

out the possibility of their unrecognized but already determined election? Was the inspired writer actually the recipient of a divine assignment to be the spokesman for the wise and the good who should assume the responsibility of civil affairs, or was he rather called to plead for the gentle handling of those precious souls whom God had already chosen?

Neither Williams nor Milton thought that man was doomed to wander aimlessly in a cruel world; rather, each believed that God had adequately provided for man's total education by furnishing him with the divine books of Nature and Scripture. Williams' and Milton's interpretive readings of these volumes emphasize their Calvinistic and Arminian views of man's nature and divine grace. Therefore, the particular roles Williams and Milton assigned to the Book of Nature and the Book of Scripture must be carefully defined if their views of the role of the "called" writer are to be understood.

The Book of Nature was more comprehensive than might at first be supposed; its study required more of its readers than an occasional interpretation of lightning bolts and earthquakes. This book contained the plenitude of God's creation, ranging from the glorious angels to the inanimate objects; and reading the book meant that man was to scrutinize its details for lessons in the management of temporal and spiritual affairs and for signs of divine approbation or condemnation. The hardships presented by nature were not to be grudgingly tolerated; they were to be read as part of a divine plan of education. To the men of the seventeenth century all of God's creation was an open book which bore witness of his existence. Regarding this, Calvin had said: "God hath not only sown in the minds of men seed of religion . . . but hath manifested himself in the formation of every part of the world, and daily presents himself to public view, in such a manner, that they cannot open their eyes without being constrained to behold him." [1]

In the second of his prolusions Milton commented on the dominant image associated with the Book of Nature, the chain of being. He believed that Homer had "significantly and appropriately" captured the universal harmony of the Book of Nature "by means of that famouse golden chain of Jove hanging down from heaven." [2] This idea of universal, divine order strongly appealed to the medieval and Renaissance minds, and it was generally conceded that God had arranged nature in a hierarchical pattern and had given each element in the ordering a specific assignment, the accomplishment of which he would supervise.[3]

The Calvinists refused, however, to accept the idea that there was a ruling aristocracy within each link of a chain. The lion might have been the ruler of beasts and the eagle may have been supreme among the birds; but for the Calvinists, who believed in the priesthood of all believers, the king was not the ruler over God's spiritual aristocracy. The Puritans rejected the religious and political hierarchies of the Anglicans and established an aristocracy of the elect who were to impose an arbitrary power over all unregenerate men in an effort to control wickedness and disorder. The Calvinists replaced this aspect of the chain of being with the "chain of command."[4] But even in this regard, such a Christian humanist as Milton can be seen in sympathy with the idea that the only aristocracy to be recognized is that of the regenerate "wise and good."

The important difference among those who were searching the Book of Nature for God's will appears only when the function of the Book of Nature is associated with the role of divine grace. For the Calvinists the Book of Nature was a valuable source of "means." The elect and the nonelect were to spend a lifetime scrupulously studying this access to God's will with the hope of learning what he had predetermined. The Christian humanists and the Arminians, however, were interested in studying nature for quite a different reason. For them nature presented the laboratory in which man perceived the vital knowledge of God's ways, the obedience to which would qualify him to receive regenerating grace; and the trials provided by nature would afford the polishing of man's dimmed virtue. Therefore, while there is little difference to be observed regarding the intensity with which Williams and Milton set about the reading of the Book of Nature, the reasons behind such reading were quite different.

Williams' university training and his writings addressed to the English Parliament and to the Presbyterian Assembly provide an interesting contrast with his frontier trading post activities and his intimate knowledge of the haunts and habits of the barbaric Indians which his peace-keeping responsibilities required of him.

This impressive breadth of experience brought him into direct contact with most of the pages of the Book of Nature, and he read them daily with care. His observations of the Indians and the New England wilderness as he recorded them in the *Key to the Language of America* are early evidence that Williams believed his examinations of the creation about him provided insights into the handiwork and will of God.

Williams believed that no part of nature was without a role to play in God's plan, and all parts together were to bear testimony of that plan to observant men. In his debate with the Quakers he argued against their total reliance upon an inner light by saying that truth was to be observed in the external world; he said: "Every wind and Cloud, and drop of Rain and Hail, every Flake of Snow, every Leaf, every Grass, every drop of water in the ocean, and Rivers, yea, every Grain of Corn, and Sand on the Shore, is a Voice or word and witness of God unto us." [5]

The confidence that Williams placed in the spark of goodness within each man, and which allowed him to give political matters even to unregenerate men, can be traced to his belief that the Book of Nature provides all men everywhere with the minimum guidance necessary for responsible moral behavior. Again and again in the *Key* he commented on the superiority of the habits of barbaric Indians to the behavior of the cultured Christians. Speaking of this universal availability of God's witness he said: "God hath not left himselfe without wit[ness] in all parts and coasts of the world; the raines and fruitfull seasons, the Earth, Trees, Plants . . . witnesseth against, and condemneth man for his unthankfulnesse and unfruitfulnesse toward his Maker." [6]

Williams found more in the Book of Nature than just a general witness of God's presence; he found specific instruction, as in an analogy he drew from the behavior of fish: "How many thousands of Millions of . . . sea-Inhabitants . . . preach to the sonnes of men on shore, to adore their glorious Maker by presenting themselves to Him as themselves . . . present their lives from the wild Ocean, to the very doores of men, their fellow creatures in *New England*." [7] A more dramatic example can be cited from his argument with the Quakers. During the first day of the debate, there was an eclipse of the sun, and Williams proclaimed that the judgment of the Lord had been made manifest. The sun had "preached aloud" a sermon to the effect that although wickedness and false teachings can "cloud" God's face from the world, man should be assured that soon God "will break forth again in his eternal brightness, splendor and glory." [8]

Williams' assurance that tribulations were intentionally given to man in an effort to discipline him had an important relationship with the Book of Nature. He believed that only by the careful observation and analysis of the hardships imposed by nature could man discern the divine messages intended for him; it was his conviction in this regard that prompted his writing of the *Experiments of Spiritual Life.* Away at his trading post and unable to go to his wife when he heard that she had been very ill, he composed and sent to her his conclusions as to why God had seen fit to afflict her at that time. He wrote: "It hath pleased the most *high* to cast downe thy *outward* man, and againe graciously to lift him up, and thereby teach us both, to examine and try the *health,* and *strength,* and *welfare* of the *inner.*" [9]

There was no place, however, in Williams' philosophy for the idea that a king or an archbishop should have power over other men because they were nearer the angels in a hierarchical gradation of men. Williams felt that hierarchies created by men should be ignored. Only God's elect could lead in religious affairs, and even they were to be restricted to the use of spiritual swords. In civil governments, no authority could be assumed by any mortal until it had been willingly given to him by his fellow men, and the retention of that power was dependent upon the responsible behavior of the civil officer and could be withdrawn whenever the people found such action necessary.

Any tendency of Williams toward Milton's Christian humanistic and Arminian interpretation of nature was clearly limited by the Calvinism that he expressed in *George Fox.* Arguing against the Quakers' idea of immediate light within, he defended the view that the knowledge of one's election is available only "from without" and that the Book of Nature had been provided for man as "means" for persuading his rational capacity that he had been chosen and for teaching him what God would have him do. His clearest statement on how the important perceptions from nature were to convince man is this one: "All *light,* or *Truth Natural, Civil,* or *Divine* it comes from without, and is received by the

Internal Faculty according to the *Capacity, Nature* and *measure* of it. All Truth or Falsehood, Light or darkness is first espied by the *watch* or *Sentinel, Fancy* or *Comprehension,* &c. From thence it is conveyed to the *Court* of *Guard,* where Captain Reason or his Lieutenant, common Sense and Experience taketh Examination, and Memory keeps a Record of proceedings which go on by degrees to Actions, &c."[10] Williams was searching the Book of Nature in an effort to determine what God had already decreed so that he might respond appropriately; this is quite different from Milton's conception of the same divine book.

For Milton, the Book of Nature played a more significant role in the regeneration of man than providing the "means" of a pre-determined election. The Book of Nature was a visible representation of God's Law of Nature which had been coassigned with his power of grace to effect the regeneration of man. The remnant of goodness within man's breast was a part of this "unwritten law"[11] of nature which was inherent in all of God's creation. And just as that remnant was active within man's breast to move him toward the reparation of his ruins, so the divine law was active within all the remainder of the Book of Nature accounting for its order and urging it to provide for man's responsibilities and trials which, in conjunction with divine grace, would effect his exaltation.

Homer's image of a golden chain pleased Milton because the idea of order was his dominant preoccupation. Again and again in the religious and political struggle he predicated the establishment of order in matters of church and state upon the necessity of order and harmony within the individual heart. It was the Book of Nature that could show to man the exemplary order which he was to follow. In one of his many exhortations to "observe the natures of all living creatures" for examples of this order, he encouraged man to continue his searching upward to the thunderbolts and then to the sun, of which he said: "Yea, follow as companion the wandering sun, and subject time itself to a reckoning and demand the order of its everlasting journey."[12]

The pattern of hierarchical order in nature represented for Milton the sequence of man's curriculum of study. The scale of nature was to be studied by man from the bottom to the top, progressing from the study of matter up to plants and from plants on up to living creatures.[13] Milton suggested, for example, that there was very little temporal knowledge that could not be learned from the careful observation of the animals. They give "illustrations of the healing art" and "prognostications of winds, storms, floods and pleasant weather." Milton also said that "household affairs owe many things to the ants"; matters of state take examples of order and industry from the bees, and the "art of war credits to the cranes the expedient of posting sentries and the triangular order of battle."[14] From the contemplation of creatures, the curriculum called for ascension to the spiritual considerations at the top of the chain: "Let not your mind suffer itself to be hemmed in and bounded by the same limits as the earth, but let it wander also outside the boundaries of the world. Finally, what is after all the most important matter, let it learn thoroughly to know itself and at the same time those holy minds and intelligences, with whom hereafter it will enter into everlasting companionship."[15]

Milton's Arminian concept that man's reparation is related to his successful resistance to temptation and his endurance of trial should be related here to his views on the Book of Nature. He fully accepted the Calvinistic principle that all of nature was in a fallen state because of man's depravity; the mortal creature deserved no better. Regarding this he wrote in *De Doctrina:* "All nature is likewise subject to mortality and a curse on account of man." However, he saw beyond nature's fallen condition to the divine purpose associated with the so-called curse: He cited Gen. 3:17, which says "cursed is the ground for thy sake."[16] Only when man ignores the light within him and refuses to try does the Law of Nature become a curse to him. Such adversities as thorns, thistles, blindness, and continuous decay were provided for man's "sake," a providential challenge to assist him in his reparation.

Like Williams, Milton fully rejected the idea that kings and archbishops had an inherent, God-given right to rule over people lower on a hierarchical scale. Unlike Williams, however, he never supported the idea of political democracy. He firmly maintained that the regenerate few constituted a spiritual aristocracy of wise and good men who were responsible for imposing order upon the depravity of willfully unresponsive and therefore unregenerate men.

Just as Williams' views of the Book of Nature tend toward Christian humanism and Arminianism when not seen in the con-

text of his Calvinistic doctrine of grace, so Milton's regard for the
Law of Nature leans toward Pelagianism unless properly associated
with his belief in the essentiality of divine grace. His curriculum
for studying the scale of nature and his beliefs on growth through
resistance and endurance were all dependent upon man's reception
and retention of God's divine, regenerating power. While the study
of the Book of Nature is a primary responsiblity of every man, it
must be accompanied with "experience at the level of grace."[17]

The second of the two divine books given for man's guidance
was the Book of Scripture. While its companion volume, the Book
of Nature, contained the unwritten law of God, this heaven-sent
guide gave to man God's written law just as he had caused it to be
recorded. Even though both books were designed to participate in
the regeneration of man, the Book of Scripture was regarded as
the "better assistance" to lead man to "the Creator of the world"
because its companion had been dimmed by the Fall of man and
because this second volume explicitly set forth God's will in such
critical matters as salvation, atonement, and resurrection.[18]

Williams and Milton were writing during a period when the
Book of Scripture was playing a more critical role in the religious
and civil affairs of Englishmen than it ever had before. Not only
had the achievements of printing made the Bible known to an un-
precedented number of people, but the authority given to individual
scriptural interpretation by the Reformation was urging the Puritans into a full-scale revolution. The anticipated concord and freedom that had been hoped for and expected as a result of widespread scriptural study had produced instead a state of chaos in
the affairs of both church and state.

The major difference between the Christian humanists' and the
Calvinists' interpretations of the Book of Scripture lay in the conclusions that they drew from the Israelite models of religious and
civil polity. The Calvinists made a literal application of these
models and thereby demanded a closer relationship between
church and state than the humanists could tolerate, despite their
own interest in the fusion of temporal and spiritual matters. The
most severe rejection of the Calvinists' use of the Old Testament
models, however, came from Williams; his typological interpretation
of the scripture caused him to separate completely the church
from the state.

The controversy between the literal and the typological interpretations of the Old Testament is a good example of the failure
of the Protestant theory that concord would ultimately result
from sincere individual study of the scripture. Certainly the dis-
putants could not have been more devoted and sincere in their
approach to their solutions; the problem lay in the fact that the
scripture seemed to justify two contradicting positions. The Calvinists believed that the pattern of civil and religious control which
had been given by God to the Children of Israel was an important
part of the covenant he had made with Abraham, and they found
no evidence that he had altered his instructions to his people in
any way since then.[19]

For the typologists, however, the dispensation of grace was to
allow only the spiritual antitypes of the physical types that had
existed during the dispensation of the Law. Old Testament types
were defined as "physical rehearsals of spiritual significances ultimately to be made intelligible in the New Testament."[20] For
example, the stories of Joseph's being cast into the pit and Jonah's
being swallowed by the whale were more than stories or physical
happenings; they were intended to serve as types for the spiritual
antitype of Christ who would descend into hell.[21] The typologists
believed that the physical coercion used by the kings of Israel in
punishing the offenders of God's chosen people was but the
shadowy type of the spiritual persuasion that Christ was to introduce during the dispensation of grace.

Williams' dispute with John Cotton on the relationship of the
church and the state, his extended debate with the Quakers concerning God's method for revealing truth, and his writings to his
wife on the proper approach to spiritual life and health illustrate
that he was an intense biblicist who took pains to document his
position on all subjects with a plethora of specific references. For
him the second of the two divine books served as the primary
source of "means" through which God revealed his mind. It contained all "the Saving Knowledge of God" that was necessary for
man to know, and it was to take precedence over customs, traditions, and supposed inner spirits—a constant message of his to the
Jews, Catholics, and Quakers.[22]

The noticeably heavy reliance upon scriptural citations, which
characterize almost all of Williams' works, cannot be attributed to

the particular responsibility of a man who had received training for the ministry. On the contrary, Williams gave no more attention to the Bible than he expected of every other Christian. He believed that individual passages from the Holy Book had to be scrutinized because God had intentionally hidden his messages behind "Skreens" and "Veils"[23] which could be removed only after relentless examination. Williams also felt that a knowledge of Hebrew and Greek was necessary so that the student could study the oldest scriptural manuscripts available; he labeled the Quaker's reasoning that such study was not necessary as *"proud Laziness"* prompted by the devil's inner light, upon which they were relying.[24]

At the heart of Williams' differences with his fellow Calvinists was his typological interpretation of the Book of Scripture.[25] These differences are important to the understanding of Williams because it was upon them that he based his defense of religious and civil liberty. To fail to understand his typology is to run the risk of seeing him further from the Calvinists and closer to Milton than he actually was. For while Williams seems to be a forerunner of civil democracy based upon individual equality, he was actually an orthodox Calvinist who had a radically different view of the relationship that God was temporarily permitting between his elect and the unfortunate nonelect during the dispensation of grace.

Approaching the Old Testament typologically, Williams believed that the kings of Israel were "all invested with a *typicall* and figurative respect,"[26] that no civil power was to have in the dispensation of grace. This meant to Williams that an Israelite king could exercise both temporal and spiritual control over the collected group of God's chosen people as a type of the antitype Christ, who would come to rule over the civil and religious affairs of the elect in a spiritual manner. The wrath of an Old Testament king against heresy and wickedness was more than a physical act; it was allowed by God as a type of the antitype spiritual sword that would be firmly but peacefully used against the violaters of God's elect during the dispensation of grace.

Williams believed that with the advent of Christ the "partition wall" that had separated the elect from those not chosen by God had been put down, and all the chosen flock had been scattered in the wilderness.[27] This did not indicate to Williams that God had abandoned his elect; on the contrary, he was to gather them again in his own due time from among the unregenerate. In the meantime He was providing them with ample "means" that they might learn of his will through diligent study. In no way did this typological interpretation cause Williams to alter his Calvinistic views of election and grace,[28] and it certainly did not make him more tolerant of doctrine that he considered heretical. Rather than advocating a peaceful democracy in matters of religion, he favored constant warfare; but he limited the weapons to spiritual swords.

What his typology did alter, however, was his views on religious and civil matters of polity. While the Old Testament kings had exercised coercion in protecting the gathered flock, no one in the dispensation of grace was permitted to exercise such authority. Williams called for the complete separation of church and state so that the scattered elect, wherever they might be, could freely search for the "means" telling of their election without the fear of being persecuted by civil authorities.[29] This preoccupation with the absolute religious and civil freedom of the scattered, unidentified elect caused Williams to reject New England Puritan ideas of Federalism as well as the Old Testament models of polity being used by the English Presbyterians.[30] When placed in this religious context, his interest in civil democracy was little more than the by-product of a system designed to defend God's elect.

Although Milton's identification with Christian humanism encouraged him to draw many of his ideas from the classics, he had no less respect for the Book of Scripture than did Williams. His *De Doctrina Christiana* is overwhelming evidence that he regarded the scriptures as more than a handy source of arguments for his tracts and ideas for his poetry. As he claimed in his Preface to that work, he urgently felt the need to "scrutinize and ascertain" his religious beliefs "by the most careful perusal and meditation of the Holy Scriptures."[31] For Milton the Book of Scripture was an indispensable aid to right reason[32] in guiding it beyond the pitfalls of custom and tradition to the truths essential to the reparation of man's fallen condition.

Rather than believing that man should make a meticulous examination of the scriptures in the hope of finding "means" which would assure him of an already determined election, Milton felt that each person was to assemble from the Book of Scripture the elements of the divine pattern of living which, if obediently followed, would entitle him to the reward of regenerating grace. Although this exemplary pattern had been made available to all, "no Man or Angel . . . [could] know how God would be worshipt and serv'd" unless he regularly and persistently sought His teachings from the sacred pages of divine revelation.[33]

Milton accepted fully the idea that every man was to search the scriptures for himself rather than relying upon the interpretations of others, clergymen in particular. With this in mind he included the study of foreign language in the academic curriculum so that more men would have the capacity to read the scriptures regularly from the originals.[34] Regardless of occupation no one was to be excused from scriptural study; of this he said: "Neither let the Countryman, the Tradesman, the Lawyer, the Physician, the Statesman, excuse himself by his much business from the studious reading thereof."[35] Even the most unlearned were left without excuse because their reason and the holy spirit would allow them to understand what was expected of them if they were "diligent" and "constant" in their reading.[36]

Milton's views on the dispensations of law and grace have certain elements in common with those of Williams. He too believed that Christ had redeemed man to "a state above prescriptions by dissolving the whole law into charity."[37] Like Williams, he refused to give an antinomian interpretation to Christ's gift of grace. In being freed from the prescriptions of Moses' Law, man had been made subject to a higher one; the "charity" of the dispensation of grace meant that the eternal morality of the earlier period was still present; but rather than being rigidly demanded by rules, moral obedience was now to be expressed willingly in the "love of God and our neighbor." [38]

Milton also expressed some typological views of the Old Testament that are very similar to Williams'. Referring to the fortieth chapter of Ezekiel, he said, "God . . . seeking to weane the hearts of the Jewes from their old law to expect a new . . . under Christ, sets out before their eyes the stately fabrick & constitution of his Church; . . . indeed the description is as sorted best to the apprehension of those times, typicall and shadowie, but in such manner as never yet came to passe, nor never must literally, unless we mean to annihilat the Gospel."[39] However, Milton's few typo-

logical references do not reject all the Old Testament models of
polity with the completeness that Williams' typology does. In fact,
Milton's view that the regenerate few should always occupy the
positions of civil leadership and his early enthusiasm for the English as a "Chosen Race" have overtones of Old Testament polity.[40]

Milton's belief that the Book of Scripture, correctly interpreted
by the guidance of the Spirit, constituted an authority superior to
that possessed by any existing religious or political group resulted
in views on the freedom of conscience and the separation of church
and state that were very near to those of Williams. However, there
remained important differences. Because he didn't share Williams'
belief that divine election was predestined, he could never tolerate
the absolute freedom of conscience that Williams advocated. Milton
required it for himself because any suppression of his scriptural
interpretation would have been persecution of truth, but he had
to insist upon the suppression of some ideas of the unregenerate
because he felt that unrestricted falsehood could jeopardize the
reparation process. In like manner his separation of church and
state[41] was never as absolute as was Williams'. While state interfer-
ence with his own reading of the Book of Scripture would have
been intolerable, his Christian humanistic fusion of the spiritual
and the temporal simply would not allow him to turn matters of
the state over to unregenerate men as Williams' typological interpretations permitted him to do.

Not only did mid-seventeenth-century Englishmen believe that
God had required ancient prophets to record his will in the Book
of Scripture, but many of them also accepted the fact that certain
men of their own day could be "called" to set forth in writing his
will on important religious and civil issues. Both the humanist and
Christian traditions had contributed to a general respect for the
gifted or inspired writer. The humanists had maintained that skill-
ful writing was capable of "civilizing mankind and sustaining the
social order" by making the "good appear not merely good, but
emotionally alluring and sensuously attractive."[42] The Christian
tradition had needed only to turn to the exemplary writings of the
Apostle Paul to observe the inspirational nature of written exhortations to righteousness.

The Calvinists and the Christian humanists shared a great deal of
confidence in the "called" writer; however, they had quite differ-

ent interpretations as to what the role of such a writer was in the divine plan of regeneration. As exponents of these traditions, Williams and Milton were required to formulate answers to the following questions: Was the chosen writer a modern-day exemplar called to explain the dependence of the plan of reparation upon man's obedience, or was he called to make a plea for man to search out the possibility of his unrecognized but already determined election? Was the inspired writer the spokesman for the wise and good who were responsible for maintaining a civil environment conducive to man's reparation, or was he called to plead for the physical protection of those precious souls whom God had already chosen?

The motivation underlying Williams' extensive writing was his conviction that he had been called to the service of God. Having searched unsuccessfully for a religious institution that embraced the divine truth as it had been revealed to him, he felt that he was a select instrument in God's hand whose writing enjoyed more than divine approbation: His writing had been commanded by God. In *The Bloody Tenent Yet More Bloody* he justified his second lengthy argumentation against the New England divines by saying, "It pleased *God* to lay a *Command* on my *Conscience* to come in as his poor Witnesse in this great Cause."[43]

While all of his writings mention God's approval of his undertakings, Williams can hardly be accused of simply using conventional references to divine help as a crutch to his arguments. The evidence that he sincerely sought for and humbly felt that he had received guidance on specific issues is quite convincing. A good example, from among many, can be seen in *George Fox* in which he declared the truth of his assertions by saying to the Quakers: "I believe the holy *Spirit of God* (in answer to my poor Petitions and Meditations) resolved and quickened my Spirit to the present *Undertake* and Service."[44] The characteristic tone throughout all of Williams' writings is one of unquestioning assurance that he had been "called."

Williams was thoroughly Calvinistic in his view of the role that was played by the "called" writer. He believed that his writing discharged two related responsibilities. The first of these was the vindication of Christ's elect who had been mortally wounded by persecutors and also the protection of Christ's elect yet living.

Referring to the elect who had been killed, Williams said: "My soul not only heard the dolefull *cry* of the *souls* under the *Altar* to the *Lord* for *Vengeance,* but their earnest *sollicitations,* yea and the command of the *Lord Jesus* for *Vindication* of their *blouds* and lives spilt and destroyed."[45] Evidence of his interest in the protection of the elect against tyrannical persecution is abundantly given in his two *Tenents.* In these he tirelessly documented his agrument that all consciences must be free from the physical sword.

His toleration of conscience, however, should not be allowed to obscure the fact that he was adamant in using the spiritual sword against all ideas which seemed false to him. In his *Queries of Highest Consideration* he told the Westminster Assembly that while most of the music that was given to them from various sources was intended to please their ears, his music would *"sound not* sweet *but* harsh" because it was the truth intended to correct their errors.[46] His debate with the Quakers provides an even better example. Williams has been frequently accused of allowing the Quakers freedom of conscience and then betraying them by attacking their religious views. In this, however, Williams was not inconsistent. He did insure their complete freedom of conscience, but at the same time he had been "called" by God to warn them of their errors. After his five-day debate with them, he set about to record all the proceedings and to give additional documentation to his views so that the entire work could serve as an effective witness for truth to Quakers everywhere.

The second role that Williams assigned to his writing was the providing of "means." Truth presented clearly and persuasively to the intellect was to serve man as "means" for achieving an inner conviction which would be granted him by the divine gift of grace. Williams' belief in the necessity of supplying man's mind with a continuous series of "means" explains his willingness to provide for his reader an almost endless sequence of scriptural exegeses. While all of his argumentative defenses of truth were intended as "means," his *Experiments of Spiritual Life* was his effort dedicated entirely to the explication of the process man is to follow in learning of God's predetermined will. He said that by writing of what God expects of man, he was "Sowing a little handfull of *spiritual seed.*"[47]

Like Williams, Milton believed that he had been called by God
to stand apart from the corruption of the existing religious insti-
tutions and reveal the divine will. He felt himself " 'toucht with
hallow'd fire' as was the prophet Isaiah."[48] Milton frequently expressed his "highest thanks to the heavenly bestower of gifts"[49]
for the calling that had come to him, but he was careful to qualify
his standing by saying that his divine guidance was dependent
upon his own industry. He required of himself not only "devout
prayer" but also "industrious and select reading, steddy observation, [and] insight into all seemly and generous arts and affaires."[50]

The role that Milton assigned to his writings had all the breadth
required by his Christian humanistic fusion of temporal and spiritual matters. As he stated in his earliest prose, he believed that
"one man endowed with knowledge and wisdom, like a great gift
of God, may be sufficient to reform a whole state,"[51] and he dedicated himself to the accomplishment of that very goal. In his
Second Defense he declared that he had been called by God to
"undertakings of the greatest magnitude" which would be "of the
highest use to society and to religion."[52] Milton committed himself to the solution of both the religious and the civil problems
because he saw them as flaws in a single fabric, and he felt "called"
to assist in the mending that was of greater service to man than
was the most laudable instance of valor among men in arms.[53]

Milton believed that his writing was performing a greater service
to man than could be accomplished upon the battlefield because
he was revealing principles of truth which would permit men to
rule over themselves, the only lasting solution to the turmoil in
religious and civil affairs. He was convinced that his inspired writing
could measurably assist in the reparation of man's fallen nature
because he had been given the gift "to inbreed and cherish in a
great people the seeds of vertu, and publick civility, to allay the
perturbations of the mind, and set the affections in right tune."[54]
No higher calling could be given a man than the endowment Milton
thought had been given to him: He was "called" to assist men in
the reparation of their ruins by teaching them the principles which
would assure temporal peace and eternal glory.

While both Williams and Milton were thoroughly persuaded that
they had been "called" to write, the views behind the service that
they felt they were performing are quite different. Williams in no

way supposed that his writings were influential in the decisions of God as to who would be designated as elect. His view of his contribution did not go beyond the vindicating and protecting of the persecuted elect and the providing of "means" that his fellow men might learn of God's predetermined will. It is for this reason that Williams fortified his lengthy arguments with a plethora of biblical documentation. Milton, on the other hand, saw his writings as playing an important role in man's reparation. He hoped to persuade erring men to prepare to receive the blessing of regenerating grace, the blessing they were denying themselves through their own disobedience. Milton's Arminianism also called for an argumentative defense of the truth, but it moved beyond the requirement to assist man in understanding God's plan to the need to motivate him to prepare himself for the reception of divine grace. This necessity of appealing to the highest sense of man provides a fascinating explanation for Milton's ambition to express himself poetically.

Without question the pens of these two persuasive Puritans had far-reaching effects upon all those of subsequent generations who were to inherit the Puritan tradition on both sides of the Atlantic. For those in America who would inherit this tradition which Williams helped to establish, however, there would always be a certain shadow of doubt cast upon the role of the writer in his society. American writers from Anne Bradstreet and Edward Taylor to Melville and Hawthorne were to feel a tension between the impulse to reach a wide audience and use their skills to improve the society and the suspicion that real change results only from prime movers more powerful than the gift of the writer.

NOTES

1. John Calvin, *Institutes of the Christian Religion,* trans. John Allen (London: Thomas Tegg, 1844), I, 43.

2. John Milton, *The Works of John Milton,* ed. Frank Patterson *et al.* (New York: Columbia University Press, 1936), XII, 151.

3. Perry Miller, *The New England Mind: The Seventeenth Century* (New York: Macmillan, 1939), p. 209; see also Arthur O. Lovejoy, *The Great Chain of Being: A Study of the History of an Idea* (Cambridge: Harvard University Press, 1936), pp. 52, 184.

4. Michael Waltzer, *The Revolution of the Saints: A Study in the Origins of Radical Politics* (Cambridge: Harvard University Press, 1965), pp. 159, 166.

5. Roger Williams, *The Complete Writings of Roger Williams* (New York: Russell & Russell, 1963), V, 290, 445.

6. Ibid., I, 186.

7. Ibid., I, p. 202.

8. Ibid., V, 64.

9. Ibid., VII, 56; see also V, 27.

10. Ibid., V, 370–71.

11. Milton, *Works*, XVI, 101. Milton's ideas on the Book of Nature are actually developed much more fully in the poetry than in the prose. The documentation from the poetry deserves a separate study, which would likely begin with Raphael's discussion with Adam: *Paradise Lost*, V, 469–90.

12. Ibid., XII, 171.

13. B. Rajan, "Simple, Sensuous, and Passionate," *Milton: Modern Essays in Criticism*, ed. A.E. Barker (New York: Oxford University Press, 1965), p. 10.

14. Milton, *Works*, XII, 283.

15. Ibid., XII, 171.

16. Ibid., XV, 217.

17. Rajan, "Simple, Sensuous, and Passionate," p. 11.

18. Calvin, *Institutes*, I, 55–56; see also Miller, *New England Mind*, p. 194.

19. A. S. P. Woodhouse, "Milton, Puritanism, and Liberty," *University of Toronto Quarterly*, 4 (April, 1935), 484; see also Perry Miller, *Roger Williams: His Contribution to the American Tradition* (New York: Bobbs-Merrill, 1953), p. 35; James Ernst, *The Political Thought of Roger Williams* (Port Washington, N.Y.: Kennikat Press, 1966), p. 178; and Irwin H. Polishook, *Roger Williams, John Cotton & Religious Freedom, a Controversy in New and Old England* (Englewood Cliffs, N.J.: Prentice-Hall, 1967), p. 86.

20. Perry Miller, "Roger Williams: An Essay," in the *Complete Writings*, VII, 16–17; see also C.A. Patrides, *Milton and the Christian Tradition* (New York: Oxford University Press, 1966), p. 129.

21. Miller, *Roger Williams*, p. 33.

22. Williams, *Writings*, V, 148–49, 335; see also Ola Elizabeth Winslow, *Master Roger Williams: A Biography* (New York: Macmillan, 1957), p. 226.

23. Ibid., VII, 198.

24. Ibid., V, 388.

25. Miller, "Roger Williams," VII, 10.

26. Williams, *Writings*, III, 347.

27. Ibid., I, 392; see also VII, 212.

28. Miller, *Roger Williams*, p. 208.

29. Williams, *Writings*, III, 150.

30. Woodhouse, "Milton," p. 490; see also Miller, "Roger Williams," VII, 10.

31. Milton, *Works*, XIV, 5.

32. H.R. MacCallum, "Milton & Figurative Interpretation of the Bible," *University of Toronto Quarterly*, 31 (Apr., 1962), 401.

33. Milton, *Works*, VI, 165–66.

34. Ibid., IV, 285; see also Harris F. Fletcher, "The Use of the Bible in Milton's Prose," *University of Illinois Studies in Language and Literature*, 14 (Aug. 1929), 308.

35. Milton, *Works*, VI, 175.

36. Ibid., XVI, 259.

37. Ibid., IV, 76.

38. Ibid., XVI, 125, 141.

39. Ibid., III, 190; see also VI, 53–54.

40. F.E. Hutchinson, *Milton and the English Mind* (New York: Collier Books, 1962), p. 75.

41. Milton, *Works*, VI, 25.

42. Miller, *New England Mind*, pp. 305–7.

43. Williams, *Writings*, IV, 41.

44. Ibid., V, 2; see also I, 79, and VII, 197.

45. Ibid., IV, 25.

46. Ibid., II, 253.

47. Ibid., VII, 52.

48. A.E. Barker, *Milton and the Puritan Dilemma: 1641–1660* (Toronto: University of Toronto Press, 1942), p. 36. Barker is here citing *On The Morning of Christ's Nativity*.

49. Milton, *Works*, VIII, 11.

50. Ibid., III, 241.

51. Ibid., XII, 259.

52. Ibid., VIII, 19, 67.

53. Ibid., VIII, 9.

54. Ibid., III, 238; see also XII, 163, 165.

TWO

The posy UNITY: Anne Bradstreet's Search for Order

EMILY STIPES WATTS

Anne Bradstreet's poetry has variously been understood as a record of a Puritan pilgrim's progress to God and hence a true expression of American Puritanism;[1] or as a statement from a poetic sensibility which did not understand the Puritan mission in the New World and hence lay outside "the continuity of American poetry";[2] or as verse rather typical of poetry by English women in the seventeenth century;[3] or as the compelling record of an American Puritan woman whose historical, familial, and sexual situation limited her poetry, either intellectually or emotionally.[4]

Most recent critics and anthologizers tend to favor her short "domestic" verses, those poems directed to her husband, children, or grandchildren, or the brief, devotional poems, such as "As Weary Pilgrim." The long "nondomestic" poems are generally ignored, even though they form the bulk of the first edition of *The Tenth Muse Lately Sprung Up in America* (1650).[5] Bradstreet herself seemed to consider these long poems, especially the Quaternions (1,617 lines) and "The Four Monarchies" (3,570 lines), as significant poetic efforts. The often anthologized and quoted "The Prologue" in which she defends herself as both woman and poet is, in fact, the prologue to the Quaternions.

These long poems are unsatisfactory to modern readers for a number of reasons. Intellectually, they seem to be eclectic, with the second part of the Quaternions ("Of the Four Humours"), for example, an apparent rehashing of the medieval scheme of man's constitution and with "The Four Monarchies," a work heavily dependent upon Sir Walter Raleigh's *A History of the World* (1612). Prosodically, Bradstreet's "heroic couplet" could not sustain the long didactic poem, although the total collapse of Bradstreet's prosody at the end of each of these long poems can be

attributed to other causes, as we will shortly understand. Historically, the poems do not seem wholly typical of American Puritan
verse, nor, really, despite critical claims to the contrary, are they
similar to the verse of contemporaneous English female poets,
such as Katherine Philips ("the Matchless Orinda") and Margaret
Cavendish, Duchess of Newcastle.

On the other hand, Bradstreet's long poems are, despite the
charge of eclecticism, certainly metaphysically and intellectually
ambitious (especially for a woman of the seventeenth century)
and, surprisingly, generally nonreligious in both tone and concept.
The kinds of intellectual concerns in these poems are varied and,
at times, even self-contradictory. These long poems, in fact, seem
to be the record of a series of independent poetic probings in
which the reader can watch the poet discovering what to know (or
not to know) in the very act or process of poetic creation. What
Bradstreet was seeking was some kind of metaphysical system of
correspondences and order which would inextricably interrelate
God, man, and the natural world. A poem such as "Contemplations"
indicates that she was well aware of her fellow Puritans' understanding of order: the immanent order of a Creator, an order
which could be discovered by reasonable man using his Bible and
studying nature.[6] And yet, of course, melancholy is only too
apparent in Bradstreet's "Contemplations" and contrasts sharply
with the vigorous and affirmative assertion of this immanent order
in poems such as those of Michael Wigglesworth and Edward
Taylor, her near contemporaries.

In the Quaternions she at least begins with confidence and
affirmation as she asserts that she has found "How divers natures
make one unity."[7] Indeed, at the conclusion of "Of the Four
Humours in Man's Constitution," she triumphantly announces
that she has discovered "A golden ring, the posy UNITY" (1. 605).
Old stuff intellectually perhaps, but nevertheless an indication of
Bradstreet's philosophical inclinations.

Bradstreet seems to have been, by nature, a philosophical monist;
she wanted the world, man, and God to form "A golden ring." She
sought "UNITY." However, as her poetry clearly indicates, she
found only a dualism (at best); she could not sustain the posy
unity. When she ended her life as a "weary pilgrim," she was only

waiting for the Bridegroom to whisk her away to a heavenly after-life and perhaps to the answer to her questions. The poem, appar-ently one of her last ones, does not indicate that she ever found the posy or the golden ring, only that she trusts that, in a heavenly afterlife, she will unite with Christ or, as in "My soul, rejoice thou in thy God," that she will be "dissolved."

In fact, profound uncertainty and intellectual insecurity (not as to her own eternal status but as to the metaphysical situation) mark the body of Bradstreet's verse. Even though in "The Four Humours" she triumphantly concludes that she has found the "golden ring," in the next sections of the Quaternions she discov-ers, in the very act of writing, that her golden ring was only brass. She came to her final position of surrender to Christ by way of a difficult and frustrating path; her surrender, her acceptance of Christ (who is hardly mentioned in her early poems) is simply that—a surrender. Intellectually, as her poetry records, she could never resolve the problem of order, even with reference to Puritan typology.

THE ARGUMENT FROM HISTORY

Bradstreet's longest poem, "The Four Monarchies," is a series of sketches of the monarchs and major events during the history of the ancient Assyrians, Persians, Greeks, and Romans. Based upon Raleigh's *A History of the World,* it is a listing of kings and queens, wars and intrigues, defeat and death. As Josephine K. Piercy notes, however, Bradstreet's history omits the creation, Raleigh's own moralism, any significant reference to Adam, or any typical Puritan moralizing.[8]

Nevertheless, Bradstreet's historiography, like Raleigh's, can generally be categorized as "providential," deriving from Augustin-ian *significatio,* with secular historical evidence demonstrating a cyclical *vanitas vanitatum* of a corrupt mankind.[9] The lesson, of course, was simple and grim: man's life is a mixture of good and bad in a divinely decreed but "fallen" world.

Bradstreet could not finish her poem. Although she mentions (3565-66) that her papers were destroyed by fire and thus she could not continue, it is evident that she might never have finished the poem anyway. At the conclusion of the third section, "The Grecian Monarchy," she is already weary and apologetic: "The subject was too high" (3417), she complains. She then manages to struggle into "The Roman Monarchy" for 135 lines before finally giving up.

As Bradstreet versifies history, the past is a series of catastrophes of individual men and women who hate and destroy not just each other but entire civilizations. Despite a judicious or loving soul who might appear from time to time, it is a dismal story which goes on and on. Although a responsible and just king (Nebuchadnezzar or even the young Alexander) might come to power, he soon became corrupt; even good parents, such as Esther and Artaxerxes Longimanus, produced cruel and despotic children (1286–89).

Bradstreet's dark vision did not allow for a redemptive or soteriological approach to history. God's various covenants with mankind, so important to the American Puritan, are not noted; even the Babylonian Captivity, a significant prefiguring or type of the New England mission,[10] is quickly passed over (416–546). Unlike her New England contemporary William Bradford, another providential historian, Bradstreet does not refer, even obliquely, to the expected redemption for the New England elect which must sometime be an end to all the human suffering. If scholars acknowledge Bradford's history as "melancholy,"[11] they can only recognize Bradstreet's as despairing. Except near the very end of her poem, when Bradstreet declares that all history "trembling stand[s] before the powerful Lamb" (3407), the Puritans' God is not mentioned. Mankind, Bradstreet suggests, can create only chaos in a wholly secular world.

Bradstreet had apparently begun her study with one clear intention: to mark the historic interactions of the ancient pagan monarchies with Israel. She begins "The Four Monarchies" by tracing Nimrod's ancestry to Ham and then, at least in the early passages, notes the points at which the Assyrian kings reflected biblical history. Her interest in the historic situation of the Jews vis-à-vis the ancient monarchies is, naturally enough, most intense at the time of the Babylonian captivity (416–546) and of Daniel's visions, which come to serve as prophesies of the destruction of the various monarchies (e.g., 2618–30 and 3392ff.). The "best" of the Persian monarchs is Esther's husband, Artaxerxes Longimanus (1215-78).

However, Bradstreet's careful awareness of the interaction of the Jewish and pagan states soon disappears, as Israel, in her view anyway, becomes only a minor kingdom with little or no historical significance, especially as Alexander sweeps through the ancient world. Engrossed as Bradstreet became with the historical significance of Alexander and the Greeks, she nearly forgets to mention Israel (brief references occur in lines 1878-84 and 2003-4).

As Bradstreet wrote the poem, she seemed to learn that Israel had played only a slight role in ancient secular history and that, except for Esther and Daniel, the Jews were as violent and warlike as other ancient peoples. Moreover, as the poem progressed, Bradstreet understood even more clearly the transitory nature of monarchies. Thus she begins her poem with a reference to man's vanity (6-7)—a favorite theme of Raleigh's (and of Ecclesiastes); after 3,374 more lines, however, she concludes:

> Thus kings and kingdoms have their times and dates,
> Their standings, overturnings, bounds, and fates;
> Now up, now down, now chief, and then brought under,
> The heavens thus rule, to fill the world with wonder.
>
> 3380-83

It is at this point that Bradstreet becomes weary of her poem and her prosody collapses.

The nation of Israel was one of central concern for the American Puritans, who saw their own community as a type of Israel; the Exodus from Egypt and from Babylon prefigured the Puritans' own exodus from England. The ancient Israelites were God's own chosen people who had fallen into apostasy, but of whom the New England Puritans were the symbolic "remnant" to whom God had granted a new beginning.

If Bradstreet had hoped to learn anything of ancient Israel from her study of history, or if she had hoped to find evidence even in biblical characters such as Daniel and Esther which might relate Old Jerusalem to her own New Jerusalem, she seemed to have found nothing.[12] At no point does her "providential" history edge toward "redemptive" history, as, for example, even Bradford's did. Unlike the early Calvinists and her contemporary American Puritans, Bradstreet did not heed Augustine's warning in Book XI of the *Confessions,* and thus she saw secular history as "a series of meaningless moments in a drama of the absurd,"[13] with man's only recourse to stand "trembling" before the paradoxically labeled "powerful Lamb." It is no wonder that the poem is unfinished and that the poetry lapses into doggerel.

In part, the lessons she learned from "The Four Monarchies" are contained in these stanzas from "Contemplations":

29

Man at the best a creature frail and vain,
In knowledge ignorant, in strength but weak,
Subject to sorrows, losses, sickness, pain,
Each storm his state, his mind, his body break,
From some of these he never finds cessation,
But day or night, within, without, vexation,
Troubles from foes, from friends, from dearest, near'st relation.

30

And yet this sinful creature, frail and vain,
This lump of wretchedness, of sin and sorrow,
This weatherbeaten vessel wracked with pain,
Joys not in hope of an eternal morrow;
Nor all his losses, crosses, and vexation,
In weight, in frequency and long duration
Can make him deeply groan for that divine translation.

33

O Time the fatal wrack of mortal things,
That draws oblivion's curtains over kings;
Their sumptuous monuments, men know them not,
Their names without a record are forgot,
Their parts, their ports, their pomp's all laid in th' dust
Nor wit nor gold, nor buildings scape times rust;
But he whose name is graved in the white stone
Shall last and shine when all of these are gone.

In contrast to "The Four Monarchies," in "Contemplations" Bradstreet does trace man's dismal state to Adam, but as she examines "ages past" (stanzas 10-16) she again omits such major (for the Puritans) historical and redemptive interactions between God and man as the covenant with Noah or the Exodus from Babylon. Beginning especially in stanza 18, she turns for consolation to nature because, at least in history, she can find no order. Her view of man and his secular situation is drastically more pessimistic than the more hopeful redemptive historiography of covenant theology advocated by her fellow Puritans.[14] Only the individual soul who has received grace, or "whose name is graved in the white stone," can find hope.

Bradstreet's inability to find "order" in secular or providential history is not so very remarkable, for even Raleigh could finally only shake his head and cast his eyes devoutly to heaven. What is remarkable about Bradstreet's historiography is her very different approach from that of even early American historians such as Bradford; except for her occasional use of Daniel's prophecies and her final acknowledgment of the "powerful Lamb," she cannot identify in any way a "course" throughout history. If such is the nature of God's providence, then indeed man can only tremble before the "powerful Lamb."

The appearance of Christ and the various covenants seem not to have signaled for Bradstreet any particular deviation in mankind's historical and secular course. Man has been miserable and constitutionally the same throughout history, as her inability to achieve any cohesive theory suggests in both "The Four Monarchies" and "Contemplations." (This is not to deny that Christ provided salvation for the individual.) In viewing secular history, Bradstreet could not identify even the modicum of progress for mankind as posited in Puritan covenant theology, nor does she examine history soteriologically. Bradstreet had difficulty comprehending any meaning in historical events in a world she seemed to have perceived as incredibly brutal and disorderly.

THE ARGUMENT FROM NATURE

Scattered throughout Bradstreet's poetry is abundant evidence that order, of some kind or another, existed in the natural world. In the Quaternions, generally thought to be among her earlier poems, she managed, at least for a time, to perceive an elaborate and intricate series of relationships between man and nature (not God) based upon Hippocratic and Aristotelian principles. With the balancing of Water/Phlegm/Childhood/Winter-Spring; Air/Blood/Youth/Summer; Fire/Black Bile/Middle Age/Autumn; and Earth/Spleen/Old Age/Autumn-Winter, Bradstreet felt that she had found the "golden ring, the posy UNITY."

Although the sixteen poems appear to form a tight and balanced unit, the four poems of the final Quaternion, "The Four Seasons of the Year," do not correspond to the other Quaternions. Moreover, "The Seasons" are each shorter than the other poems of the group, and Bradstreet apologizes: "My subject's bare, my brain is bad,/Or better lines you should have had:/The first fell in so naturally. . . ." The Quaternion immediately preceding "The Four Seasons" is "Of the Four Ages of Man"; and clearly in this Quaternion Bradstreet's elaborate scheme collapses, apparently in the process of creation, as the poet is forced to make adjustments in her scheme in the following "The Four Seasons."

Some of Bradstreet's finest poetry is contained in "Of the Four Ages of Man," in which the speakers cease to be personified abstractions and tend to resemble real people. If, for example, we examine "Childhood" (paralleled first with Phlegm and Water and then, quite awkwardly, with Winter-Spring), Bradstreet's problems become eminently clear. Phlegm/Water (Childhood) are characterized, in the traditional manner, as unstable and tame, yet patient, the opposite of Choler/Fire (Middle Age). The baby in "Childhood" may be unstable, but he is certainly not tame or patient. Water is characterized as a life-giver (spring rains and floods), but the parasitic baby thrives as the mother wastes. In fact, unlike the balanced portraits of Water and Phlegm previously drawn to parallel the Child, the baby has little to recommend him, and the reader can only sympathize with the mother, who "With weary arms . . . danced and 'By By' sung."

Moreover, the middle-aged man (Choler and Fire) turns out not to be the angry man predicted by "Choler" and "Fire." Although "fired" to some extent by ambition and vanity, he is, nevertheless, a good provider and father, a patient pastor, and an unselfish worker. In short, the golden ring of unity simply cracked. The four-part correspondence of nature and man seemed to be to Bradstreet a most inclusive scheme until she attempted to fit human characteristics into the abstract design. Bradstreet could fit together the elements and the humours, but the four ages of man simply did not correspond. Thus, in the fourth Quaternion, "The Four Seasons," Childhood becomes part Winter and part Spring; Old Age part Autumn and part Winter. Somehow man himself does not "fit" into the general scheme of things.

The conflict between the abstract and the personal, between the pattern or "order" and the individual, is undoubtedly the source of Bradstreet's problem. Unflinchingly, Bradstreet, in the very act of writing her poem, realized that the individual, as she realistically examined him, was in conflict with the abstract pattern. "UNITY" could only confront "diversity." Indeed, Bradstreet's predicament in this poem is quite similar to that of Emily Dickinson, who, as Allen Tate has observed, *"perceives abstraction* and *thinks sensation."*[15]

The Quaternions is a surprisingly non-Puritan poem. Although the Child traces his difficulties to Adam, Old Age hopes to see his Redeemer, and Spring recalls Eden, the general scheme of the world, the general sense of order, is nowhere traced to the immanence of God. One must assume that Bradstreet understands this nature-man order as having been established by God at the Creation, for, as Bradstreet observes in "To My Dear Children," a very late autobiographical letter, "That there is a God my reason would soon tell me by the wondrous works that I see, the vast frame of the heaven and the earth, the order of all things, night and day, summer and winter, spring and autumn, the daily providing for this great household upon the earth, the preserving and directing of all to its proper end."

It was not Bradstreet's interest or ability which disintegrated as she wrote the final four poems of the Quaternions: it was, apparently, that man and nature could not be closely interwoven or united—a perception which Bradstreet more clearly and sorrowfully expresses in "Contemplations." The Hippocratic-Aristotelian static situation of the elements, humours, ages, and seasons—a thesis neatly ordering the "diversity" into a "unity"—had collapsed for Bradstreet, as correspondingly the prosody, diction, and poetic images disintegrate in the final four poems.

"Contemplations" contains elements of both "The Four Monarchies" and the Quaternions, with references to Puritan natural typology evident throughout the poem. In "Contemplations," Bradstreet has not used her poem as a vehicle to discover (or to fail to discover) order and unity. The poem itself is consistent in tone, prosody, diction, and meaning. The poet more clearly knows what she is going to say as she begins her poem, and the reader is the explorer, not the poet. Nevertheless, the title "Contemplations" suggests the meditative nature of the poem, the process which the poet had experienced before she wrote the poem.

Bradstreet early introduces Puritan typology in stanzas which
declare that the natural world is directly reflective of the divine, as
in stanza 4:

> Then higher on the glistering Sun I gazed,
> Whose beams was shaded by the leavie tree;
> The more I looked, the more I grew amazed,
> And softly said, "What glory's like to thee?"
> Soul of this world, this universe's eye,
> No wonder some made thee a deity;
> Had I not better known, alas, the same had I.

After further "contemplations" of the Sun,[16] she concludes, with
typical Puritan reasoning, "How full of glory then must thy Creator
be, /Who gave this bright light luster unto thee?" (stanza 7). Such
a conclusion that God's decrees have become objectively real
certainly represents a sense of immanent order existing in the
natural world. Such a typological argument is Puritanism at its
most conventional.

However, at least for the poet, there remains an unbridgeable
chasm between herself and nature; nor is there any solace in the
knowledge that nature is reflective of God. In stanzas 22–28, with
the examples of the river, the fish, and the bird, the poet realizes
that she cannot follow the same kind of "course."[17] Nature is
aligned with God and can participate in His orders; man cannot.
Only in death can man find "security" (stanza 32). The Puritan, of
course, looked upon his earthly life as only temporary, a pilgrim's
path to heaven. Puritan typology was one means of discovering the
order and man's place in it; for Bradstreet, however, the typological relationships in nature only made more evident man's inability
to partake in any order, at least while he is on earth. It is a grim
poem, often cited by critics as melancholy and (falsely, I think)
understood as a preromantic poem. The melancholy, it seems to
me, is the result of the poet's inability to discover metaphysical
"UNITY" at two separate points.

Historically, as I have pointed out, from Adam's time to the
poet herself (stanzas 10–18), the poet can find only death and sin.
The Puritans' redemptive sense of God's interaction (and covenants) with man is not mentioned; the course of history in "Contemplations" is actually not very different from that in "The Four
Monarchies," although one deals with pagan civilizations and the
other with the Puritans' biblical forefathers.

Perhaps even more amazing is Bradstreet's inability to find affirmation and comfort in Puritan typology. Man's mind can recognize the sun as a "type" of the divine, but at least for Bradstreet, man is separate from and does not participate in the order inherent in the natural world. In fact, in stanza 18, she appears to be recalling the lesson she learned in the Quaternions—that natural order cannot apply to man:

> When I behold the heavens as in their prime,
> And then the earth (though old) still clad in green,
> The stones and trees, insensible of time,
> Nor age nor wrinkle on their front are seen;
> If winter comes and greenness then do fade,
> A spring returns, and they more youthful made;
> But man grows old, lies down, remains where once he's laid.

This chasm isolates the poet, it seems to me, and creates the tone of lonely melancholy.

Unlike Puritan poets such as Edward Taylor, who could at least in mystical moments participate in God and in His order (e.g., "The Experience"),[18] Bradstreet could recognize the immanent order, but could not participate and could not intellectually place man within any order which she could identify. As Bradstreet wrote in her prose letter "To My Dear Children," "I never saw any miracles to confirm me." Order must lie beyond man's understanding and knowledge.

Thus Bradstreet was able to find "UNITY" in the essences of God and the natural world, but man was isolated. Diversity was again the result of Bradstreet's attempted affirmation of "UNITY." It is true, of course, that for the Puritans the dichotomy between man and God was absolute: Infinite and finite, Perfect and imperfect, Glory and sin. Nevertheless, the Puritan could find his place in God's order through God's communications of himself, whether they be direct, or through the Bible, or through nature. Bradstreet claims never to have had any direct communication with God; man's history, as recorded in the Bible and elsewhere, seemed to show no pattern, at least no pattern comprehensible to the poet; and when Bradstreet turned to nature, whether she used ancient theories (the Quaternions) or Puritan typology ("Contemplations"), she could see some kind of order manifest in nature, but it was an order (or kinds of orders) in which the poet at least could not participate.

At the same time that Bradstreet was probing her universe to discover "the posy UNITY," she was writing another, very different series of poems, most of which were kept in her notebooks. These poems are of emotional desperation, pleas to God to relieve her of sickness or fear. Like many Puritans, Bradstreet turned emotionally and directly to God in times of desperation, in sickness or during her husband's journeys across the sea.[19] In fact, Bradstreet's earliest extant poem, "Upon a Fit of Sickness, Anno 1632 *Aetatis Suae,*19" is only the first of this series. Overly emotional at first, such poems develop in dignity and conclude with "As Weary Pilgrim." We should, however, note that the poet's prayers to God develop from a "let me live" to a "let me die."

After 1650, Bradstreet no more sought to affirm "the posy UNITY." As she noted in item 67 in her prose "Meditations Divine and Moral," she had concluded "how unsearchable are [God's] ways and His footsteps past finding out."[20] No more ancient kings or intellectual probing; after 1650, devotional poems and "domestic" verse. Yet even in her domestic verse can be traced the difficulty and tension of such a surrender. Especially in the two children's elegies, "In Memory of My Dear Grandchild Elizabeth Bradstreet" and "On My Dear Grandchild Simon Bradstreet," the adjustment is tenuous: "Let's say He's merciful as well as just."

Most critics welcome Bradstreet's turn to domestic and simple devotional pieces. These brief lyrics are more satisfying in terms of theme and structure; the images are integrated, the poems more polished. However, as historically significant as the domestic poems are in terms of theme and image exploration, these poems remain "not very imaginative," as Pearce observes.[21] What is lacking in these poems, it seems to me, is the poet's imaginative and intellectual tendency to understand and know through her poetry. Although graceful, the love poems to Simon Bradstreet are uncomplicated and direct and say very little about the nature of their love. The devotional poems are direct entreaties to God; no longer has the "weary pilgrim" energy to grapple with metaphysical problems. The poems concerning her children have not even the compelling reality of underlying tension of the earlier "Childhood" (poem nine of the Quaternions).

Bradstreet's use of her long poems to know and understand, that is to learn in the act of writing, ended in failure and disintegration, as she discovered, even while writing, that she could not find that sense of order she sought. The Quaternions, "The Four Monarchies," and "Contemplations" are not comforting poems. The poet's own arguments—not to mention the prosody itself—disintegrate as the poem is being written. In the Quaternions, Bradstreet moves from certainty to uncertainty; in "The Four Monarchies," she could discover no hopeful pattern in the course of secular history as she worked her way through it; in "Contemplations," her melancholy is the result of her inability to find her place in the historical and typological order.

To read Bradstreet's devotional and domestic poems is to understand only half a poet. Her long poems give evidence of a mind searching for some system, some comprehensive order by which to grasp the world and God. She sought secular, intellectual answers for questions which ultimately became for her religious and emotional. It is possible to see her passage as the inevitable Puritan's progress, for in the end she could only surrender and trust that some transcendent order existed in the hereafter. Yet her final poems of "rejoicing" that death is at hand represent the words of a submissive and surrendering woman who had once hoped to affirm, through her poetry, "the posy UNITY," but who could, in mind and soul-rending reality, find only diversity.

NOTES

1. Josephine K. Piercy, *Anne Bradstreet* (New York: Twayne, 1965), p. 41. Also, Robert D. Richardson, Jr., "The Puritan Poetry of Anne Bradstreet," originally published in *Texas Studies in Literature and Language*, 9 (1967), 317–31, and reprinted in *The American Puritan Imagination: Essays in Revaluation*, ed. Sacvan Bercovitch (Cambridge: Cambridge University Press, 1974), pp. 105–222.

2. Roy Harvey Pearce, *The Continuity of American Poetry* (Princeton: Princeton University Press, 1961), p. 24.

3. Elizabeth Wade White, *Anne Bradstreet: "The Tenth Muse"* (New York: Oxford University Press, 1971), pp. 273–82.

4. Such a view appeals to both sides of the sexist spectrum, from John Berryman's macho "Homage to Anne Bradstreet" to Adrienne Rich's slightly feminist essay, "Anne Bradstreet and Her Poetry." See also Piercy, *Anne Bradstreet*, p. 72, and Ann Stanford's "Anne Bradstreet: Dogmatist and Rebel," *New England Quarterly*, 39 (Sept. 1966), 373–89.

5. Two articles concentrate on specific aspects of the long "nondomestic" poems. In "Anne Bradstreet's Poetic Voices," *Early American Literature*, 9 (Spring 1974), Kenneth A. Requa has noted that "The Four Monarchies" fails because of "the conflict between. . .historian and housewife, the Raleigh-like master of times past and the self-conscious poet who doubts her

abilities as historian poet" (p. 6). He further concludes that the Quaternions is flawed "by the failure of the creating poet to provide a satisfactory structure" (p. 9). On the other hand, in "Anne Bradstreet's Quaternions and 'Contemplations,' " *Early American Literature*, 8 (Fall 1973), Anne Hildebrand discerns an affirmation of order and "divine unity" in the Quaternions (p. 119) as well as "suggestions of transcendence" in "Contemplations" (p. 125).

6. As Perry Miller has pointed out in *The New England Mind: The Seventeenth Century* (Cambridge: Harvard University Press, 1954).

7. "To Her Most Honoured Father Thomas Dudley Esq. These Humbly Presented," *The Works of Anne Bradstreet*, ed. Jeannine Hensley (Cambridge: Harvard University Press, 1967), l. 35. All subsequent quotations to both poetry and prose will be lines from this edition.

8. See Piercy, *Anne Bradstreet*, chap. 2.

9. Sacvan Bercovitch, *The Puritan Origins of the American Self* (New Haven: Yale University Press, 1975), pp. 41–42.

10. Sacvan Bercovitch, "Horologicals to Chronometricals: The Rhetoric of the Jeremiad," *Literary Monographs*, ed. Eric Rothstein (Madison: University of Wisconsin Press, 1970), III, 7 *et passim*. See also Bercovitch, *Puritan Origins*, p. 42.

11. Bercovitch, *Puritan Origins*, p. 45.

12. Bradstreet did discover something of woman's history: several of the ancient queens she discusses in "The Four Monarchies" reappear in "In Honour of Queen Elizabeth."

13. Bercovitch, "Horologicals to Chronometricals," pp. 15–16.

14. Bradstreet's only historical, hopeful voice is "New England" in "A Dialogue between Old England and New; Concerning Their Present Troubles, Anno, 1642." In this poem, the major turning point in history is the Reformation ("After dark Popery the day did clear"). It should be noted that the glorious prophecy ("Then fullness of the nations in shall flow,/ And Jew and Gentile to one worship go") with which the poem concludes is qualified by two "ifs" (ll. 296–97).

15. "Four American Poets: I. Emily Dickinson," *Reactionary Essays on Poetry and Ideas*, ed. Allen Tate (Plainview, N.Y.: Books for Libraries, 1936), p. 13. The emphases are Tate's.

16. This stanza might further suggest Bradstreet's affirmation of the divine immanence throughout nature in another way, if Sun is read as a pun for Son. Child of the Renaissance that she was, Bradstreet might well have expected her readers to make this association. The possibility of this reading was suggested by my colleague Allan Holaday.

17. These stanzas remarkably intimate Emily Dickinson's #1510 ("How happy is the little Stone").

18. Such mystical moments seem to have provided that instant of "unity" with the divine for the otherwise personally isolated Puritans. Norman S. Grabo has noted that such ecstatic moments are more common in Puritan literature than we have been willing to admit; see Norman S. Grabo, "The Veiled Vision: The Role of Aesthetics in Early American Intellectual History," first published in *William and Mary Quarterly*, 19 (1962), 493–510, and reprinted in Bercovitch, *The American Puritan Imagination*, pp. 19–33.

19. As she wrote "To My Dear Children": ". . . He [God] hath never suffered me long to sit loose from Him, but by one affliction or other hath made me look home . . .—which most commonly hath been upon my own person in sickness, weakness, pains. . . ."

20. Hensley, *Works*, p. 288. Bradstreet's "Meditations" do indeed suggest, by her occasional use of simple moral analogies from nature, that she was able, at least when she wrote the "Meditations," to see correspondences between nature and man. However, a large proportion of her analogies are between one man and another man, or between one kind of human experience and another, or between man and food. Moreover, her meditations do not have the metaphysical and transcendental scope (analogies between heaven and earth) which Jonathan Edwards' *Images or Shadows of Divine Things* exhibits.

21. Pearce, *Continuity of American Poetry*, p. 23.

THREE

The Jawbones Schema of Edward Taylor's *Gods Determinations*

WILLIAM J. SCHEICK

Although Norman Grabo's conclusion that *Gods Determinations* will become "the fixed star in Taylor's critical firmament" strikes me as very dubious, his call for a change in the emphasis of scholarship on this long poem warrants attention.[1] Discussions of such possible influences as morality plays,[2] Theocritan song contests (as well as other classical works),[3] Ignatian meditative practices,[4] Lorenzo Scupoli's *The Spiritual Conflict* (among other writings),[5] and homiletic tradition[6] contribute usefully toward a description of interesting features of Edward Taylor's poem, but they ignore the question of whether or not the work possesses an autonomous inner dynamic of the sort present in sophisticated expressions of literary art. Similarly, although Michael Colacurcio's insightful consideration of Taylor's sense of audience and Sargent Bush's thoughtful inquiry into Taylor's use of paradox extend the perimeter established by earlier descriptive criticism of the poem,[7] even they finally furnish little more than a suggestion of the artistry of the work.

In an effort to broaden our appreciation of the aesthetic achievement of *Gods Determinations,* I shall focus on an underlying schema and its supportive motifs[8] in the poem in order to demonstrate that the work is considerably more unified than has been previously suggested. This organization chiefly derives from the poem's structural imagery pertaining to the shape of a pair of jaws. The upper and lower extremities of this jawbones design serve Taylor as coordinates for Christ (the manifestation of Mercy, the Gospel) and Satan (the manifestation of Justice, the Law), respectively; caught between these two adversaries, descending from above, are the elect souls who dramatically experience an emotional ebb and flow between despair and presumption as they, collectively as the church, are carried by these jawbone forces from their natural house to a heavenly mansion.

Let me begin somewhat unconventionally with a diagram of the underlying schema of *Gods Determinations:*

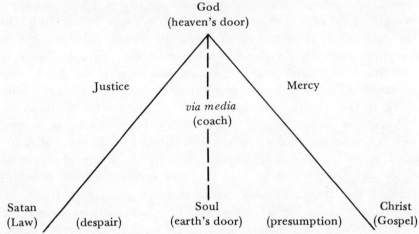

Perhaps the first step in arguing the validity of this design is to mention a remark in the poem in which Satan speaks of the distressful plight of souls caught between the divine and demonic factions. "Flanckt of by him before, behinde by mee./ You'st stand between us two," Satan reminds the harassed souls, whom he then asks, "What will you do when you shall squezed bee/ Between such Monstrous Gyants Jaws as Wee?" (p. 404).[9] The image Satan employs does not merely reflect his fiendish attempt to deceive his victims into an easy capitulation to the bleak implications of his question; contrary to what one might expect, Satan is not wrong, nor is he at a fundamental level ever mistaken in *Gods Determinations.* Regardless of his personal intentions and the peripheral distortions of what he says, Satan must intrinsically speak the truth in some essential manner because the reality of God defines everything in creation and thus determinatively establishes an ineluctable context for every remark made by the devil.

In the sermons of the *Christographia,* Taylor refers to this idea when he explains that God "gives a permit to Satan . . . to bring forth his uttmost Diabolicall Subtilty into its highests, and magnificent exploits to Subvert, and overturn the Glorious Work of God in the Creation"; yet "the Wisdom of Divine Grace hath made the

Old Serpents Wisdom a pen in the hands of his own Envy writing himselfe, whether he will or no, to be an Utter *foole*," for "God makes this Design of Satans, destructive to Satans design and promoting of the whole Creation to a greater Glory."[10] Satan, in short, unavoidably serves as a divine agent, in which capacity everything he says is informed by and reinforces divine truth. On the surface, of course, Satan's sophistry presents this truth in a beguiling manner. As the first author of sin—sin, for Taylor, is nothing more than a privative mental inversion of the good order of creation[11]—Satan tends at a superficial level to distort divine facts. In the specific instance of his hectoring the saints about the "Monstrous Gyants Jaws," what he says is true as far as it goes; perversely he emphasizes only one feature of the divine reality behind man's present circumstances, namely the wrathful aspect of God, and prevaricates by omitting any mention of the merciful side of the Deity. Because Satan distorts truth in this fashion, Christ calls him a liar (p. 405). Satan lies primarily by means of a false emphasis on some facet of divine reality, but always detectable beneath the surface of his warped rhetoric is the complete truth. Satan's language can finally only point to God's verities and thereby functions as a divine instrument because, as Taylor comments in one of his meditations, "Words and their Sense within [Christ's, the Logos'] bounds are kept" (2. 106, 15).

Satan's role as an agent of God is an important feature of *Gods Determinations,* one which helps explain the meaning of Sargent Bush's apt observation that "at times it becomes difficult to distinguish between comments by Satan on this subject [the paradox of man's predicament] and those by Justice."[12] In fact, Satan echoes Justice not only concerning the human dilemma but time and again in the poem because Taylor presents him as the temporal manifestation of divine wrath. Taylor's association of these two characters is not surprising when one considers that since the expression of divine justice was necessitated by the perversity of sin, its manifestation in the temporal world quite appropriately evinces a counter deformity.

Had the Fall never occurred, Justice would never have been aroused in relation to man; initially a latent attribute of the Deity, divine wrath was provoked into temporal expression by the distortion of sin and, in turn, purgatively mirrors that distortion in the postlapsarian world. Consequently, not only does Taylor have Satan descant in the same terms as does Justice (for example, in the passage noted by Bush regarding man's mountains of sin [pp. 397, 409]), but he also carefully introduces both characters by means of similar imagery. Of Justice, Taylor writes:

> Offended Justice comes in fiery Rage,
>   Like to a Rampant Lyon new assaild,
> Array'd in Flaming fire now to engage,
>   With red hot burning Wrath poore man unbaild.
>
>   p. 391

Satan too is described as a lion (pp. 407, 434) and portrayed in a fashion which Taylor intends to remind the reader of Justice:

> Then Satan in a red-hot firy rage
> Comes belling, roaring ready to ingage
> To rend, and tare in pieces small all those,
> Whom in the former Quarrell he did lose.
>
>   p. 403

As the surrogate of Justice in the deformed postlapsarian world, Satan assumes the role of the divine lion, revealing in his roaring sophistry the distortion of sin, which had incited God's wrath. As the temporal representative of the divine lion descending upon mankind, Satan fittingly torments his victims with an image of their destruction by a pair of jaws consisting of himself and the Deity.

Taylor amplifies the jawbones schema of his poem by developing a dog motif, the imagery of which corresponds to that of the lion references. Because of the corrupt proclivity of their affections to "range/ As yelping beagles doe" (p. 416), Taylor explains, many of the elect initially worry over the plausibility of Satan's assertion that they are merely the Deity's canines running "unsent for" and responding "to an Empty Whistle" (p. 407). In actuality, however, Satan knows of such futility because, as the saints eventually recognize, he is God's dog, in which capacity he represents the deformed manifestation of Justice in the postlapsarian world. Harried by Satan, the elect soul calls out to Christ: "He bayghs, and barks so veh'mently at mee./ Come rate this Cur, Lord, break his teeth I pray" (p. 414). In response to the soul's request to be

free of Satan's jaws, Christ elucidates the meaning of its encounter
by explaining that when "This Yelper fierce will at thee bark:/
That thou art mine this shows":

> But yet this Cur that bayghs so sore
> Is broken tootht, and muzzled sure,
>   Fear not, my Pritty Heart.
> His barking is to make thee Cling.
>   p. 414

In this reply Christ reveals the radical truth underlying Satan's
earlier reference to the fearsome jaws in which the captive soul
seems doomed to perish. The jaws of death do indeed betoken a
genuine threat to most men, as Satan indicates, but these same
jaws function as a means of shepherding or carrying the elect to
eternal life.[13] In accentuating the broken teeth of these jaws,
Christ unveils the distortion Satan perpetrates whenever he implies
the jawbones consist of himself and Justice—the evasive *him* in
the statement "Flanckt of by him before, behinde by mee" is
typical of Satan's duplicity in shaping the immediate context of
his remark so that the soul will understand Justice to be the referent of the pronoun. Christ makes clear that in reality Satan and
Justice constitute a single force counterbalanced by Mercy. Christ's
answer stresses the unitive dynamics of the jaws, the fact that apparently contrary forces combine in all-encompassing, integrating
divine reality. Satan, as the temporal manifestation of Justice, and
Christ, as the temporal manifestation of Mercy, ultimately function in terms of a single harmonious divine purpose resulting in the
salvation of the elect. When the saint realizes that in this sense
"wrath is full of Grace," his terror of God's jawbones schema
metamorphoses into praise of the unitive divine reality informing
its extremities: "My Front! my Rear!" (pp. 417, 418).

Taylor's Satan, in fact, performs as an inverted Christ, even as
Justice opposes Mercy and even as sin, which necessitates the
temporal expression of Justice and Mercy in Satan and Christ,
reverses goodness. Pretending to serve as man's mediator—Taylor
may have been influenced by Augustine's characterization of the
devil in this guise (*Confessions,* X, 42)—Satan parodies Christ's
roles as Logos and Redeemer. Originating from a perverse Logos,
Satan's words do not create but aim to invert the order of creation,
a notion Taylor indicates throughout the *Preparatory Meditations*

whenever he refers to sin through imagery suggesting creation retrograde. Creation, the central stage of the soul's encounter with the downwardly cast jaws of Justice and Mercy, possesses an inherent vertical principle, a chain of being to which Taylor refers as "the Scale of nature" and a hierarchy of glory,[14] in accord with which everything in nature inclines upwardly toward its Creator. Taylor suggests this principle of order in the first preface of *Gods Determinations*,[15] in which he observes that the Logos "spake all things from nothing" and that, since God "Gave All to nothing Man indeed,whereby/Through nothing man all might him Glorify," everything in creation worshipfully tends back toward its divine source (pp. 387–88).

Whereas Christ's role as man's Redeemer reasserts this natural order, Satan's sophistry encourages men to reverse the principle of ascent and to look downward toward the earth. In one notable instance Satan argues that "Nature shows that Life/ Will strugle most upon the bloody Knife/And so will Sin," specifically concluding that "The North must wake before the South proves Kind./ The Law must breake before the Gospell binde" (pp. 408–9).[16] Just as sin overturns good, Satan's advice inverts the fundamental law of nature's chain of being, for Satan entices his victims to consider nature rather than its source as their only ground of being. Throughout *Gods Determinations* Satan consistently resorts to natural law as the exclusive basis of his arguments. Satan insists on natural law—in scholastic theory that part of the divine law known to men through reason—because he represents Justice, who if he had his way would abandon man, as a consequence of the latter's violation of the "Morall Law" (pp. 395-96). He would thereby leave man to the futile effort of trying to read the Book of Nature in the dim light of postlapsarian human reason. So abandoned, man would be doomed before Justice because, as Taylor makes clear early in the poem, nature "scarce gives/Him life enough, to let him feel he lives" (p. 390).

As an advocate of natural law, Satan appropriately designs his arguments, based on nature, so that they will appeal to human reason, the faculty of the rational soul which in prelapsarian times was (along with the will) man's crowning attribute but which in postlapsarian times barely functions. Adam possessed both intuitive wisdom (*sapientia*) and experiential knowledge (*scientia*);

after the Fall, only a weakened form of the latter remains in
Adam's descendents. By directly touching a soul with saving
knowledge (Taylor's term in the *Christographia* for what he
speaks of as "Inherent Grace" [p. 393] and the gift of faith in
Gods Determinations), Christ can restore something of Adam's
intuitive wisdom; Satan, however, can only appeal to man at the
level of common knowledge (Taylor's term for information derived
from the sensorium), through information he derives "as an Eaves
dropper gets the knowledge of what is said in the house."[17]

Taylor carefully indicates in his poem that Satan can influence
someone's mind only through the vehicle of the senses:

> Hence in their joy he straweth poyson on,
> Those objects that their senses feed upon.
> By some odde straggling thought up poyson flies
> Into the heart: and through the Eares, and Eyes.
> Which sick, lies gasping: Other thoughts then high
> To hold its head.
>
> pp. 406–407

Like everything else in nature, even in postlapsarian nature, the
senses are radically good, but they fall subject to Satan's sway
because the body, of which they are a part, is inadequately disci-
plined by the corrupt rational soul:

> So in the judgment Carnall things Excell:
> Pleasures and Profits beare away the Bell.
> The Will is hereupon perverted so,
> It laquyes after ill, doth good foregoe.
> The Reasonable Soule doth much delight
> A Pickpack t'ride o'th'Sensuall Appitite.
>
> p. 409

The rational soul should guide the senses rather than take its
direction from them. Deprived of saving knowledge and in possession only of some form of common knowledge—the condition
which Justice believes fallen man unremittingly deserves and
which Satan argues is indeed man's inescapable destiny—the human
race can only despair as it tries rationally to decipher the Book of
Nature. Although sufficient for man's indictment, natural law
proves inadequate for his salvation; for the world subsequent to
the Fall is a place where the human "senses do inveagle" the soul
"to tend the Beagle," God's cur (p. 415). As Luther had explained,

summarizing his Augustinian sources, "since human nature and natural reason" readily imagine "that righteousness must be obtained through laws and works" and "since they are trained and confirmed in this opinion by the practice of all earthly lawgivers, it is impossible that they should of themselves escape from the slavery of works and come to a knowledge of the freedom of faith."[18]

Satan asserts "Natures Law: which Law he [God] Gave" and concludes from that law that "Though Grace is Gracious; Justice still is just" (pp. 424, 422), but in fact the covenant of grace has replaced the convenant of works and the Gospel now balances the Law. Telling but half the truth, Satan inevitably implies the other half. His words, all of which have their source in the Logos, unwittingly suggest the whole truth underlying their rhetorical surface distortions. Consider, for example, Satan's willingness to "anatomize" the interior of the people he is tempting so that they can "Believe [their] very Eyes" (p. 409). Although such scrutiny is correct, the mode of perception urged by Satan is inadequate; that is, as an advocate of natural law and as a perverse mediator inclining downward toward the earth rather than upward toward God, Satan promises to externalize the soul's interior so that it can be discerned by the fleshly eyes. The devil can tempt man only in terms of the sensorium, and Taylor's audience would readily have recognized that Satan has reversed the procedure, that properly one should internalize his outward actions for assessment by the eye of reason in accord not only with the Book of Nature but also and, more important, with Scripture.

Satan compounds his warped emphasis when he further remarks, "You want Cleare Spectacles: your eyes are dim" (p. 409). Volunteering to interpret the evidence—parodying Christ's revelations—he will set before man's fleshly eyes, Satan unknowingly implies the whole truth by reminding the saint that in the postlapsarian world one sees through a glass darkly, that not only are the body's eyes unable to read the Book of Nature directly, but also the rational eye (informed by the senses) likewise requires assistance. As Taylor makes abundantly evident throughout the *Preparatory Meditations,* and as he doubtless expected the audience of *Gods Determinations* to realize, the eye of reason requires the lens of faith:

Mine Eyes are dim; I cannot clearly see.
Be thou my Spectacles that I may read
Thine Image, and Inscription stampt on mee.
1. 6, 8–10

Although thy Love play bow-peep with mee here.
Though I be dark: want Spectacles to prove
Thou lovest mee: I shall at last see Clear.
2. 96, 50–52

Thus Satan's comment intrinsically betrays to an attending Christian its warped emphasis as well as the inadequacy of its forensic procedure.

Taylor develops this Pauline (see especially Galatians) opposition between the Law and the Gospel by extending the implications of the human need for the spectacles of faith and by suggesting other deficiencies in man. Not only does man "Lisp," but "A Cripple is and footsore" (pp. 453, 399; cf. 410): "He'th broke his Legs, yets Legs his stilts must bee" (p. 393). Whereas under the covenant of works man had legs, now "For all he hath, for nothing *stand* it shall" (p. 396; italics added). Because in the postlapsarian world man must "stand bent," he cannot manage to "stand at Glories room" until he first learns through faith to "stand on" Christ (pp. 426, 456, 394), meaning that he must wait upon and depend on Mercy; for "Faith will *stand* where Reason hath no ground" (p. 436; italics added).

Near the conclusion of *Gods Determinations,* Taylor combines this motif with another pertaining to the hands of the elect and of God:

But as they stand
Like Beauties reeching in perfume
A Divine Hand
Doth hand them up to Glories room.
p. 457

Just as before the Fall man possessed legs, he likewise could exercise his hands in compliance with the covenant of works. Subsequent to the Fall, however, Justice indicts man "for want of hands" and warns: "Whosoever trust doth to his golden deed/Doth rob a barren Garden for a Weed" (pp. 393, 396). Man now finds himself "leaden heel'd, with iron hands" and, consequently, helplessly dependent like a child to whom Mercy must extend a guiding hand and point the way (pp. 395, 396, 449). At the beginning of his work, Taylor refers to the engagement of God's hands in the act of creation (p. 387) and throughout the poem stresses his salvation of the elect as a re-creation, an act whereby he "Doth with his hands hold, and uphold the same" (p. 399); Mercy thus promises, "I'll make him hands of Faith to hold full fast" (p. 394). Satan inadvertently alludes to man's current need for hands of faith in his remarks about the monstrous jaws threatening man-kind: "You'l then be mawld worse than the hand thats right/ Between the heads of Wheelhorn'd Rams that fight" (p. 404). Although the immediate context of his comments about human hands distorts truth, Satan similarly unwittingly cues the true saint to the underlying verity of the following assertions: "God doth not Command/ Such things of us as had are of no hand" and "Hence sprouts Presumption making much too bold/ To catch such Shaddows which no hand can hold" (pp. 424, 425). When-ever arguing from the Book of Nature, appealing to reason through the senses, or stressing the Law, Satan unavoidably uses language which alerts the informed reader to Scripture, faith, and grace.

The primary premise of all of Satan's rhetoric is the notion that an eternal dichotomy characterizes reality. He believes this idea because, as the author of sin, he mentally rebels against God and because, deprived of saving knowledge, he derives his sense of things from natural law, which, as the Book of Nature, seems to the distorted vision of the sinner to reflect irreconcilable warring factions. Satan's *raison d'être* arises from a Manichean belief in a permanent dichotomy; his sense of personal reality depends on the continued existence of the world in the divine jaws, and his unilat-eral emphasis on nature not only affirms this basis for his own existence but also, as a result of his position as a mediator invert-ing the order of creation, represents his effort to increase the dis-tance between God and man in order to intensify commensurately the span between himself and Christ. In terms of the jawbones schema of *Gods Determinations,* in other words, Satan endeavors to invert the chain of being, especially with regard to man, who is the crown of creation, because the extremities of the jawbones would increasingly widen in direct proportion to his success in directing creation away from the divine unitive point where the jaws join. In this way man's awareness of irreconcilable oppositions in the temporal world would be augmented, and, it follows, Satan's sense of personal reality would be reinforced. Satan thrives on dichotomy; he has no other mode of existence. He fears the true order of creation, inherently inclining upwardly to God, because it implies the end of time, when God's temporal manifestations of Justice and Mercy will cease and everything in creation, except the nonactive damned, will return to the unitive reality of its Creator. Then, as a surrogate of Justice in the natural world, Satan will no longer have a role to play. His sense of personal reality will dissolve even as the notion of an eternal dichotomy, on which that sense had been based, will disintegrate.

However mistaken Satan's emphasis on conflict and opposition as an eternal verity finally is, it proves a limitedly accurate description of a temporal world in which "All mankinde splits in a Dichotomy" (p. 400).[19] That some people are saved while others are damned is the central, most worrisome concern for the soul caught between Justice and Mercy. The soul's fateful suspension between damnation by Justice and salvation by Mercy defines the innermost dramatic core of *Gods Determinations*. This pivotal anxiety explains why, after setting the stage by means of a brief statement on creation and the Fall of man, Taylor commences his poem with a dialogue between Justice and Mercy. No interruption of dramatic action, as Norman Grabo has suggested,[20] no mere concession to the influence of English pamphlet dialogues or to Ramist method, this section of the poem serves as a touchstone to all that follows. It establishes the dichotomy of salvation and damnation as the basis for everything presented in the body of the poem touching God's temporal response to earthly matters.

The saint experiences his natural life in terms of this transitory dichotomy. He not only must contend with Satan's tempting notion of a permanent macrocosmic dichotomy but also must counter the terrifying implication of an apparent irremediable split within himself. Satan refers to this internal conflict when he accuses man of wearing a "Double Face," as evidenced in the tension between his "Outs, and Inns" (p. 409). Referring to the human tendency toward hypocrisy, Satan emphasizes the seeming disparity between the internal and external aspects of one's self. What can one do when the very forces of creation participate in an eternal contention and when man, as well, is so helplessly divided against himself?

Satan intends his rhetoric of dichotomy to make the beleaguered victim ask this question. If the tempted individual fails to affirm that "Faith will stand where Reason hath no ground" (p. 436) and succumbs to Satan's double-talk about assessing one's self in relation to postlapsarian nature and reason, then he will emotionally drift toward the lower part of the divine jaws. This polarization leads to despair, for Justice and the law of nature offer no hope for mankind. If, on the other hand, one counters Satan's argument overconfidently, he will tend too presumptuously toward the opposite extremity of the divine jaws. Each Christian experiencing the two forces of the divine jaws must beware "this or that extream," Taylor warns, he must strive not to range "too low or high"; rather, he should endeavor "to keep on either side the golden mean" (p. 447; cf. Satan's unwitting indication of this idea [p. 411]).

Taylor does not suggest that the saint can attain a perfect balance between despair (Justice) and presumption (Mercy) while on earth. Time and again in *Gods Determinations* and in the *Preparatory Meditations* he explicitly indicates that the elect normally experience an ebb and flow of the affections. Thus, to Satan's question of whether or not one can demonstrate repentance "By those salt Rivers which do Ebb, and Flow" (p. 412), the saint should answer that he cannot do so with certitude at the moment but that this emotional vacillation truly presents a favorable sign insofar as it is typical for the elect to undergo this experience in the temporal world. As the saint makes his way back to God (in the schema of the poem the point where the jawbones meet), he experiences a fluctuation between presumption and despair. While on earth he can at best limit these affective waverings, which decrease as his progress toward God commensurately diminishes the gap between Justice and Mercy. By striving to remain "on either side the golden mean" instead of trying the impossible task of toeing the mark perfectly, by using his "hands of Faith" instead of only the fleshly ones of nature (i.e., good works) in order to grasp the "Bridge, and Raile" of Christ's example, the saint proves that "Faith will stand where Reason hath no ground," circumvents excessive emotional vacillations, and finally escapes "Sins Gulph each way" (pp. 394, 436, 420). Just as Justice and Mercy, Satan and Christ, the Law and the

Gospel, represent only apparent antagonists in the temporal drama to be resolved in God's unitive reality, just as the divine jaws which these seeming adversaries comprise do not devour the elect but carry them to eternal life, so too the fluctuations between presumption and despair become for the saints "blessed motions" (p. 432) rhythmically conveying them to heaven.

Taylor cleverly devises a house motif, possibly suggested by Augustine's concept of earthly and heavenly cities, to depict the elect soul's journey, conducted between the extremities of the divine jaws, from this world to eternity. In the opening lines of *Gods Determinations* Taylor presents nature or the earth as a home with "Pillars" and a "Corner Stone," an architectural wonder with a beautiful inner décor (p. 387). Developing the earthly context of these images, Taylor refers to the human body as a cottage and a hall (pp. 388, 417, 421), as well as to the heart as a castle or fort of life (pp. 388, 389). Subsequent to the Fall, Taylor explains, man dwells in a "Lapst Estate," his house in ruins; he finds himself "turned out of Doors, and so must stay,/ Till's house be rais'd against the Reckoning day" (p. 399). Dispossessed of the secure homely comforts of nature, his body, and even his heart, man is now a crippled "Traveller," a wandering, helpless, footsore pilgrim "a trudging hard" in search of a new house (pp. 421, 410). Satan, in his effort to reverse the chain of being and thereby to widen the gap between himself and Christ, tries to lure man back to nature, as if man had never been ousted at all. But the saint, seeking to "stand at Heavens Doore," journeys toward the point in the divine jaws where the extremities meet and where he is eventually admitted "to Glories room" (pp. 451, 457).

Because this movement through the divine jaws is terrifying for the elect, because no one can "track Gods Trace but Pains, and pritches prick/ Like poyson'd splinters sticking in the Quick" (p. 399), God provides the security of the church, a home which travels with the saints and protects them from a too dangerous exposure to the extremities of temporal dichotomies. In *Gods Determinations* Taylor depicts the church as an architecturally sound (recalling his portrait of prelapsarian nature) coach which carries the handicapped saints from their earthly home to a heavenly abode:

A Royall Coach whose scarlet Canopy
O're silver Pillars, doth expanded ly:
All bottomed with purest gold refin'de,
And inside o're with lovely Love all linde.

                                    p. 400

Those who decide "they'le abide/ At home before they'l pay so
much to ride" (p. 400) in this moving house, those who "gaze on
ruine, but refuse the hand" (430), foolishly harken to Satan's
double-talk about nature as the secure ground of their being.
Choosing to dwell at the point where the apparent conflict between Justice and Mercy is maximally manifest, they will encounter doom in terms of either presumption or despair. Those
who abandon earthly concerns and, together with the proper order
of creation, journey toward God will lodge comfortably and safely
within the church, which in a collective sense progresses as steadily
as does the elect soul's individual growth in grace. As these saints
near their destination, they undergo a final metamorphosing experience of an internal dichotomy as they "Stand gazing much between two Passions Crusht/ Desire, and Feare at once which both
wayes thrust" (p. 455); but as the elect pass through heaven's door,
the last vestiges of apparent temporal dichotomies dissolve into
the unity of God. In heaven each saint discovers that whereas
formerly his heart was "once a Stall" for God's cur, it has now
been transformed into a "Tabernacle" of the Holy Spirit (p. 416).
As Taylor makes clear through imagery related to his house motif,
heaven is the hive Justice and Satan would close to man (p. 392);
it is "the Hony Comb" prepared for the souls ("lately Wasps,
made Lady-Bees") who make the journey, the saints whom Christ
addresses as "my Hony" (pp. 394, 452, 414).

The consideration of such motifs as that of the hive or house,
especially in relation to the jawbones schema to which they contribute, allows for a fuller appreciation of *Gods Determinations*.
Even the prevalent military imagery as well as the legal and sea
motifs, all three of which are too conventional to warrant exegesis
in the preceding remarks, function in terms of the poem's internal
structure. Although the imagery of warfare seems at times to convey a sense of irreconcilable opposition between divine and satanic
forces, Taylor in fact intended it to serve as a means of dramatiz-

ing the dynamic between Justice and Mercy in the temporal world. Taylor, in my opinion, occasionally fails to keep this context perfectly evident, partly, I suspect, because the weight of convention behind these military images exerts its own impetus, wresting them out of the poet's full control. Nevertheless, with regard to the entire poem even the military imagery falls into its proper place and finally focuses on the resolution of all conflict by God's reclamation of the dwellings and territories lost through man's evil. Although not everything in *Gods Determinations* can be completely explained in terms of the jawbones schema, recognition of its structural function elevates our appreciation of the poem's aesthetic merits. It is to be hoped that future considerations along similar lines of analysis will reduce the impression, as expressed by Donald Stanford, that the work is "an anthology of poems all written on the same subject but in different styles at different times rather than a coherent composition."[21] *Gods Determinations* may not be perfect and it may not be Taylor's best poem, but it represents a more accomplished aesthetic achievement than most of Taylor's critics have perceived.

NOTES

1. "*Gods Determinations*: Touching Taylor's Critics," *Seventeenth-Century News*, 28 (Summer 1970), 22–24. An opposite view is expressed by Karl Keller, *The Example of Edward Taylor* (Amherst: University of Massachusetts Press, 1975), pp. 127–38.

2. Nathalia Wright, "The Morality Tradition in the Poetry of Edward Taylor," *American Literature*, 18 (Mar. 1946), 1–17.

3. Willie T. Weathers, "Edward Taylor, Hellenistic Puritan," *American Literature*, 18 (Mar. 1946), 18–26.

4. Norman S. Grabo, *Edward Taylor* (New York: Twayne, 1961), pp. 166–67.

5. Donald E. Stanford, *Edward Taylor* (Minneapolis: University of Minnesota Press, 1965), pp. 26–29.

6. Jean L. Thomas, "Drama and Doctrine in *Gods Determinations*," *American Literature*, 36 (Jan. 1965), 452–62.

7. Michael Colacurcio, "*Gods Determinations* Touching Half-way Membership: Occasion and Audience in Edward Taylor," *American Literature*, 39 (Nov. 1967), 298–314; Sargent Bush, "Paradox, Puritanism, and Taylor's *Gods Determinations*," *Early American Literature*, 4 (Winter 1970), 48–66. John Gatta, Jr., has recently made an interesting case for the function of humor in the poem in "The Comic Design of *Gods Determinations touching his Elect*," *Early American Literature*, 10 (Fall 1975), 121–43.

8. Arguments for the presence of structural motifs as an aesthetic device in Puritan literature are made in my "Anonymity and Art in *The Life and Death*

of That Reverend Man of God, Mr. Richard Mather, " American Literature, 42 (Jan. 1971), 457-67; "The Widower Narrator in Nathaniel Ward's *The Simple Cobler of Aggawam in America,"* *New England Quarterly,* 47 (Mar. 1974), 87-96; and *The Writings of Jonathan Edwards:Theme, Motif, and Style* (College Station: Texas A & M University Press, 1975).

9. All quotations from Taylor's poetry are from *The Poems of Edward Taylor,* ed. Donald E. Stanford (New Haven: Yale University Press, 1960). Page references for *Gods Determinations* are cited parenthetically in the text; for the *Preparatory Meditations* series, poem, and line numbers are given.

10. *Edward Taylor's Christographia,* ed. Norman S. Grabo (New Haven: Yale University Press, 1962), pp. 117, 24-25, 96.

11. See my *The Will and the Word: The Poetry of Edward Taylor* (Athens: University of Georgia Press, 1974), pp. 56-66.

12. Bush, "Paradox," p. 57.

13. Satan's windy sophistry, those "Canons" which "Shoot onely aire" (p. 406), separates the wheat from the chaff. He "Doth winnow them with all his wiles, he can,/ As Wheate is winnow'd with the Sieve, and Fan" (p. 407; cf. the soul's fear that it is full of chaff [p. 435]).

14. Taylor, *Christographia,* pp. 22, 159-60.

15. The importance of the two prefaces as an indication of Taylor's approach to *Gods Determinations* in terms of thematic divisions rather than with regard to dramatic conventions is suggested by Robert D. Arner, "Notes on the Structure of Edward Taylor's *Gods Determinations,"* *Studies in the Humanities,* 3 (June 1973), 27-29.

16. Christ can argue from nature as well, but whereas Satan reads the Book of Nature from Justice's point of view ("Soon ripe, soon rot" [p. 407]), Christ interprets it in the light of Scripture ("These White Frosts and the Showers that fall/ Art but to whiten thee withall./ Not rot the Web they smote" [pp. 417-18]).

17. Taylor, *Christographia,* p. 369.

18. "The Freedom of a Christian," in *Three Treatises,* trans. W. A. Lambert (Philadelphia: Muhlenberg Press, 1960), p. 315. Taylor, incidentally, cites Luther (see, for instance, *Edward Taylor's Treatise Concerning the Lords Supper,* ed. Norman S. Grabo [East Lansing: Michigan State University Press, 1965], pp. 72, 125, 139), as do Increase Mather (*The Life and Death of That Reverend Man of God, Mr. Richard Mather* [1670], [Bainbridge, N.Y.: York-Mail Print, 1974], pp. 61-62) and other Puritan divines.

19. And so, once again, Satan's distortion reveals a truth. Although the sort of apparent dichotomies Satan emphasizes do vanish with the end of the world, the difference between the saved and the damned does persist. However, whereas in the temporal world demonic and divine forces seem engaged in dramatic contention, at the end of time everything will clearly be defined in terms of God's unity; which is to say, that the damned, albeit separated from God, will not contend against Him as a force but, in their nonactive privative condition, be defined simply by their exclusion from the beatific vision. The damned's privative selflessness parodies the elect's unitive selflessness in God; but both are defined finally in relation to God—the saints positively, the condemned negatively—not in regard to any ultimate dichotomous forces. Taylor does not delve into this complex notion in *Gods Determinations* because he directs his poem at the elect, for whom indeed in every sense apparent dichotomies dissolve in eternity.

20. Grabo, *Edward Taylor,* p. 162. It should be noted that Grabo tends to dismiss the validity of his analysis of the five-act division of the poem which had led him to construe the dialogue as an interruption.

21. "Edward Taylor," in *Major Writers of Early American Literature,* ed. Everett Emerson (Madison: University of Wisconsin Press, 1972), p. 86.

FOUR

The Example of Edwards: Idealist Imagination and the Metaphysics of Sovereignty

MICHAEL J. COLACURCIO

Edwards' "modernity"—let us begin by stipulating—is a dead issue. It might be possible for a person with a *very* strict philosophical conscience to argue that the question was never properly settled because it was, from the first, a question *mal posé*; that Perry Miller's habit of always saying more or less than he meant touched off, in this instance, a great deal of misplaced precision about "medieval" and "modern." From such a premise such a person would go on to a process of sympathetic redefinition, reassessment, and reevaluation. A thankless task, surely. For the case was argued with as much vigor and intelligence as such things usually get. Eventually it even got its own casebook.[1] But then criticism inevitably moved on to other, less nominal (if also less exhilarating) topics. And though the old question lurks around the edges of my own essay on how precisely to come at Edwards, it will enjoy direct discussion only in footnotes.

Let me then state my own first premise at once: modern or medieval, advanced or retarded, for good or ill, Edwards was a "Christian Philosopher." However we might *feel* about the fact, no approach to his thought which does not take a fairly complex account of it can possibly have historical validity.

The significance of my preliminary formulation may be clearer to some readers than to others. Obviously Edwards was, what Hawthorne once called him, a "very eminent Christian." And just as obvious to readers of *The Nature of True Virtue* or parts of *The Freedom of the Will* is the fact that he often reasoned with careful precision in a philosophical way. But somewhat more is intended. In the tendentious formulation of Vincent Tomas—borrowed from

H. A. Wolfson, and made rather too gleefully back against Miller—
Edwards' philosophy was one which "placed itself at the service of
Scripture and was willing to take orders from it."[2] More sympathetically: to call Edwards a Christian Philosopher is to associate
him with the great scholastics of the Middle Ages and to recognize
that for him, as for them, philosophy could not go on as if a revel-
atory (and sacrificial) divine interposition into history had never
occurred. Whether or not things like metaphysics, or natural
theology, or rational ethics could be considered valid disciplines
in themselves, they could not be, for the Christian Philosopher,
completely self-motivated activities. In Edwards' mental world,
clearly, the data (to him the "truths") of the Christian Revelation
still functioned as the given source of primary certitude on questions of ultimate human significance.

In this simple, preliminary, and nonevaluative sense, it is not
unfair to call Edwards "medieval": the continuity between his
basic position on the problem of "Reason and Revelation" and
that of, say, Thomas Aquinas seems evident. Edwards' key passages on the subject are already well known, and much of what
modern Thomists (Etienne Gilson and others) have said about
Aquinas and his contemporaries holds equally for Edwards. In
both cases philosophy could hold only a second place: it might
not be reduced to the status of "handmaiden of religion," but it
does seem something of a helpmate in the study of revealed
theology. One rarely senses that he is hearing, in either case,
elegant rationalizations got up to "prove" what he suspects is
already "known." The problem is somehow more complicated
than that; and most instances of such transparent epistemological
sleight of mind pass rather quickly from the history of thought.
Nevertheless, in both cases we are dealing with the traditional figure of "faith seeking understanding"; and, more problematically,
with a very vigorous and powerful philosophy which is yet sub-
sumed by something *else*. By Thomistic definition, Edwards'
proper subject and mode is that sort of "theology" in which
philosophy goes naturally to work on the supernaturally given
data of Scripture. [3]

The result is often hard to get at. Strictly *philosophical* address
to Edwards' thought has to face the problem of abstracting the
purely rational elements away—not only from poetically given

truths of Scripture, but also from the total system, whose primary impulse or rationale may not be philosophical at all. Any *larger* sort of address would have to face the touchy problem of discovering the laws by which his total system assimilates philosophical strategies to biblical idioms; and the cogency, or at least the coherence, of that assimilation would surely provide an important index to Edwards' value, or at least his elegance, as a thinker.

This last operation is by no means an easy one. But it is, in my view, the essential task of Edwards criticism. To be sure, most interpreters of Edwards have had some theory of how the various elements in this system are hierarchically arranged, or how they articulate with one another. Very few commentators, for example, have missed the implication that the crucial definition of "will" (as inclination) and the powerfully argued theory of "freedom" (to *do* but not to *will* as one wills) have something radically to do with a Calvinist theory of predestination. But such correlations are not usually made with much precision. And no single modern study of Edwards has taken as its leading theme the problem of the cooperation between explicit philosophical argumentation and prior Scriptural attitude.[4] It is part of my argument that such an approach to Edwards is absolutely essential. And it is toward such a study that the present essay is preliminary.

Very preliminary. For all sorts of difficulties concerning the state of the arts of both philosophy and scriptural interpretation in the eighteenth century must be handled summarily and in footnotes. And, more obviously, there are too many Edwards texts, even excluding the "Miscellanies," to be treated in a brief essay. Potentially at least, each of these texts presents us with a different configuration or model of the cooperation between revealed certitude and rational analysis; potentially, at least, there are as many variations as there are problems and occasions.

Still, the situation is not hopeless. One very important continuity seems assured by the nature of Edwards' audience, largely defined. We might think of it as American latter-day (and perhaps backslidden) Puritan; or American, Scottish, and English (Low-Church) Calvinist; or Atlantic-Community Protestant.[5] It is each or all of these at various times. But in any case Edwards can legitimately imagine that many pious souls want or need to hear what he has to say against those Arminians or other "supernatural rationalists" who, having agreed with John Locke that reason must sit in judgment on any supposed revelation, are in fact corrupting the Pauline-Augustinian-Calvinist-Reformed reading of the Scriptural economy of salvation. Towards them Edwards' task is always to show that a sound philosophy supports or ratifies the "orthodox" religious teaching as surely as an unsound one perverts or revises it. Those who can both *read* and *think,* he argues, have no trouble—not with Calvinism and not with the Unity of Truth.

And if the rhetorical task does (undeniably) change somewhat in the course of his career, it does so intelligibly and in ways that are both limited and predictable. Edwards' dismissal from Northampton in 1750 would mark an almost-clear division of his career into two phases. Before that date Edwards' philosophy almost always has a pastoral context: we find it—*passim,* as needed, and largely by implication—in works basically designed toward the conversion of souls, for whom bad reasoning could only be a sign of bad faith. This is so whether the souls are those of Northampton or of some wider evangelical world, interested and perhaps participating in a season of grace; and whether they are, as events develop, likely to be on the side of Davenport's enthusiasm or of Chauncey's rationalism. After 1750, however, the philosophical problem becomes more prominent and direct. As Edwards goes to work, one by one, on the various parts of his projected summa, the philosophy can no longer remain implicit. His audience must now be thought to include not only the unwary and the perplexed but also the rationalistically and determinedly hostile: Davenport and Chauncey may be supposed to regard themselves as good Calvinists but Taylor and Whitby may not. Still, even these men imagine themselves to be within the pale of Protestant consensus. And so their doctrines of freedom and of original sin can (indeed from Edwards' point of view *must*) be met on the complicated ground of what the orthodox inheritance and the best rational analysis conspire to teach the mind about the divine economy.

In the pages that follow, then, let us briefly review a few of the major Edwards texts, including some from the earlier period which are not on the surface very metaphysical. After we have acquired some sense of Edwards' situation, problems, and strategies as a Christian Philosopher, it may then be instructive to conclude with special emphasis on Edwards' treatise of *The Great Christian Doctrine of Original Sin Defended.* Whatever Edwards may have believed about the strategic importance of his *Freedom of Will* in his polemic against the Arminians, a fair number of interpreters have sensed that it is the *Original Sin* which "leads us to the very secret of Jonathan Edwards" himself.[6] And I heartily agree. Here is where the whole system comes to a sort of vexed completion—at a point which is, theologically, fairly appropriate for a latter-day Calvinist trying to rescue the *rational* validity of God's *sovereign* decision to treat with all men in Adam; and at a point which is, philosophically, fairly predictable for an idealist who had begun by discovering that God is the only substance and that His stable ideas and efficient will are all we can ever know our "world" to be.

2

The first problem concerning the relation between philosophical speculation and theological tradition in Edwards' early publications is to discover that philosophy matters *at all*. Herbert Schneider, himself a professional historian of philosophy, has concluded that it does not. More convincingly than any commentator since, he traces Edwards' early discovery that Locke's "power" and Newton's "atom" both lead the mind to the same immaterialist "point"; and that whether we start with Locke's "substance" or Newton's "space," we always end up discovering that the world exists "no where but in the [Divine] mind." But then, according to his view, Edwards "practically discarded" his early insights "in his later and maturer thought." Thus Schneider reads Edwards' career from 1731 to 1750 without reference to his early idealism; and when he comes to the later, explicitly philosophical works, he proceeds on the understanding that these "are based on an entirely different set of categories."[7]

Moreover, contradictory assumptions have led to similar embarrassments. Most critics have felt that Perry Miller vastly overemphasized Edwards' early philosophical debt to Locke and Newton, as opposed to his reliance on ideas available within an established theological tradition. Miller himself—distinguishing things that may ultimately belong together—concluded that nineteenth-century commentators had made entirely too much of Edwards' similarity to Berkeley. And this latter verdict has received fairly widespread endorsement.[8]

All of this is a way of saying that the figure of Edwards' philosophy—within, around, or behind his early theology—has not proved easy to discern. A Calvinist theory of sovereignty there is, abundantly and from the first: to begin with "God Glorified in Man's Dependence" is to begin with the premise that man depends on God *absolutely,* for all his being and all his good, both material and spiritual, both before and after the gracious work of redemption. And, once the Awakening is fairly under way, a "pietist theory of love" forces itself on our attention: implicit in the experiences recorded in the *Narrative of Surprising Conversions* and well worked out in the psychological distinctions which make up the first part of the *Treatise Concerning Religious Affections* is Edwards' constant theory that our willings can be only as our experiences have been.[9] But a theory of the universe equal or appropriate to these forms of piety does not immediately announce itself, explicitly and as such. At first glance one is indeed tempted to conclude, even as Edwards and Berkeley both suggest, that after the idealist reduction of the world has been made, everything really does go on just as before,[10] including theology.

And yet the double premise, that everything human depends *absolutely* on God, and that man can (and must) have a profoundly affective *sense* of this state of affairs as the highest reality, seems powerfully indicative of a reality-principle lurking somewhere. And I suspect that students who follow the progress of Edwards' thought from his early "Notes" on to his "Miscellanies" will always be a little uncomfortable with the premise of a divorce between philosophy and theology in Edwards' early career. For in those unpublished works new insights confirming the ideal status of the world are constantly being correlated with biblical affirmations that it is in God that we "live, move, and have our Being."[11]

Perhaps the real problem is knowing exactly what to look for. It may be that the essential task is not to discover rational extensions of biblical knowledge; in fact we find very little of this. Nor even to locate specific philosophical supports for embattled theological doctrines, though here Perry Miller's sense of the occasional loaded word is probably accurate. But the simpler and more pervasive question may be more revealing: can we identify a large "metaphysic" which needs to be true for Edwards if the theology he is espousing is to be coherent? What view of the world does

Edwards seem to be taking for granted? What, given Edwards' theological positions, might his major philosophical insight be?

It might well have something to do with a special understanding of "cause." Surely Miller is right to see that Edwards' radically Protestant scheme of salvation must sooner or later develop some "non-efficient" theory of the relation between man's faith and God's gracious gifts; and surely this occurs in his early treatise on "Justification by Faith Alone." Obviously faith and justification go together, but the problem is one of mechanics; and, more subtly, faith cannot be the cause or even the "condition" of salvation in any sense implying that man forces God. The terms of Edwards' solution could indeed have been suggested, even as Miller proposes, by one peculiar, nonmechanist sentence in Newton. Or, just as plausibly, they may have been influenced by the parallelist "occasionalism" of Malebranche; or they might be powerfully proleptic of Hume's radically empiricist theory of cause as repeatedly observed sequence. But in any event, Edwards wants to say (among many other things, of course) that, in general, "cause" is a very tricky notion; and that, in particular, there is plenty of "reason" to deny that man's choices compel God's responses in a mechanical chain of events.[12]

To be sure: it is hard to feel that Edwards ever does solve his basic problem of showing how (in the formulation of Conrad Cherry) faith can be at once a completely free gift and a fully human act—not in this essay at least. In terms of perception alone, as we shall see, he does very well. But in terms of cause or condition, no matter how subtly conceived, his argument seems to imply an inelegant reduplication of the orders of grace: grace has to mean *both* an offer of salvation freely made *and* the power of acceptance, also given with equal freedom. In short, the "Calvinist" problem of God as the Giver, the Gift, and the Power to Receive remains a problem.[13] Nevertheless, the moves Edwards makes in this essay are philosophically revealing. At the very least we see him assuming and operating according to some "way of ideas" in which the nexus between any event and any other is more arcane and rather more mental than we ordinarily imagine.

Or perhaps we sense that Edwards' root problem involves the competition (not to say the contradiction) between the Lockean and other, less empirical (more illuminist) epistemologies in his early theories of grace. According to what philosophical scheme, we might wonder, can grace be called both a "sense" and a "light"? The problem exists not only between "God Glorified" and later works, but within most of these later works themselves. "A Divine and Supernatural Light," which Miller singled out as containing the whole of Edwards' system in a kernel, is a particularly revealing instance. The title points one way, and we can easily find our way to the Cambridge Platonism behind it. But the emotionally crucial passages point quite another: identifying *idea* with *sense,* and epitomizing sense as *taste,* they lead us just as directly to John Locke.[14]

Evidently all sorts of roughly approximate psychologies and systems of metaphors can be reconciled if one's metaphysics is large enough. Granted that something not unlike Edwards' movement of thought may occur in Thomas Shepard—or elsewhere, at large, in the Puritan emphasis on "experimental" religion—still the precise model for his doubly sensationist reduction occurs in a famous section of Book II of the *Essay Concerning Human Understanding.* And when all the dust of "source" and "influence" settles, surely this fact counts for something.[15] Evidently Locke is not so hard to reconcile with Plato if one has already interpreted him as the thoroughgoing idealist which his definitions threaten to make him, rather than as the stubbornly dogmatic believer in objective "qualities" and hidden "substrates" he imagined himself to be. And evidently Puritans, Neoplatonists, and Really Radical Empiricists can all help one say that grace must be nothing *but* an idea if he has already demonstrated that, between God and man, ideas are all that ever *can* be.[16] Biblical precedent would be significant, of course; but even there the tolerance of diverse idioms might have to be accounted for in terms of the nature of things. And evidently some form of idealism has, all along, provided Edwards with just such an account.

What we seem to sense, therefore, at least in a general way, is that when Edwards writes about the Calvinist (and pietist) theory (and experience) of grace, he is keeping the terms of his early idealist speculations absolutely before him; that they provide him, quite simply, with the rational support and even the philosophical counterpart of the theology of grace. He never makes the parallelism completely explicit, of course. And the reason surely has less to do with any growing speculative timidity than with a perfectly just perception that such a comparison or translation of idioms would be confusing or irrelevant to his primary audience of anxious souls. The problematic saint who is having trouble putting aside all causal reliance on his own moral works and sensuously apprehending the perfect omnipotence of God as *the* saving psychological truth will probably not be helped by being told that, after all, his entire world exists nowhere but in God's "determination, his care, and his design."[17]

Theoretically, of course, the insight might be very helpful. If God is, in the last analysis, the *"ens entium"* and the only "real existence," then how can the first moral quibble fairly arise? If philosophy is always running up against the discovery—in perfect validation of the Divine Name—that "God and real existence are the same"; that "in metaphysical strictness and propriety, He is and there is none else"; then why should the situation be any different in piety?[18] If God is, properly speaking, the only true substance and the only truly efficient cause in the history of that process we call the universe, then why should anything *but* God be supposed to matter in the history of the process of salvation? Why should God's determinations touching his elect be any less spiritual than his primary ontological determination? It seems clear, for example, that this idealist version of sovereignty came to Edwards himself, as a sort of philosophical "preparation for salvation," well before the spiritual experiences recorded in the "Personal Narrative." Indeed, one could even argue that the philosophical insights *were* that salvation and that the doctrines and piety came (later) only as a sort of psychological corollary.

But however that case might be, it is easy enough for us to see that Every Christian is not necessarily his own philosopher; and no more so, certainly, in the Northampton of the Williamses and the Hawleys, the Bartlets and the Hutchinsons than elsewhere. If, philosophically, as we may already begin to sense, the problem with the correspondence between idealism and Really High Calvinism is that it is altogether too close; that the two are, essentially, too nondifferent to be truly useful as explanation, the one of the other; still, practically, the matter is much simpler: the Evangelical Christian regards Pauline (and not quasi-Berkeleyan) language as normative; and the eighteenth-century inhabitant of the Connecticut Valley would probably find the terms of the philosophical solution more difficult than the religious problem itself. And with intellectual frustrations added to his already desperate moral and psychological ones, he might well cry "metaphysics!"

And so—as I read the documents of this first public period—Edwards goes on, never *explicitly* using his original philosophical premises, never *overtly* invoking his radically idealist insight, and yet never for a moment ceasing to think of the world exactly as he had in his early "Notes" and in his essay "Of Being." What we see, essentially, is the figure of a man who can easily swallow the gnat of sovereignty because he has already fairly devoured the camel of pure idealism. Surely Edwards needed to be an idealist to assure himself that his theory of sovereignty was more than a pious fiction or feeling, that the totality of man's dependence on God was as direct and unmediated as it was absolute. Would not material substance be just as much a troublesome intermediary in a psychological theory of grace as it was a needless and operose hypothesis in the theory of being? And, even more fundamentally, how could God really be ALL IN ALL if it were necessary to ascribe fully real being to anything else? This cluster of ideas might threaten to have serious consequences, of which both the Christian and the Philosopher may want to keep track. But surely the literary critic, reading for the implications of structure and tone, may fairly point to the perfect congruence between a theology of sovereignty and a metaphysics of idealism in even Edwards' *least* philosophical works.

If anything, those works tend to be even less philosophical after the "surprising" events of 1734–35 than before. The successive versions of the *Faithful Narrative* give us very little more explicitly to go on, as Edwards becomes less and less a framer of theses about salvation and more and more a psychological sociologist, not to say a "novelist." Yet even when he is being most particular, Edwards never lets us lose sight of the kind of universe we are in.

The four-year-old Phebe Bartlet retires into the "closet" of her own mind and speaks directly to God. She speaks of heaven and prefers it to earth—preferring God to mother, father, and "little sister Rachel." But she has not "been in heaven," and it is not "any imagination of any thing seen with bodily eyes that she called God"; her experience is not memory or fancy of anything earthly, but a direct idea or sense of the divine order. And after her remarkable experiences she cares for the "plums" of this world not at all; her true satisfaction is merely "to sup with God." What most people would call a metaphor is to her more real than what most people would call substantial nourishment. Accordingly, Scripture and catechism become more real to her than anything else; and she is well prepared for death.[19] She is already living out of time and in that true space which saints—of whatever age, and with or without the aid of Sir Isaac—know as God's body.

Metaphysics may be a grown-up pastime, but evidently the sense of reality can come to anybody; so that Edwards' adult accounts add scarcely anything at all to the childish paradigm. Abigail Hutchinson is not a well woman. But she is no enthusiast of diseased imagination; the only effects of her "direct intercourse" with God is that the healthy wish to become "meek and lowly in heart" replaces her sickly tendency always to be "murmuring at God's providence"; and that she now has a "sense of glory of God in the trees." She dies "without and struggling."[20] Sarah Pierrepont Edwards does not die but lives, gloriously, in a crescendo of "extraordinary transports" and as the crowning literary glory of Edwards' *Thoughts Concerning the Revival*. By now Edwards is distinguishing his truly spiritual cases from those involving "distempers catched from Mr. Whitefield and Mr. Tennent"; and, among other things, one catches hints of metaphysical distinctions. Mrs. Edwards' experiences are not those of an "enthusiastical season" but of "the eternal world." For a time, indeed, our own shadow-world entirely disappears: "All that is pleasant and glorious, and all that is terrible in this world, seemed perfectly to vanish into nothing, and nothing to be left but God." She does not become "antinomian" in after-moments, of course, but the essence of her experience is that a sense of "the awful majesty of God" serves not only "to take away her bodily strength" but also, at times, to "overwhelm body and soul." She knows she is nothing, and the all-sufficiency of God comes to her in the divine definition: "I AM THAT AM."[21]

This is piety, of course, and not philosophy; experience and not metaphysics. Sarah can scarcely be thought to have reflected on

the implications of Locke and Newton any more than Phebe Bartlet. But Edwards' idealist imagination shines through the experiences of his literary creations: in grace God is perceived to be ALL
IN ALL because in metaphysics it is only to him that real being
can be ascribed.

Edwards' own experiences, recorded so passionately in the
"Personal Narrative," could easily be made to yield the same
"philosophical" conclusions. The ardent man who learned to
worship Sovereign Authority in the awful voice of the thunder,
and who prayed for a complete self-abasement so "that God might
be ALL ," is clearly related—whatever Edwards' later theory of
identity might imply—to the excited adolescent who intuitively
knew that Newton's occult atoms and Locke's occult substance
could be nothing *but* the omnipresent, regular, and powerful will
of God. And no doubt the two descend in about equal parts from
the precocious boy who studied spiders, spinning and being blown
out to sea, and who dared proclaim design to govern in a thing so
small. Spiders, material substance, and even (as the self-abnegating
piety of the "Personal Narrative" spiritually forecasts the literally
self-destructive philosophy of the *Original Sin*) the substantial
self: all must be sacrificed to what Melville might call "the ever-
encroaching appetite for God."

3

But before we create for ourselves the impression that Edwards'
Calvinism and his idealism are *nothing but* the (perfectly inter-
changeable) theological and philosophical counterparts of one
another, and that there is in his career neither chronological
development nor any meaningful disposition of aboriginal convictions or basic insights or root metaphors into philosophical discourse, we should remind ourselves that the pious narratives of
the Awakening lead us directly into the rational distinctions of
the *Religious Affections* and, indirectly, across our line of period-
ization, to the strenuous argumentation of *The Freedom of the
Will.* It is one thing frankly to doubt that Edwards' "conversion"
to sovereignty actually constituted so radical a change of mind as
the "Personal Narrative" would have us believe. But it is quite
another to imply that nothing new *ever* happens to Edwards. There
may well be, even as Perry Miller insisted, only one fundamental

perception in Edwards, repeated over and over again, in a variety of idiomatic approximations and with various degrees of indirection.[22] But it is impossible to deny that, after the public challenge offered by the writings of Chauncey (and others) in the 1740s, Edwards began a process of more and more careful philosophical explanation.

The *Religious Affections* is, clearly the "transitional" work: by the time Edwards has got down to cases (in Parts II and III), we are back in the sociological world of the Awakening and back on that meta-psychological terrain known as "the distinguishing of spirits"; but before we get there, we must pass through a moderately technical discussion of the human "faculties." And it is here, precisely, that we have to begin to take account of Schneider's second large assertion about the presence of philosophy in Edwards—namely, that the later works introduce us to a philosophical terminology entirely different from that of his early idealist deductions.

Once again, it is easy to see what he means. What we have now, in place of bold speculations about the ultimately mental character of reality and the logical primacy of the divine mind within that system (in place even of pious echoes or analogues of such theories), is a set of argumentative observations about the relation of affectivity and action; or, equally, the nonrelation of speculation and action. The shift seems radical indeed, but we would do well to resist the immediate conclusion that Edwards has drastically altered his basic views. On the one hand, Edwards is taking up a problem as posed by the scholastic or relatively rationalistic challenge of Chauncey; at this level of debate, all he feels called upon to show is that, within the very "world" supposed by Chauncey's common sense, a better case can be made for the religious use of affection or will rather than of reason. And, on the other hand, the explicit "faculty psychology" of Part I does eventually lead us on, later in the work, to the same sort of "ideal" hints we have heard before.

At issue, initially, is not the absolute problem of BEING, in which *of course* everything threatens to fall back upon God—and on which, incidentally, Edwards would be as hesitant to instruct Chauncey as he would his own Northampton parish. At issue, rather, are the relative problems of human perception and motivation which must, on premise, presume a certain reality for human affections and motions. Challenged by a rationalist on his "pietist theory of love, Edwards responds with an "affective theory of will": to will means no more than to be affected or attracted or inclined; to be free (as he will repeat with greater force and clarity later) is merely to have the power to execute inclinations, whatever they may be, and however they may be thought all complicatedly to have come about. Philosophy, in his view, can tell us no more. So that what remains to be said is, theoretically at least, very simple—as evident to common sense as it is patently the meaning of Scripture: true religion consists in having and executing holy inclinations. Chauncey, therefore, will please desist from embarrassing the work of God's powerfully inclining Word and Spirit on the basis of either his attenuated scholastic sensibility or his tediously reiterated philosophical misapprehensions. For his own part, Edwards will get on with the main theological business of providing a detailed explication and elaboration of the affections or inclinations which Scripture teaches are the direct and proper work of the Spirit in conversion.

And yet if Edwards is impatient here, dealing with the preliminaries of philosophical psychology, and using tools which touch only the structure of human motivation as it may be observed by anybody who will pay close and unbiased attention to what consciously occurs, he is nevertheless very expansively and lovingly detailed when he arrives, in his first "distinguishing sign," at his own peculiar, Lockean definition of grace. After he has dismissed certain affective states as inconclusive signs of saving spiritual influence, and before he is well launched into his lengthy and sensitive (but finally circular) excursion into the true science of spiritual semiology (which may also be read, more simply, as his phenomenology of the Christian life),[23] he once again reminds us that grace can be, after all, nothing but an idea.

Some have called grace a "light," and though this may confuse "the common and less considerate and understanding sort of people," such a usage is perfectly proper; in speaking of spiritual things "we are forced to use figurative expressions" and, of course, "scripture itself abounds with such like figurative expressions." But if we may usefully think of grace coming to us as, metaphorically, a light to illuminate our darkened spiritual perceptions, still in strict philosophical propriety we receive it as an *idea*—once again identified with a *sense,* and once again epitomized as a *taste.* The Lockean paradigm reappears unchanged from the "Divine and Supernatural Light," and Edwards now publicly signals this context by suggesting that grace might most properly be defined (generically, at least) as a "new simple idea"; it is a "nucleus" or "kernel" of experience, unitary and indivisible, a cornerstone and building block of consciousness which is not to be had by what Locke and Edwards both call "composition."[24] And once again we are forced to ask why—according to what ultimate scheme of things?—this must be so.

In fact, this is the only really useful direction our analysis can take. For, on the one hand, all our explicitly theological questions are answered in advance. Edwards has already taken great pains to explain that a "spiritual" idea is not an idea of the soul as opposed to the body; that it is a special rather than a common communication from the Spirit; that having this utterly simple but remarkably new idea is equivalent to an actual indwelling of the Spirit; and that (accordingly) it makes possible a whole new range of affections or inclinations, even as the *new* simple idea joins with other (old) simple ideas in an endlessly rich "composition" of complex ideas, themselves all made now apocalyptically new by that very composition.[25] And on the other hand, we are shut off from asking "modern" or experimental psychological questions about the sensory mechanisms by which all this comes about, as effectively as we were in the "Supernatural Light." Edwards is appropriating Locke to his own purposes, of course, and we can argue about the legitimacy of his use. But clearer than anything else is the fact that he is taking Locke in a Berkeleyan rather than a Hartleyan direction. He simply does not care to ask mechanistic or materialistic questions about whether the Spirit-as-Idea can more properly be said to enter at the eyes, the ears, the taste, or the touch, or about what physiological motions might be thought thereafter to occur.[26]

All we can say for sure, apparently, is that the experience is *like* that of a person seeing color for the first time; or even more appropriately, tasting honey for the first time. Though Edwards seems to fuss inordinately (and even to contradict himself) about whether the persons in his analogies are supposed to be equipped with the general power of sight or taste before their new experience, he nevertheless makes it quite clear that in his primary, theological case no new "faculty" is given; there is, physiologically, no "sixth sense" which might be described by analogy with the other five. It is merely that, experientially, the saint has a new, subjective awareness of divine things, sensory and affective in kind.[27] It is simply that—by a process we cannot begin to understand, but with effects which the saint cannot fail gloriously to confess and which the impartial observer is constrained however reluctantly to admit— an entirely new relation to reality has come about. Some power- fully regenerating experience has changed everything. Some radi- cally simple insight into the way things are has made reality secure and the economy of salvation intelligible—and both lovable, as God's stable idea and sovereign will.

If we are willing to take Edwards seriously here, we can, I think, grasp the insight that holds his whole world-view together. And unless we are willing to take Edwards this way, the various argu- ments of the *Religious Affections* (and of the other works as well) must always seem factitious, a congeries of separate propositions, got up on the ground, *ad hoc* and *ex parte,* for the essentially reactionary and arguably obscurantist purpose of rescuing a deeply embattled orthodoxy. At issue is not only Edwards' philosophical elegance but also his spiritual coherence.

To pursue Edwards in the single direction he would consider legitimate is to ask why grace can be explained entirely according to a "way of ideas" and in no other way. Grace has always been a double sort of divine influence—which enlightened the mind *and* strengthened the will; a special infusion of knowledge *and also* a special aid in the will's somewhat separate struggle to love and enact the good and to hate and avoid the evil. Here there is only *one* influence: a new sense of reality, from which everything else immediately and automatically flows. According to the new and simplified paradigm, all God has to do to convert (and progressively sanctify) a man is to grant him, by his Spirit, some sense, some sight or taste—by Lockean conflation, some *idea*—of the way He truly is. To know BEING at all is to know enough.

In one respect, internally, Edwards' elegant simplification of the logistics of grace is accomplished, obviously, by means of the very relationship Edwards has posited between intellect and will; or, more precisely, between consciousness and affectivity. The will "is *as* the last dictate of the understanding"; or, more simply, we love according as our signficant experiences have been. And it is toward this radical simplification and psychologizing of grace that Edwards' much discussed and celebrated unification of the "faculties" ultimately points.[28] But this is hardly Edwards' ultimate consideration. With BEING ITSELF always before him, how can he be other than impatient with the question of whether accidental man needs only light or both light and heat in order to love the essential God? What concerns Edwards far more deeply, it seems to me, is the "objective" status of grace as a constituent principle in an essentially "ideal" world. What kind of "thing," after all, could grace be in the stubtle world Locke and Newton have implied?

To admit the legitimacy of this placement of the question is to see the answer at once. If "nature," as we ordinarily understand it, has no true existence anywhere "but in the divine mind"; and if it comes to us as a communication of "his determination, his care, and his design, that Ideas shall be united forever, just so, and in such a manner, as is agreeable to such a series";[29] then how can that "grace" which theologians know to be its counterpart be thought of any less simply? If nature is nothing but so many of God's ideas regularly communicated to all men's minds, then what could grace *conceivably* be but one very special idea communicated to the saints alone? If all God does ordinarily is maintain a stable sequence of simple ideas, then surely it is philosophically illegitimate to suppose that his extraordinary or supernatural activity involves anything more than the unique communication of his Spirit as a "new simple idea." Any separate form of spiritual "strengthening" would be as quaint a premise in divinity as that of material substance in metaphysics. Entities are not to be multiplied. And if the so-called "corporeal" word "is to no advantage but to the spiritual,"[30] then surely no one will imagine that the spiritual world itself need turn back to the corporeal for help.

This insight takes us, then, close to the heart not only of Edwards' system but also to his sense of life in the world. By itself, the premise that God obtrudes Himself, as a simple idea, into the normal order of human consciousness and affectivity seems merely odd, a strangely pious guess at what Poe would call the "Plot of God." By itself, it suggests the magical rescue of a bad romance rather than the inevitable effect of a well-made tale—or of a really elegant proof in higher geometry. But taken together with an idealist epistemology and metaphysics, it comes to seem not only sleek and efficient but really inevitable. All God does in grace is all God does in nature—furnish ideas to other minds.

At the same time, however, this insight takes us to the precarious edge of intelligibility. And it leaves us, for the moment, with some very nasty problems. Granted, now, that grace is only a special idea in the midst of a nature which is, as it were, "already" ideal. And granted that the prime effect of this very special idea is to give any man or woman (or child) who receives it the sense of a direct and absolute dependence on God's continuous activity at least as compelling as any philosopher's reasoning. Still we may want to ask where all this really does leave the human creature, considered in himself. A man may know, from the virtual conversion afforded by the idealist revolution in metaphysics, that his world is God's will and idea. And he may come to sense, from the conversion effected by one very special idea, that God is just what Scripture says, BEING ITSELF; and that he must be affectively *to man* what he effectively is *in reality,* ALL IN ALL. But what, in the long aftermath of these surprising conversions, can he say about himself? If God is the only substance, and if ideas are His only form of creative expression, what can Edwards say about the ontological status of that human form of consciousness which regularly receives those ideas called nature or, by a different law no less regular, the special idea called grace, and which reflects on the conditions and meaning of that reception?

Common sense or pragmatism is, here, no solution. Furthermore, to weaken and grant a truly "substantial" (even if purely "spiritual") existence to man is to sin against sovereignty; it is, very likely, to commit the "unpardonable sin" against the Spirit whose intimations of sovereignty have seemed to complete the guesses of metaphysics. What remains, I should judge, is pantheism—which seems a very reckless philosophical gambit indeed. While it may be impossible to show that Edwards ever consciously adopted such a position, still it is in that direction he seems bound to move; and it is with a position very like pantheism that we will see him struggling when, in the crucial work on *Original Sin,* he is forced to face the tendencies and limits of his system.[31]

4

In order to provide an adequately "conclusive" account of the *Original Sin,* it is necessary to treat other major works (and other significant dimensions of Edwards' career as a Christian Philosopher) somewhat briefly and indirectly. From one point of view this must seem a very dubious strategy indeed, for we are just now arrived at the "period" of Edwards' more full and explicit, public philosophizing. *The Freedom of the Will* completes the analysis of volition begun in the *Religious Affections,* and it can be argued that this effort constitutes Edwards' principal claim both to modernity and to serious consideration as a major figure in the history of philosophy. Moreover, the brief but brilliant *Nature of True Virtue,* which also intervenes, is in fact the single work by this "very eminent Christian" which is purely philosophical in structural essence. At issue, over all, might be the justice (and the relevance) of the claim that Edwards' philosophical terms change "in his later and maturer works."

At the same time, however, to place concluding emphasis on the *Original Sin* is more than an abbreviating convenience or an argumentative strategy. For several reasons. On the one hand, according to the model of the Edwardsian career I am proposing, the *Freedom* and the *Virtue* both amount to species of polemical delay: in both, it seems to me, Edwards argues penultimate points against peripheral persons. Only in the *Original Sin* does he come back, once again and perhaps inevitably, to the very heart of his *own* problems—which, as we have seen, loom everywhere in the early works, palpably present in their visible absence. And on the other hand, according to the model of Edwardsian criticism I am proposing, it is only in the *Original Sin* that philosophy and theology assume their most "exemplary" roles and relations. There, most clearly, a whole metaphysic is explicitly brought to bear on a crucial theological issue. Let us look at this second, more formal problem first.

The *Virtue* tries to exclude specifically Calvinist (or even Christian) theology altogether. But it preserves its philosophical purity "artificially," as it were, by maintaining a strict "academic" separation of "disciplines" in which the author himself does not ultimately believe, and which may not reflect the true state of mind or soul of any actual believer, or any doubter either. The case is not without instructional value to modern Christian academics who might wish to see, for example, Thomistic philosophy established on a secular basis alone; and less tendentiously, it does represent, *de facto*, one of the models according to which a Christian can "do philosophy"—with his Christianity as glaringly absent and obvious as his metaphysics might be in a work on grace.[32] But it does not, quite evidently, introduce us into the psychological or imaginative mixture at the heart of that Christian Philosopher we call Jonathan Edwards. From this personal center he himself deliberately holds us off.

From this point of view—that of persons as against disciplines— the *Freedom* is clearly more instructive. It is, in its aggregate, explicitly some sort of Christian-Philosophical hybrid; and, in that regard, its mixed mode is a somewhat fairer model of Edwards' own mixed mind, as he struggles with opponents who are finding some brand of common-sense philosophy sufficient to overturn the venerable teachings of the reformed tradition. At the same time, however, we are likely to find its peculiar mix just a trifle odd—as, formally, at least, theology is brought to the aid of philosophy rather than the other way around. The Christian problem of "Freedom" may take its ultimate beginning in the literary interpretation of St. Paul; but Edwards' own book begins in a very strict (and modern) philosophical manner. Edwards defines the area of freedom through a careful analysis of the terms used in moral discourse and then tries to show that other analyses will always prove incoherent. So far so good: it is Arminianism and not (as charged) Calvinism which is introducing unintelligibility into the moral world. But obviously Edwards feels challenged to meet another charge as well—that Calvinism is inconsistent with Christian revelation as well as with man's ordinary sense of the moral life. And so theology enters as Edwards begins to appeal (as if to a "fact") to that perfect sort of "virtue," perfectly consistent with moral determinism, which Scripture forces its adherents to suppose as the moral habits of God and Christ. It is at this point that the modern reader, fairly addressed at the beginning in terms of his rationality alone, may begin to have difficulties with the validity of his own presence in Edwards' audience.

I do not mean to suggest that nothing like this ever happens in the *Original Sin*. Early in that work, indeed, something even more

troublesome seems to occur: Edwards begins with that much discussed and much heralded purpose of presenting a fully empirical
and fully historical account of the moral state of mankind relative
to depravity or its opposite, but he proceeds immediately to treat
the Judeo-Christian scriptures as if they were a neutral account of
the problem, and (what is probably worse) he presents an analysis
which is thoroughly infected with definitions of depravity and integrity which it is the very purpose of many books of that Scripture
all tendentiously to prescribe. The procedure is worse than circular,
and so no one should ever claim that Edwards' *Original Sin* is notable
for its academic or disciplinary purity.[33] All I mean to suggest is that
by the end of the *Original Sin,* things have got themselves very
instructively straightened out. Thus, when all the chips at last are
down, and that ultimate Christian premise of a universal Fall in
Adam is placed rationally on the line, the full weight of Edwards'
reason is brought to its defense. For this once, at least, Edwards
tries to prove that what his tradition holds most sacred in faith is
inescapably true according to the highest reason of things.

Which brings us around to one other, less formal consideration—
the degree of "ultimacy" which the varieties of "reason" in
Edwards' later works may be supposed to possess. Here the *Freedom* is the more obvious case.

In spite of Edwards' repeated insistence that the *Freedom* was
his absolutely crucial work *contra* the Arminians, and notwith-
standing the high valuation placed on *parts* of it by modern philosophical commentators, it is really impossible to feel that it is a work
in which all of Edwards' intellectual cards are out on the intellectual
table. We may utterly reject the hostile view (of Conrad Wright)
that Edwards does no more than throw sand in the eyes of his
already dim-sighted opponents by tacitly adapting their confused
terminology to his own special use, and then utterly demolishing a
position which no one really held; but still we are left with our
feelings about what the book's most able and sympathetic critic
(Paul Ramsey) calls its "bracketing." Seeking "to catch the agent
in the very act of willing or choosing, and to give an accurate report
of what goes on in the soul or mind in the state of willing and at
the time of willing," Edwards consistently excludes from analysis
("brackets") everything which goes before that very act—including,
of course, the process by which the strongest inclination has come

to be the strongest.[34] Even if we leave aside the opportunity to question the ultimate usefulness of this procedure in producing any clarification beyond the tautological discovery that yes, indeed, we always do pretty much will what we will; and even if we decline to object that the sense of "will" emerging from such a procedure amounts to something like "motor signal sent by the brain to the limbs in walking" and is, at very least, most unlike the more passive sense proposed in the initial conflation of will with affection, inclination, desire, and preference; even if, in short, we feel Edwards solves the problems he elects to face, we may still be left a little unsatisfied.

Possibly we even feel defrauded, in a way we never do in, say, "A Divine and Supernatural Light." Edwards is now "doing" philosophy: let him really do it. Obviously he *has* a theory of what goes before the act of willing. Obviously, as I have already suggested, every reader senses that his theory has something to do with his Calvinism. And obviously, as we are now in a position to observe, it has very much to do with the kind of simple ideas with which a person has been furnished. But none of this comes out. What we get instead—to fill up a whole book—is, negatively, the furious attack on the incoherence of other supposed theories of will and, just a bit more positively, the elaborate demonstration that it is those supposed theories and not Edwards' own which are inconsistent with the ordinary moral life and the extraordinary virtue of God and Christ. We can understand the human and the rhetorical situation perfectly: Edwards is defending as much of his total system as has been challenged by Arminian writers on the will. And we come to the end (I think) less assured that either moral action or Christian virtue requires us to will our willings than we might naively have asserted at the outset. But surely our main response is that Edwards has left out some important pieces of his own intellectual puzzle. Things we easily infer and kindly supply in works of piety we begin to hold out for in works of technical philosophy. It requires an effort of judiciousness to avoid hostility.

It is easy to see that Edwards' terms have indeed changed. But an adequate understanding of this fact involves our seeing that they change in the same way and for the same impatient reasons they had changed in the opening of the *Religious Affections:* the pressure of somebody else's bad "anthropology" is distracting Edwards away from his own proper study—the metaphysics of sovereignty. If we sense any of that higher and more imaginative science amid the empirical observations and logical (or Scriptural) argumentations of the *Freedom,* it is only, implicitly, in Edwards' denial that man, however "free" to execute his intentions, is nevertheless not possessed of any originating "power" over them. That "power"—which Locke had suggested might be all we really mean by substance, which Newton had imagined to hold atoms together and apart, and which Edwards had identified as the continuous, regular, and creative "will" of God—belongs to God alone. Man may be said to possess "freedom" but never the "power" which is the same as BEING.[35] And so, whatever the *Freedom* may say to historians of philosophy, its literary meaning (provoked by and expressed with reference to misguided and inept "men of God," such as Whitby and Watts, who imagine that something like autonomous power in man is necessary to the cause of religion) is something like this: For God's sake hold your tongue about "the freedom of the power of the faculty of will" and let me love BEING.

Accordingly, the most sympathetic view we can take of the *Freedom* is that it is not the book Edwards most wanted to write. It may have aroused his polemic instincts, but it did not draw out his imagination. Those arrogant Arminians needed to be answered; and, in the end, *faute de mieux,* the task fell to Edwards. He would answer them on their own terms and, for the most part, *only* on their own terms; that would, of course, involve changing his own. And while the process of learning to meet worldly adversaries on the empirical grounds of rational psychology might be part of a philosophical maturation, it is utterly wrongheaded to think of the *Freedom* as a work in which Edwards begins to work himself out of his childish, imaginative idealism.

The *Virtue,* at first glance, seems an entirely different sort of work: it is much less exasperated in tone and (as I have suggested) much more "pure" to the modern mind. Much more coolly now Edwards sets about the task of trying to say what kind of "beauty or excellence" both "natural" and "true" virtue may amount to. The search-and-destroy polemics have largely disappeared, even though Edwards clearly has certain ill-considered and/or sentimental users of Francis Hutcheson very much in mind. Nor is there any overt attempt to correlate his proofs from natural ethics with scriptural teachings which everybody is supposed to know and accept, even though it is perfectly plain that Edwards' prime law of "benevolence to Being in General" is intended as a precise counterpart of the first great "commandment"—to love God with one's whole mind, heart, and soul. In short, Edwards seems totally in control: the argument seems to be, if not metaphysical, nevertheless exclusively *his own*. And to the extent that one can agree (with Roland Delattre) that the section on "Excellence" in Edwards' "Notes on the Mind" provides us with his key term, to that extent one would have to posit the fundamental importance of the *Virtue*.

But though it can be argued that "excellence" is the highest name for the expressive activity of God on the practical or moral side; and though "beauty" may be the primary attribute by which He is apprehended by other minds, still it cannot be maintained that this is His highest name or the ultimate aspect under which the metaphysician must regard His essence as such. That of course must always remain the name and the aspect of BEING. And so, however useful we may find the *Virtue* to our own situation in ethics or aesthetics; or however satisfactory we may judge its methodological purity, to which I have already referred; it seems clear that it is not *quite* the book which takes us back to the ultimate and essential Edwards. And we must be very careful, at some level of criticism, not to confuse our academic judgment that Edwards may have done his most effective philosophical thinking when he was provoked, by the fashionable ideas of others, into the subsidiary disciplines of psychology, ethics, or aesthetics, with our personal perception that his own organizing insights and most fundamental intentions lay in the area of idealistic metaphysics.[36]

We may sense, perhaps, that we are on the verge of something crucial in this area when we find Edwards stressing that the "analogy" between "secondary" (or, as it were, material) and "primary" (or, as it were, spiritual) excellencies may be perceived only by those who have already had experience of the latter, more real sort; that "saints" (to use the language Edwards here strictly excludes) can see the world as God's perfect poetic body, whereas others see only forms and relations. Thomists, we may remind ourselves, would teach otherwise—that the analogy of being works "up" as well as "down," before as well as after the operation of grace; that analogy beginning all innocently with the natural constitutes, in fact, the natural man's most natural and direct road to God. But all Platonists (including, not incidentally, Edgar Poe) think otherwise; the ability to make significant poetic or theologic sense of the appearances or "shadows" of the world seems absolutely to depend on one's having first got out of the cave and seen the "divine and supernatural light." Edwards, however, is totally unwilling to go into such matters here. He never frankly raises the question of *why* analogy should work one way and not the other. For our present, limited, ethical purposes it is enough to be *told* that no sense of proportion between the shadow-beauties of the creation and the spiritual excellencies of the Creator can be perceived by the mere amateur of natural harmonies; such a proportionate sense is "the consequence of the existence of [true] benevolence, and not the ground for it."[37]

Edwards knows perfectly well that he is flirting with the edge of his own metaphysical abyss, and he very consciously pulls himself back. He allows himself to imagine that his reader may be worried about that absolutely first question of why the natural and the spiritual worlds should be analogous or "correspondential" *at all*. But he raises the question only to "bracket" it: "Why such analogy in God's works pleases him, it is not needful now to inquire."[38] Followed out, such a problem would lead to metaphysical questions about BEING ITSELF, perhaps to the ultimate theological question of its Trinitarian structure; and all such questions are being put off, presumably, for a more direct and comprehensive treatment elsewhere in Edwards' many-mansioned summa. For the present inquiry it is sufficient to observe that it did *in fact* please God to establish analogy or correspondence of the secondary with the primary beauty as a "law of nature," just as He was pleased to establish, at the secondary level itself, gravity. What we could possibly understand by "gravity" or what a "law of nature" might signify in the physics of idealism, Edwards will not tell us here. Once again we are put off.

It is just this sort of deferral or bracketing or evasion which does *not* occur at the embattled conclusion of the *Original Sin*. There, finally, where Edwards' theological difficulties are deepest, he brings forward his most fundamental, original, and authentic metaphysical insight. The "distinguishing mark" of the *Original Sin* is that in it, alone among the published essays and treatises, Edwards is willing to bring the full weight of his idealistic metaphysics—preserved intact from his earliest unpublished works—explicitly to bear on a problem that has taken its rise in the traditional interpretation of a specific Scripture by a historical community of believers. And that, I take it, is a rather perfect model of the faith-and-reason problem as most commonly apprehended: rational speculation to the aid of traditional belief.

In writing about the *Original Sin* one is tempted to suggest (in imitation of Henry Adams, writing about Aquinas) that here Edwards placed the last stone in the bold, aspiring, and majestic arch that was his own Christian-Philosophic summa. What holds one back, chiefly, is an ironic sense of an opposite sort of truth—namely, that the place where Edwards' theology and his metaphysics come most tellingly together is the same place where his whole edifice comes tumbling down. Or, to change the metaphor, when he brings his highest reason to the rescue of his deepest faith, we see how profoundly problematic both are, and for precisely the same reasons. In any event, it must be with some such sense of ultimate catastrophe or embarrassment, shadowing an ultimate imaginative triumph, that we approach the conclusion of the *Original Sin*.

5

For the purpose of displaying Edwards' daring but disastrous rescue of theology's embattled first premise by an almost wildly imaginative appeal to philosophy's last word on idealism, it is not particularly necessary to judge, or even carefully to trace, the progress of the admittedly "impure" argument that winds its way through *The Great Christian Doctrine of Original Sin Defended*. It is absolutely necessary, however, to see exactly where we are when—in Part Four, chapter III—Edwards makes his fervent "appeal to such as are not wont to content themselves with judging by a superficial appearance and view of things, but are habituated to examining things strictly and closely."[39] We need to understand not only the specific intellectual issue which occasions but also the contextual pressures which motivate this remarkably direct (and for Edwards nearly unique) appeal to a strictly philosophical audience. The terms of this address are so unlike those of the *Freedom,* which makes its decisive appeal to the meaning of "freedom" in ordinary moral discourse, that we can hardly fail to sense a state of intellectual crisis.

At issue, most specifically, is "that great objection against the imputation of Adam's sin to his posterity [namely] that such imputation is unjust and unreasonable, inasmuch as Adam and his posterity are not one and the same" (p. 389). It is perfectly true, of course, that the legalistic or "forensic" idea of God's "imputing" Adam's sin to anyone else will always present serious *rational* difficulties. And nowhere, I suppose, will these be greater than within a "Calvinist" emphasis on God's *voluntaristic* sovereignty, where God's will or word or wisdom (as distinguished from some universal rationality) is held to be the sole, the essential, and even the "constitutive" rule of justice. Furthermore, since imputation is one of only two principal explanations of the relation between Adam's original sin and our sinful origination available to Edwards, and especially since it is the one most relied on in his particular tradition, he seems bound to face the problem in a fairly direct way.[40] To "bracket" this question would amount to a very serious sin of intellectual omission. And so when Edwards does face the question of trying reasonably to explain God's sovereign decision to regard all men as having sinned in Adam, that moment, whenever it occurs, must be fraught with a certain tense excitement.

But in addition to these "traditional" difficulties, Edwards has some specific rhetorical and even logical problems of his own making. One almost imagines they are deliberate, to make the chapter in which he appeals to his first philosophy as dramatically climactic as he senses it is intellectually crucial. And these emplotted difficulties also add to the interest of what turns out to be, for a Calvinist, a remarkably rationalistic attempt to prove that what God declares to be the case in "imputing" Adam's sin to each and all of his individual children is also highly consistent with the nature of "things," as that scheme can now be understood according to certain "late improvements in philosophy" (p. 385).

Edwards is not, of course, going to assert that "the great Christian doctrine of original sin" is, in all its Calvinistic ramifications, a self-evident truth, like an axiom in logic or geometry; from the proposition that "it is necessary some being should Eternally be," for example, nothing follows relative to Adam and us. Edwards even seems willing to concede that our own situation, as corrupted children of Adam, might have been otherwise, had God thought, declared, or "constituted" things otherwise. As a contingent arrangement, that complicated economy is (unlike the necessary economy of the Trinity) incapable of rationalistic proof *a priori*.[41] But Edwards is going to assert that to understand and rationally accept the justice of God's imputation of Adam's personal guilt requires no *special* invocation of divine voluntarism, and no understanding of the nature of reality, beyond what any decently reformed (i.e., idealistic) metaphysics will furnish. In order to show this, Edwards seems to have arranged his book so that he will have to appeal to his metaphysics—and to an audience willing to witness the appeal—only once, and at precisely the right time. So that if our sense of personal engagement and embattled challenge is strong, our sense of strategy is even stronger.

Edwards has been arguing (as the burden of Part One) that all men do fall to sinning, seriously and repeatedly, almost as soon as they are able; and as for the rivalry between sin and virtue, who will seriously contend (he asks) that there is much *true* virtue in all the world? As a literary inventory of the human scene, Edwards' gloomy survey matches anything in Ecclesiastes, or Augustine, or Melville; as poetic invention, his myth of the Fall can fairly stand beside that of Plato and Cardinal Newman. And whatever we may think of the moral or sociological "science" involved, it is necessary to "grant" (even if we do not "concede") a universal tendency to sin if we are to follow Edwards' strategy. From such a "steady tendency" he imagines any reasonably empirical person will necessarily infer a "steady cause." An adequate cause, he argues, could only be corrupted principles of perception and inclination, a corrupted "nature"; and, as it seems evident to him, Scripture's "genetic" explanation of this natural given would seem to be Adam's Fall (rather than any malign creativity on God's part).

That Scripture actually does teach, clearly and throughout, such an interpretation of the human condition becomes the exegetical substance of the argument in Parts Two and Three— as the *Original Sin* begins to reveal quite clearly that its basic mode is scriptural theology and not rational philosophy; and certainly not empirical science. With impressive learning and marvelous hermeneutical clarity, Edwards argues that Taylor and other liberals are making literary nonsense out of both Testaments; that to reject the premise of original sin as Scripture's basic *donnée* and initial plot-event is not only to reject Paul's masterful exegesis of Genesis and everything since, but also to render the account of redemption literally as irrelevant as the redemptive act itself would be, on liberal premises, spiritually "nugatory."[42] In short, the Christian Scripture makes no decent literary sense unless universal depravity is a fact, with Adam figuring as somehow the cause or root explanation.

And so by the time Edwards comes to his last part—"Containing Answers to Objections"—he understandably supposes that very much is already accomplished: liberal sociology has been denied *de facto;* and liberal hermeneutics have been vigorously disputed, from the structural integrity of the text itself. Edwards' implied audience, let us recall, is entirely Christian in professed loyalty; whatever the exact state of its relation to the reformed tradition, it still honors Scripture as God's uniquely revealed word. To show, therefore, that the very coherence of Scripture depends on the perfect parallelism of Adam and Christ as root cause and root cure of the human condition would be, to them, somewhat more than the exemplar in literary structuralism it may be to us. And by the end of Part Three, Edwards imagines he has essentially proven the complex original-sin case by showing just that. But though his work as moral sociologist and as exegete is now completed, his work as Christian Philosopher is just beginning. Far more than mere odds and ends of left-over reflections, his "Answers to Objections" are identically that work.

Edwards' liberal or "supernatural rationalist" opponents are objecting, most simply, that Scripture could not *possibly* teach what Calvinism says it teaches because such a "truth" would be radically inconsistent with all the rest of reality. Adam *cannot* be the cause of our sin because the sinful choice, like any other human choice, is an absolutely free and completely personal thing: God could not make a man sinful in Adam any more than he could make him a carpenter through his father's election of that calling. Example might count for something, but there must always be personal choice or "sin" makes no rational sense. Hence any religious system founded on the premise of sin prior to individual human choice utterly disqualifies itself. Scripture *cannot* teach that and still be Scripture. Reason must judge: God himself cannot reveal what is unreasonable, cannot declare the inherently unintelligible to be true.[43]

Or, alternately, if we supposed that somehow He could, He would not be God to us. A "god" who could make us guilty in Adam, thousands of years before our birth, would be in effect a devil-god, a poisonous moral monster worse than any Dr. Rappaccini. He and not we would truly be the "author of depravity." The only proper response to such a god would be an Ahab-like defiance. God must be good as well as reasonable or life is absurd and not worth living.

The question of how such a full-bodied rationalism came to have widespread credibility within a basically voluntarist tradition is a fascinating one, as Perry Miller has shown; but it need not detain us here.[44] Probably it is sufficient to observe that here, as elsewhere, Edwards felt the popular threat of philosophical objections to the religion of his tradition. Or perhaps we may want to observe that a thinker who began his intellectual career with certain "ontological" (perhaps even "Cartesian") reflections on the rational necessity of ABSOLUTE BEING within a universal system of noncontradiction is probably not the man to ask whether his opponents can draw Leviathan up with a hook and let it go at that. What concerns us, much more fundamentally, is the strategic disposition of the answer Edwards gives to the many-headed but really single-minded liberal objection against the rational justice of the Calvinist scheme.

How, we might ask ourselves, has the problem of "imputation" come to be *the* great objection? Clearly it is *one* such. Arguably it is the one to which many others might be reduced. But such a reduction would have to be *made*. And my own penultimate point is that Edwards has, quite specifically, made things just this way: so that, when the last or greatest objection is made—about Calvinism and reality—he can respond with a single metaphysical proof of their utter consistency.

As a "first" objection, Edwards gives the obvious and humanly very telling liberal protest in its moral form: "men's being born in

sin, without their choice . . . is inconsistent with the nature of sin"
(p. 375). Surely this might be the last or climactic objection in
somebody's scheme, but Edwards treats it (here at least) in a per-
functory way. To be sure: he has answered it at very great length
elsewhere, in the *Freedom*, by arguing that the premise of choice
before choice is an incoherent theory of human action; that to
avoid the trap of positing an infinite regress of choices we must
come at last not to an *ur* choice but to some principle of nature
(of perception and inclination) from which all choices can be
thought to proceed. He has alluded to this performance earlier in
the *Original Sin* and he merely mentions it here; he does not mean
to repeat himself. This might be simple weariness. Or it might be
intellectual economy: explicit reference to careful work done elsewhere is, as all scholars must know, not the same as "bracketing."
But still this psychological and moral problem might have been
presented as an ultimate one. We can easily imagine how, if the
Freedom case really were the intellectually crucial and not just the
polemically prominent one, Edwards might come around to this
place at the last, and end by showing—once more, with feeling—
that "it all" hinges on the observable structure of human motivation. Patently it does not, as Edwards' strategy shows.

Somewhat longer and more energetic is Edwards' answer to a
"second" objection—that to suppose a corrupted nature as the
fountain of all men's sinful choices is "to make him who is the
author of their being, the author of depravity" (p. 380). Edwards
presumes that this objection implies some active "corrupting" on
God's part, and so he answers with the essentially Thomistic (and
surely borrowed) theory of the *dona superaddita,* the reinvention
of which some critics have taken as a major accomplishment.[45]
Simply put: Adam had certain "gifts" or "principles" which we do
not now naturally possess (which are, in the simplified Edwardsean
economy of grace, nothing but the fruits of a certain simple idea
of God); when Adam sinned God withdrew those "principles"—
necessarily, since God's own Spirit-as-Idea could not be supposed
to maintain residence in a house of sin. All we inherit from Adam,
therefore, is a *lack;* and hence the whole course of man's depravity
can be explained without for a moment imagining *"God's putting*
any evil into the heart, or *implanting* any bad principle, any
corrupt taint, and so becoming the *author* of depravity" (p. 383).

Under this negative hypothesis all we need to explain (according
to Edwards) is why God might be thought to have *withheld* from
us the principles he *withdrew* from Adam. It is *not,* emphatically,
an Augustinian case of "rotten root and rotten branch"; that inelegant (arguably Manichean, blatantly materialist) paradigm drops
away even before Edwards brings forth his idealism. It is much
more nearly a case of "imputation," though Edwards lets us know
that this formulation is "vulgar" rather than philosophically precise; and if Edwards assumes the burden of the traditional term, he
changes its meaning even as he does so. Under his "Thomistic"
hypothesis of gifts-withdrawn, "imputation" is less accurately
understood as a case of God's "thinking" guilt "onto" or "into"
his posterity than of God's regarding Adam and his posterity as
sufficiently identical to "justify" the decision to withhold from
the latter what was positively forfeited by the former—so that,
without gracious protection, men universally become the sinners
we observe them historically to be. Quite obviously, questions of
rational justice are still deeply at issue here; but the tendency of
Edwards' argument is to minimize them by shifting the ground
from legal or moral theory to metaphysics. Given Edwards' subtle
redefinition of the problem, "imputation" turns from the moralis-
tic question of how, in all justice, God could make or declare all
men to be sinners before any human act on their part into the
ontological question of how, in all reason, God could possibly
treat Adam and all other men as the same moral person.

What happens over the course of Edwards' several "Answers to
Objections" is that the various meanings which are subtly merged
in the simple but powerful liberal protest that God "*cannot* make
another man sinful in Adam" are subtly taken apart into three
very discreet objections, each of which can be met on its own
proper philosophic grounds. The protest from freedom is answered
in terms of Edwards' own "necessitarian" theory. Then comes the
argument concerning what Channing would call "God's moral
character"; and Edwards easily exonerates God from the charge of
active malfeasance. What this analytic scheme leaves for last—
strategically, so that the last confrontation will take place on
Edwards' own most sovereign territory—is the question of identity.
To a carefully set up "great" objection, that "Adam and his posterity are not one and the same," Edwards thinks he has just the
right reply.

The notion of Adam's "federal" headship, his status as human-ity's "parliament man," might have satisfied certain Puritan lawyers who, in their struggle against Tudor and Stuart monarchs, may have thought legal models were perfect paradigms for reality; and who, in the heat of revolution, did not adequately consider that Adam might be holding his place without benefit of universal suf-frage.[46] But it would not satisfy Edwards the Cartesian, the Cam-bridge Platonist, the Newtonian, the Lockean (perhaps, by now, the Berkeleyan and the Humean); certain "late improvements in philosophy" have persuaded him that legalism is as quaint as Ramism. Above all it will not satisfy Edwards the great rationalizer of sovereignty, who thinks he knows a perfectly metaphysical reason according to which Adam and his posterity can be "one and the same." To be sure: any perfectly sovereign, voluntarist, "Calvinist" God might simply "think" Adam's guilt "onto" or "into" the rest of the race with as little embarrassed concern for pitiful human standards as any perfectly sovereign, nominalist, "Lutheran" God might declare a man "just" without any discern-ible reference to the actual state of the ethical case. And although Edwards is perfectly capable of making the nominalist-voluntarist statement that reality is, after all, only what God declares or wills it to be—and of backing it to the hilt with an idealism powerfully suited to the purpose—he does not *merely* say that.

What he says most generally, in his climactic chapter III of Part Four, is that "no *solid* reason can be given, why God, who consti-tutes all other created union or oneness . . . may not establish a constitution" whereby Adam and his natural posterity "should be treated as one" (p. 405). The privileged modern reader, who has made his survey of Edwards from the 1829 text of Sereno Dwight, hears the Edwardsean pun on *solid* and knows where he is at once: back in the world of Edwards' early essays, especially that "Of Atoms and of Perfectly Solid Bodies," where (as Wallace Anderson has shown) Edwards' "immaterialism" began. It began in the perception that "solidity" means nothing other than "resistance," which is the same as God's immediate "power", so that—however incredible it seems to the imaginations of the vulgar—perfect "solidity" is nothing but the atomic unity of divine creativity.[47] Anyone who hears the pun on "solid" hears Edwards asserting that those who are "habituated to examining *things* strictly and closely" will know that the problem of unity and multiplicity is, like the problem of solidity which underlies it, a rational problem in divine "constitutionality" and not a sensory problem of touching or counting. And, ultimately, the mystery of the "atomic" unity of the whole race is not much more (or less) subtle than that of the "powerful" constitution of what appears to us as material substance. Like Emerson, Edwards can make reality "oscillate a little and threaten to dance" whenever he wishes; but most unlike him, Edwards most needs that magical power in reference to the corporate sinfulness of the whole "body" of man.

Critics have given the impression that Edwards' philosophical solution to the theological problem of original sin was to create, *ad hoc,* a perilously outré theory of identity, which his successors (understandably) refused to touch with a very long pole. The alternate and more favorable theory would be that Edwards brilliantly—but "metaphysically," somewhat in the manner of John Donne—imagines an original defense of the humanistic unity of the whole "mainland"of mankind.[48] The truth, I think, is somewhat simpler, though it may imply just as great a degree of intellectual desperation as either of the existing suggestions; and this in spite of the very deliberate strategy we see at work.

What essentially happens in the answer to the liberals' "great" objection is that Edwards reminds his readers how utterly and literally true it is that all reality depends on the creative idea, will, and power of God. Taylor and others have appealed to this idea in an attempt to show that Calvinists blaspheme by imagining that God, who creates every soul directly, brings forth every man in sin. Having evaded this criticism with his theory of the gifts-withdrawn, Edwards now turns the idea powerfully against his adversaries, in a philosophical way they could scarcely have expected, but with a problematic force that threatens to leave them, as Christians, speechless—whatever their sensitivities as to "solidity." Nothing created, Edwards argues, can in the last philosophical analysis be validly considered as *anything but* God's will and idea. What we ordinarily refer to as the "law of nature" must appear to the view of those not content with judging things "by a superficial appearance" as *merely "God's Sovereign Constitution"* (p. 404). "Constitution," which might well be a crucial term in anyone's definition of the idea of "Covenant" as a stipulated or immediately willed form of causality, is now being applied to the entire range of reality. If events like faith and justification go together only because God has fitly decreed or constituted affairs so that this is so, the same can be said of all other events which men perceive as sequential or lawfully causal. The world proceeds because and *just as* God immediately constitutes it, without any sort of material or other troublesome, substantial intermediation.

Such an insight, obviously, has powerful implications for the theory of "identity." The appearance we call "the moon" remains identically itself, from moment to discrete moment, not by any causative virtue in its "substance" which, not being an inherent part of God's Trinitarian essence, it utterly lacks; but only by virtue of God's creatively willing its phenomenal continuance at every instant of man's perceptual time. We might say it continues relatively unchanged because "atoms" continue so; it is, presumably, *still* as proper to say that "God, in the beginning, created such a certain number . . . of such determinate bulk and figure" as it was in the early essays; but only if we still remember that atoms are, essentially, ideal loci of God's creative will.[49] How much more evidently, then, the case of acorn and oak; and the child that fathers the man: how can we account for the identity of these through time without supposing an "immediate *continued* creation of God . . . out of nothing at each moment"? (p. 401). To suppose otherwise is to give "substantial" existence to things other than God and so to deny his inspired and exhaustive self-definition as BEING ITSELF. To suppose that created existences *in any sense* cause the effect of their own continuance from one instant to the next is not only (stupidly) to fail of complete application in Taylor's own "Newtonian" premise that "God, the original of all being, is the *only cause* of all natural effects" (p. 401); but also (blasphemously) to contradict the biblical teaching—well supported by idealist philosophy—that in God "we live, move and have our being" (p. 404).

Even the stubborn problem of "the personal identity of created intelligent beings" yields to the keen analytic reduction: Occam's razor, sharpened by Edwards' idealism, is cutting down unreality left and right. Will anyone suppose that human memory exists apart from the continuous divine volition? That the remembrance of things past can "continue to exist, but by an arbitrary constitution of the creator"? (p. 399). Can *sameness of consciousness* really explain what causes Adam to remain Adam? Or Jonathan, Jonathan? Taylor might indeed be guilty of the fondly self-flattering thought that his own self-awareness at a human point "n" is somehow causative or predictive of a similar awareness at "n + 1"; but this psychological sense of self-identity can be maintained, apparently, only at the sacrifice of philosophical self-consistency. A sufficiently reformed ontology knows the idea of a "substantial" human identity to be illusory; and no such thought would ever, we must suppose, occur to Phebe Bartlet or Sarah Pierrepont.[50]

And so the conclusion relative to Edwards' "present purpose" is almost too obvious to rehearse: since there is no identity or oneness "but what depends on the *arbitrary* constitution of the creator . . . no solid reason can be given, why God . . . may not establish a constitution whereby the natural posterity of Adam . . . should be treated as one with him" (pp. 403-5). And that really is as far as reason can go. In a world where the solidity of the resistance of the power of the atom figures—indeed embodies, except that there are no "bodies"—the all-creativeness of the everywhere-active and immediate will of God, it is not surprising that neither material substances nor human integers really are exactly what they appear. In such a world, Edwards asks, who can give any "solid reason" why Adam and Jonathan are not just as much "one and the same" being as are the excited boy observing spiders and the philosopher in exile ministering to Indians?

Edwards does not claim, we should note, that any John or Jonathan may have ordinary experience of that particular order of divine "constituency" under which a man is, in the creative thought and by the sovereign will, and for the powerful purposes of God, united to Adam. We might infer that intimations of this order of ideal unity come in the same way as does the sense that a person-as-branch may be united to Christ-as-vine; indeed the negative or preliminary part of conversion might be the literary perception (which the idealist philosopher might then explicate) that, indeed in the sight of God I am *nothing but* the old and fallen biblical Adam. But such speculations—which might lead us to the suspicion that the order of our union with Adam is a literary order only, an order of meaning and not at all of being—are well beyond Edwards' present, valid, and unbracketed purposes. He is not, let us recall, required to do it all on the strength of reason alone. He has observed, as he assumes any person may observe, a universal depravity. He has powerfully argued that his opponents cannot really consider themselves Christians unless they admit, on revelation and in faith, that the true name for this state of affairs is an Adamic original sin. And then, finally, against the objection that this cannot, in all reason, possibly be the case, he has shown that in the highest reason our being united to Adam is no less possible than anything else in this whole unsolid and "oscillating" but lawful world. And there the argument stops, where it must.

To be sure, Edwards provides us, in a footnote, with a highly baroque image in which, despite the phenomenal obstacles offered to the vulgar imagination by a show of time, space, and substance, we seem to see "the heart of all the branches" of mankind universally and as one being concur "when the heart of the [Adamic] root, by a full disposition committed the first sin" (p. 392). But we make a very serious mistake, I think, if we take this offering for more than it is: a baroque image, offered in a footnote, by an imagination which apparently does not let imagistic absurdity embarrass or hinder its idealist purposes. The image will not "explicate" in such a way as to tell us more than we already know. If it works at all, it is only as most of Edwards' more famous "Images" work—to illustrate the already understood truths of a philosophy of sovereignty. The ultimate fact about Edwards as "poet" would seem to be that his imagination can use instances of the "secondary" beauty or harmony to illustrate truths arrived at by his modern philosophical "way of ideas," but it can never simply get to God through nature.

However that may be, Edwards rests his case at the end of the *Original Sin* not in an image but in a metaphysical argument, *contra* a complicated but pseudo-philosophical objection offered by his humanistic, liberal, and imaginatively "vulgar" opponents: since all reality is a "constitutional" expression of God's lawful power, and since not even human identity is an exception to this principle, philosophy can never be invoked to invalidate the obvious scriptural teaching about Adam's sin and man's depravity. His argument may be, in the end, only a special way of saying that reality is whatever God says it is; and this, philosophically, may be about as desperate as the purely Calvinistic teaching that "the will of God is the highest rule of justice, so that what he wills must be considered just, for this very reason, because he wills it."[51] But it is an argument which, in its idealistic form, Edwards held back for a long time, however consistent it may have been with his earliest idealism. It came out when he thought it had to, when he faced an objection proportionate to it in seriousness: it came out as a sort of desperate, last-ditch maneuver of Christian Philosophy, precisely when the very intelligibility of the Christian Scripture's first premise was most deeply embattled. Rational objections against the legitimacy of God's sovereign dealings with His individual creatures and literary objections against the typic organization of his Adamic plot are both answered with a philosophical definition of God's "definitive" relation to all other reality.

6

When we come to review the station and stature of Edwards as a Christian Philosopher, it seems fairest to regard him as one of the last of a familiar type, perhaps *the* last arguably major Christian thinker to deal with the problem of reason and revelation according to its classic and confident formulation, just prior to the onset of the higher criticism. By the end of Edwards' century, or certainly by the beginning of the next, Christian thinkers were discovering, to their dismay, that the status of Scripture was itself the major problem they had to face. Often it turned out to be an all-engrossing one, and everywhere Christian intellectual energy fairly consumed itself in the attempt to make sense out of the very idea of a "supernatural" revelation. This might be somewhat more true for Protestants than for Catholics, for whom "tradition" had always played a major role in defining the "content of faith" which the religious community embraced and the Christian Philosopher defended. But then it would also follow that the Protestants were, with their more psychological understanding of faith, better prepared for the new task; Evangelicals, perhaps, best of all. So that Edwards might have helped: not the Edwards of the *Freedom* and the *Virtue,* but surely the Edwards of the *Religious Affections.* That this did not happen probably has much to do with the account Edwards gives of himself at the end of the *Original Sin.*

Whatever we might decide about the Christian sociology of Part One, or the Christian structuralism of Parts Two and Three, it remains true that Part Four of the *Original Sin* is a deeply problematic piece of Christian philosophizing. Without being *particularly* medieval, it is, nevertheless, definitely "old-fashioned" from a nineteenth-century point of view; finally it is still part of the older, simpler effort to rescue intellectually something we have been "given" with supernatural authority. Within this frame of reference, Edwards' procedures are perfectly "valid," even perversely brilliant; but they do not quite meet the newer need of explaining the rational possibility of revelation as such. In what may be one of Edwards' most personally attractive formulations, he nevertheless clearly defines his project as "old style": we've all been saying we believe this difficult doctrine about Adam, he suggests; and so we should, it being God's word; now, if we really do believe it, it behooves us "to get over the difficulty, either by finding a solution, or by shutting our mouth and acknowledging the weakness of our understandings" (p. 395). And then he does indeed find a solution—brilliantly and in accord with the best "modern" philosophers, who, as recent histories are showing, were nearly all idealists in one form or another. But the nineteenth century would change the Christian problem from "the reasonable support of revealed doctrine" to "the philosophy of faith." And in this effort, philosophical procedures based on the cosmological implications of Locke and Newton would be entirely irrelevant.

And beyond the problem of procedures lies a very serious question of substance: does not Edwards' philosophical rescue of original sin create more difficulties than it relieves? At very best the crucial issue (of identity) is merely raised to a higher level, with ghostlier demarcations: our inability to understand a moral oneness with Adam is rationalized by the invocation of our inability to say very much about human identity at all. The net effect of Edwards' logic is not to answer but merely to annihilate questions about the ontological status of man, considered as a "created intelligent being." To the extent that such questions continue nontrivially to occur to our natural experience—and are not once and for all "answered" in a pietistic experience of the Divine ALL—to that extent Edwards' empiricism must strike us as less than radical. And to the extent that a theory of creation that is total, continuous, active, and ideal makes it hard to think of man as ever really very far "off" from God, to that extent the ordinarily gripping Christian question of how to get "back" may lose some of its compelling fascination. Whether panentheist or *merely* neoplatonic, the Edwardsean metaphysic solves the problem of man by making it disappear.[52]

Above all else, therefore, the example of Edwards provides the absolutely appropriate opportunity to observe that Christian Philosophy is valid and interesting only so long as its practitioner can keep the world from collapsing back into the mind of God. The premise that "God so wills" (or "so constitutes reality") will always suffice as a last explanation, but the game of philosophy requires that all other plausible and non-self-contradictory movements toward explanation be tried first; when the obviously last gambit is made, the game is clearly over.

It is to Edwards' credit, no doubt, that he held off from his own special form of the final appeal as long as he did—not only temporally but also intellectually, so that his *Freedom* and his *Virtue* could be written at all, and make the penultimate clarifications they do. Edwards' "delay" may seem especially impressive when we remember that nowhere has Edwards ever availed himself of any form of the Aristotelian philosophy of material substance, the single tool used most effectively in the Christian West to open up a little space between God and everything else. And yet if my instincts are right, we sense everywhere that Edwards' apocalyptic mastermove is coming, that his own footnote to Plato can hardly wait to be written; that it is proximately grounded in the traditions of nominalism and voluntarism that so thoroughly inform the tradition of Protestant intellectuality; and that it is given a powerful and appropriate new motivation by the idealism Edwards adopted so early. In short, I sense that it is toward the end of the *Original Sin* that Edwards' imagination and his system both inevitably tend. We should allow, perhaps, that even when he ends there, he provides the only really satisfactory explanation of the nearly universal Christian (and specifically anti-Aristotelian) teaching that the world would disappear if God for a single instant withdrew His willful support—that being, in Edwards' system, all the reality it ever really enjoyed. And we might even suggest that the Protestant emphasis on sovereignty achieves a sort of satisfactory or necessary last phase in Edwards' system—where the Lutheran *sola gratia* and the Calvinist *soli Deo gloria* are both swallowed up in a pietistic and metaphysical *Solus Deus*.[53] But irony and a sense of completion may be small recompense for the disappearance of philosophy and the end of man. To my conscience it seems "safer" (in Luther's own sense) to sound the cautionary note: Occam's razor can be a double-edged sword. Or: beware of explanations which prove too much.

If there is any other concluding observation to be made about our "example," it may concern, less grandly, the relation in Edwards of theology, philosophy, and imagination. It may be appropriate to suggest that the problem—and finally the harmony— of theology and philosophy is only part of the story; that what controls that relationship, from deeper down, is some intuitive grasp of reality which (like Kierkegaard's leap of faith) occurs somewhere beyond the legitimate boundaries of biblical interpretation, and which (like Poe's guess about God's plot) is quite different from both induction and deduction. Though I have no wish to end by discrediting my own estimate of Edwards' stature according to the categories of Christian Philosophy, I do wish to suggest that a less intellectualized view is just as true. The categories are necessary to maintain a steady view of Edwards' intentions at every point, and so to make "valid" interpretations. But as insistence on the personal location of those categories was itself meant to suggest, the soundest approach to Edwards is holistic and personal, and not strictly academic or categorical.

If we find ourselves asking, as we might fairly think to do, which *really* came first for Edwards, the theology or the philosophy, the faith or the reason, the religious commitment or the intellectualization, we may find ourselves with an unanswerable (and perhaps an irrelevant) question. Calvinism was clearly a "given" of his childhood and early adolescence. He may indeed have had early intellectual troubles about sovereignty, as he says in the "Personal Narrative," but he never rebelled; and if he places his conversion relatively late in his young manhood, still we might not want to write off the significance of his early pietistic experiences, in the history of his imagination, as easily as he might, in the progress of his soul. What we can see is a young person being authentically religious in a perfectly Puritan way; then discovering

the all-creative power and all-encompassing nature of God in precocious intellectual speculations; then experiencing a powerful
but hardly instantaneous conversion which completed and transformed the early piety even as it gave further validation to the
most problematic elements in the early speculations. The public
life, thereafter, is spent first in promulgating and explicating the
piety; then in defending it with available philosophical idioms
which are both appropriate and yet not too far removed from the
common understanding of things; and finally in rescuing it with
his own very first insights, however problematic to the "vulgar."
Throughout the whole career it is hard not to sense that Edwards'
"ego" has a very compelling organic or imaginative unity.

Deepest down in Edwards, accordingly, we seem to find not a
metaphysics (which "prepared" for a conversion), and not a piety
(which found its way inevitably to just the right intellectual
idioms), but rather some capacity of idealist imagination. Its quality
is best described in the negative, but from Edwards' own early
writings: it is most unlike that materialist imagination whose "prejudices" seem naturally to grow in every man "by every act of sensation" and which, unless opposed by mental culture or spiritual
discipline, cause men to "roar out, upon the mention of some very
rational philosophical truths."[54] Overcoming the prejudices of
that sort of imagination would, of course, be the first step on the
road to a consistent idealism. But possessing an opposite sort of
power—imaginative still, but not really sensory in origin—would
seem to guarantee Edwards' whole career. A capacity to suspect
that reality might be very subtle, and a power to suspend belief
long enough to wonder *how* subtle, may tell us more than anything
else about the unity and the priorities of a mind which saw spiders
and thought "teleology," which learned of atoms and guessed
"power," which experienced both nature and grace and leaped to
"idea," and which ultimately contrived to hand the whole world,
including its own consciousness and that of every other man, over
to *God Alone.*[55]

Such an imagination can seem, as it did to Perry Miller, impres-
sively scientific; but it is not, therefore, without a fundamental
flaw or besetting vice. As it maintains, in its intuitive phase, an
almost mathematical purity; so, in its expressive phase, it tends to
be not only "angelic" but even "deific." It can discover, every-

where, images of an ideality already guessed, but nowhere can it construe phenomenal nature as the mind's road to God. As such, it is an imagination which Emerson—so like Edwards in so many ways—would have to outgrow before he could become an effective natural symbolist. And it is, one might argue, a form of imagination which Poe never outgrew.[56]

But whatever the problematic consequences of the Edwardsean imagination for the literature of the American Renaissance, the consequences for Edwards' own systematic thought are fairly clear. Edwards may have been, even as Miller claimed, a poet who happened to work in ideas, but he was a poet whose imagination could do some things and not others; and, equally important, his imagination expressed itself in some ideas and not others. Again and again it availed itself of idioms—both theological and philosophical—more satisfactorily expressive of propositional simplicity than of substantial complexity. As one critic has observed, Edwards' neoplatonism deals more effectively with Being than with change. It is just as true and revealing, I think, that he is infinitely more interested in the ideal structure of matter than in its phenomenal feel. And a strong case could be made that his perceptions about Being-in-general count for more than those about God Incarnate.[57]

Most of Edwards' idioms are meaningfully related to existing Protestant options or to the developing style of philosophy, in the early "modern" period, as it paralleled or deliberately tried to mock the ideal patterns of early "modern" science. Back beyond that they are Platonic, idealist *a fortiori*. To quibble about the real influence or supposable reduplication of Berkeley is as quaintly aside from the main point as to argue about whether the revolution in thought effected by Descartes, Locke, Newton, and other "Giants" of the seventeenth century is "modern" in a full or only in a self-styled "period" sense. The main point about Edwards is surely that some given of nature or some existentially first "project of being" everywhere bent him toward one "way" of explanation. Along that way Edwards can give essentially Christian ideas, like grace and creation, a perfectly respectable standing within an idealist metaphysic. Or, alternately, he can offer, within that same metaphysic, a perfectly "Christian" understanding of secular ideas like cause, sense, analogy, necessity, and identity. "Philosophically," we can argue, it all flows from an insight into "substance" considered as that which enjoys the privilege of self-existence. And "theologically," we can easily sense, such an insight readily supports, or is supported by, Scripture's treasured revelation of the Divine Name. But about which came first it seems "safe" not to decide.

In short, to sense that there is, deep down, only one clue to all of Edwards, only one major insight being expressed again and again, is to sense only half of the one clear truth about the example of Edwards. The other half rests in the perception—out of tone and structure, style and strategy—that what makes Edwards everywhere Edwards is some absolutely fundamental bias of imagination in favor of idealism. And that perception must, in spirit, guide all our investigations of the body of Edwards' Christian Philosophy.

NOTES

1. See John Opie, ed., *Jonathan Edwards and the Enlightenment* (Lexington, Mass.: Heath, 1969); dominating the book is the argument about "modernity" between Miller and his critics.

2. Vincent Tomas, "The Modernity of Jonathan Edwards," *New England Quarterly*, 25 (1952), 70.

3. Edwards' basic text on the problem of "Reason and Revelation" is "The Insufficiency of Reason as a Substitute for Revelation," which constitutes chap. VII of his *Miscellaneous Observations on Important Theological Subjects;* it appears in Vol. VII of the Sereno Dwight edition of *The Works of President Edwards,* 10 Vols. (New York: Converse, 1829). For discussion, see Tomas, "Modernity"; and Claude A. Smith, "Jonathan Edwards and the 'Way of Ideas,'" *Harvard Theological Review,* 59 (1966), 153–173. Other relevant texts would be the sermon on "Christian Knowledge" (Dwight, *Works,* VI) and that portion of the *Miscellanies* edited by Harvey Townsend under the title "Mysteries" (see *The Philosophy of Jonathan Edwards* [Eugene: University of Oregon Press 1955], pp. 210–235). For the "medieval comparison, see Etienne Gilson, *Reason and Revelation in the Middle Ages* (New York: Scribners, 1938). And for Aquinas' definition of the "science" of the rational study of Scripture, see the *Summa Theologica,* Part I, Question 1, on "The Nature and Domain of Sacred Doctrine."

4. The "theological" limitations of Miller's study of Edwards are well known (see Tomas, "Modernity"). Douglas Elwood's *Philosophical Theology of Jonathan Edwards* (New York: Columbia University Press,1960) has a promising title but actually makes Edwards more unembarrassedly rationalistic than Miller; and A. O. Aldbridge's *Jonathan Edwards* (New York: Washington Square Press, 1964) is an unambiguously philosophical account. The principal attempt to right this uneven balance by treating Edwards as a "Calvinist theologian" is Conrad Cherry's *The Theology of Jonathan Edwards* (New York: Doubleday, 1966); it does not ignore philosophy as such, but it does pass over the problem of the *relation* of rational analysis and scriptural certitude. More recent studies have tended to be partial to

some *aspect* of Edwards' thought. See, for example, Clyde A. Holbrook, *The Ethics of Jonathan Edwards* (Ann Arbor: University of Michigan Press, 1973). The same is true of Roland Delattre's schematic study of *Beauty and Sensibility in the Thought of Jonathan Edwards* (New Haven: Yale University Press, 1968). Delattre claims to be coming at the very heart of Edwards, but to me he seems to be constructing a special plea for the "help" Edwards can give us in "Aesthetics and Theological Ethics." In a way, the best model we have of how to come at the whole of Edwards is Edward H. Davidson's *Jonathan Edwards: The Narrative of a Puritan Mind* (Cambridge: Harvard University Press, 1968); Davidson does not make the preliminary distinctions I insist upon, but he does allow for the variety of activities engaged in by Edwards' unified mind.

5. The character of Edwards' primary audience is brilliantly evoked by Perry Miller. See Perry Miller, *Jonathan Edwards* (New York: Sloane, 1949), esp. pp. 101–63.

6. Ibid., p. 276. Tomas agrees with the formula but denies that Miller himself knows the "secret" ("Modernity," p. 82). Miller's remark is cited with full approval by Clyde A. Holbrook in his "Editor's Introduction" to the *Original Sin* (New Haven: Yale University Press, 1970), p. 101.

7. Herbert Schneider, *The Puritan Mind* (New York: Holt, 1930), pp. 136–41.

8. Impatient with an old positivistic argument about the possible influence of Berkeley, Miller set aside the problem of idealism almost totally, calling it a "stratagem" (Miller, *Edwards*, pp. 61ff.). His uneasiness about the moral seriousness of idealism is shared by a number of later commentators. For example: Loren Baritz, *City on a Hill* (New York: Wiley, 1964), pp. 47–90; Claude A. Smith, "Edwards and the 'Way of Ideas'"; George Rupp, "The 'Idealism' of Jonathan Edwards," *Harvard Theological Review*, 62 (1969), 209–26. Even Wallace E. Anderson, who argues hard and technically for Edwards' "immaterialism," is slightly wary of the "idealist" label; see Wallace Anderson, "Immaterialism in Jonathan Edwards' Early Philosophical Notes," *Journal of the History of Ideas*, 25 (1964), 181–200.

9. See Herbert W. Schneider's other important treatment of Edwards: *A History of American Thought* (New York: Columbia University Press, 1946), pp. 11–18.

10. Miller strenuously cites Edwards' affirmation that we can continue to speak, properly, "in the old way" (*Edwards*, p. 63). But he fails to point out that Berkeley makes exactly the same sort of disclaimer; or that Edwards himself goes straight on to say we may speak of atoms and motions *even though* "all this does not exist anywhere perfectly but in the divine mind"; see "The Mind," in Townsend, *Philosophy*, p. 39.

Miller's essential philosophical error, it seems to me, was in arguing for a "naturalism" according to Locke and Newton *as against* the "idealism" of Berkeley, when clearly, as Schneider shows, those earlier thinkers could themselves be read in a perfectly idealist way. Though I have been profoundly influenced by Miller's book, and though I am specifically quarreling with Schneider's failure to apply his analysis of early Edwards, I am basically aligning myself with Schneider and against Miller. The "idealist" school of interpretation would also (significantly) include the following: G.P. Fisher, "The Philosophy of Jonathan Edwards," *Discussions in History and Theology* (New York: Scribners, 1880); A.V.G. Allen, *Jonathan Edwards* (Boston: Houghton Mifflin, 1889); E.C. Smyth, "Jonathan Edwards' Idealism," *American Journal of Theology*, 1 (1897), pp. 950-64; H.N. Gardiner, "The Early Idealism of Jonathan Edwards," *Philosophical Review*, 9 (1900), pp. 573-96; J.E. Woodbridge, "The Philosophy of Jonathan Edwards," *Exercises Commemorating the Two-Hundredth Anniversary of the Birth of Jonathan Edwards* (Andover, Mass.: Andover, 1904); I. Woodbridge Riley, *American Philosophy: The Early Schools* (New York: Dodd, Mead, 1907); Townsend, *Philosophy;* Elwood, *Philosophical Theology;* Leon Howard, ed., *"The Mind" of Jonathan Edwards* (Berkeley: University of California Press, 1963); and Paul Conkin, *Puritans and Pragmatists* (Bloomington: Indiana University Press; 1968).

11. This specific correlation, which will turn up at the climax of the *Original Sin,* is first made in a "Corollary" to a "Proposition" about atoms in the essay "Of Being." Edwards here identifies "body" with "solidity," "solidity" with "resistance," and "resistance" with divine "power"; he proceeds with the reflection that, strictly speaking, "there is no proper substance but God himself," so that He is very aptly called the *"ens entium"* (the very being of other beings); and then, extending his idealistic reduction to "motion" as well, he concludes: "How truly then is it in Him that we live, move, and have our being." See Townsend, *Philosophy,* pp. 17-18.

12. See Miller, *Edwards,* pp. 71-99. For more "orthodox" readings of Edwards on "Justification," see Thomas A. Schafer, "Jonathan Edwards and Justification by Faith," *Church History,* 20 (1951), 55-67; and, more important, Cherry, *Theology,* pp. 90-106. The suggestion about the likely relevance of Malebranche, which is entirely alien to all these interpreters, was a commonplace among earlier critics: see, for example, F.H. Foster, *A Genetic History of New England Theology* (Chicago: University of Chicago Press, 1907), pp. 47-81.

13. See Louis Bouyer, *The Spirit and Forms of Protestantism* (New York: World, 1954), pp. 136-65.

14. For Miller's view of the centrality of the "Divine and Supernatural Light," see Miller, *Edwards,* pp. 43-68. For the influence of the Cambridge Platonists, see the unpublished doctoral dissertation of Emily Stipes Watts, "Jonathan Edwards and the Cambridge Platonists" (University of Illinois at Urbana-Champaign, 1963). The basic studies of Edwards and Lockean epistemology are Miller, *Edwards,* pp. 52-67; and E.H. Davidson, "From Locke to Edwards," *Journal of the History of Ideas,* 24, (1963), pp. 355-72.

15. The principal "revisionist" attempts to modify our sense of the absolute primacy of Locke, in favor of established Puritan epistemology, are Cherry, *Theology,* pp. 12-24, and John E. Smith, "Editor's Introduction" to *A Treatise Concerning Religious Affections* (New Haven: Yale University Press, 1959), pp. 52-73. The passage in Locke referred to is Book II, chap. 1 and 2 (supplemented perhaps by related matter on simple ideas in Book III, chap. 4); for the comparable portion of the "Supernatural Light," see Faust and Johnson, eds., *Jonathan Edwards* (New York: Hill and Wang, 1962), pp. 106-7.

16. The idea that God's communication of Himself can *only* be "ideal" is the main theme of Edwards' "The Mind"; see, for example, Townsend, *Philosophy,* pp. 32, 36-41; 42-44, 52. Edwards' answer to Locke's dogmatically maintained belief in some occult "substratum" of material substance (in spite of his own suggestive theory of "power") is the burden of par. 61 of "The Mind," (ibid., pp. 60-63). And for Edwards' association of Plato with the empiricist way of ideas, see par. 40 (ibid., pp. 42-44).

17. Par. 34 (ibid., p. 39); the passage follows Edwards' disclaimer about speaking "in the old way."

18. Quoted variously from "Of Being" and "The Mind" (ibid., pp. 19, 33, 48).

19. "A Faithful Narrative," in C.C. Goen, ed., *The Great Awakening* (New Haven: Yale University Press, 1972), pp. 199–205.

20. Ibid., pp. 191–99.

21. *Some Thoughts Concerning the Revival of Religion in England*, ibid., pp. 331–47.

22. See Miller, *Edwards*, pp. 44–51, and *passim*.

23. For a reading of the *Religious Affections* which stresses the convertability of its argument about how "The presence of the divine Spirit [may] be discerned" into the somewhat less epistemologically problematic one about "What is true religion?"—see Smith, *Affections*, pp. 1–51.

24. Ibid., pp. 205–12.

25. Ibid., pp. 197–205.

26. The closest Edwards *ever* comes to embarrassing questions about the "mechanics" of sensation in an idealist system is merely to reject as improper (and faintly silly) the temptation to press the notion that the senses and the brain are essentially ideas. And this he does from the outset; see "The Mind," par. 35, 40, 51 (Townsend, *Philosophy*, pp. 40–41, 42–44, 52).

27. Smith, *Affections*, pp. 205–6. And compare "A Divine and Supernatural Light" (Faust and Johnson, *Edwards*, pp. 106–10).

28. For Edwards' simplification of faculty psychology, see Miller, *Edwards*, pp. 181ff.; Paul Ramsey, "Editor's Introduction," *Freedom of the Will* (New Haven: Yale University Press, 1957), pp. 47–65; Smith, *Affections*, pp. 12–18; Cherry, *Theology*, pp. 12–24; and Delattre, *Beauty and Sensibility*, pp. 1–11, 41–44.

29. "The Mind," par. 31 (Townsend, *Philosophy*, p. 39). Elsewhere Edwards calls this insight—in his best Perry Miller fashion—"the secret": "that which is truly the substance of all bodies is the infinitely exact and precise and perfectly stable idea in God's mind together with his stable will that the same shall gradually be communicated to us" (ibid., par. 13, p. 32).

30. Ibid., par. 34, p. 40.

31. The possibility of a near-Pantheism in Edwards is seriously proposed by Douglas J. Elwood; what Edwards needed, he argues, is some panentheistic "third way" which should possess the advantages of both traditional pantheism (Immanence) and traditional theism (Transcendence) and which would, thereby, place the Calvinist doctrines of sovereignty on a firm metaphysical basis (*Philosophical Theology*, pp. 12–64). The suggestion was treated "cautiously" by Anderson, "Immaterialism," p. 190, and was sharply attacked by Robert C. Whittemore in "Jonathan Edwards and The Theology of the Sixth Way," *Church History*, 35 (1966), 60–75. A recent reviewer of Edwards scholarship has concluded that Elwood's book "lacks both seriousness and conviction" and that Edwards is far better described (by Whittemore) as a Christian Neoplatonist than (by Elwood) as a panentheist; see Everett H. Emerson, "Jonathan Edwards," in Rees and Harbert, eds., *Fifteen American Authors* (Madison: University of Wisconsin Press, 1971), p. 177. About such learned matters the learned may judge. To me Elwood's book seems both serious and convincing. Both in and out of so many words Edwards repeatedly makes the point that "speaking most strictly, there is no proper substance

but God himself" and that this proposition, being absolutely universal, includes even "the substance of the soul" (see "Of Being" and "The Mind" in Townsend, *Philosophy*, pp. 17, 78). In Edwards the premise that in God "we live, move, and have our being" is more than a "cliché" (Whittemore, "Theology of the Sixth Way," p. 63); and the discovery that very many Neoplatonists (Christian and otherwise) say things very like some of Edwards' sayings is nothing to the purpose. At issue, essentially, is whether or not Edwards does in fact develop a special philosophical idiom, the rationale of which is to support Scripture's absolutist definitions of God with an utterly serious literalness that is virtually unique among "modern" Christian thinkers; and whether or not the tendency of this system is to rationalize Calvin in such a way so that his God-as-absolute-Will becomes also a God-as-unconditioned-Being; to move in a direction which Calvin himself would have recognized as "pantheistic"; and, most practically, to reach an almost self-destructive denial of significant being to man at the end of the *Original Sin*. Such are the cases I imagine myself competent to argue and feel content for the reader to judge.

32. For the Catholic-academic argument, see Anton C. Pegis, *Christian Philosophy and Academic Freedom* (Milwaukee: Bruce, 1955); Jacques Maritain, *An Essay in Christian Philosophy* (New York: Philosophical Library, 1955); and Maurice Nédoncelle, *Existe-t-il une Philosophie Chretienne*, translated by Illtyd Trethowain, O.S.B. as *Is There a Christian Philosophy?* (New York: Hawthorn, 1960).

33. Most recent critics have been uncomfortable with Miller's praise of the purely scientific character of "Part One" of the *Original Sin (Edwards*, pp. 266ff.). For the newer consensus, see Holbrook, "Editor's Introduction," *Original Sin*, pp. 27–41.

34. Ramsey, *Will*, p. 16. For Conrad Wright's less forgiving view, see *The Beginnings of Unitarianism in America* (Boston: Starr King, 1955), pp. 91–114.

35. For the sake of agreeing with Locke's basic sense of "liberty" as the capacity of a human agent and not of a "faculty," Edwards permits himself certain cautious use of the word "power" in *The Freedom* (see pp. 137–38, 163, 171–72, 175, 204); and similarly in "The Mind" and the "Miscellanies" (see Townsend, *Philosophy*, pp. 38, 155–65). But everywhere he makes it clear that this power is one of execution and not of authentic origination. Even in a rare passage on man's "likeness to God," Edwards stresses that the "soul of man" has the "power of motion" rather than of self-determination; and the passage ends with this curiously constrained formula: "If there be anything amongst all the beings that flow from [the] first principle of all things, that have any sort of resemblance to it or have anything of a shadow of likeness to it, spirits or minds bid abundantly the fairest for it" (ibid., p. 81). Carefully protected in all of this—obviously, as it seems to me—is that sort of "bare" power which Locke (Book II, chap. 23) hinted may be all we really know of substance.

36. It is probably correct to argue that beauty is, for Edwards, "the first principle of being" (Delattre, *Beauty and Sensibility*, pp. 27–41). But this should not be permitted to obscure the fact that Edwards' primary speculations are—in the "ontological" manner of Anselm and Descartes—about the idea of Being" (Delattre, *Beauty and Sensibility*, pp. 27–41). But this should not be permitted to obscure the fact that Edwards' primary speculations are— in the "ontological" manner of Anselm and Descartes—about the idea of

Being Itself. From which it would seem to follow, incidentally, that Descartes was indeed as powerfully formative an influence on Edwards' eclectic mind as Locke and Newton; see Howard, *"The Mind" of Jonathan Edwards*, pp. 28, 48.

37. *The Nature of True Virtue*, William K. Frankena, ed. (Ann Arbor: University of Michigan Press, 1960), p. 38.

38. Ibid., p. 30.

39. Holbrook, *Original Sin*, p. 405. Further references are given in the text.

40. See H. Shelton Smith, *Changing Conceptions of Original Sin* (New York: Scribners, 1955), pp. 1–35. Also relevant is Conrad Wright's contention that it is Adam and not Will which really divides Edwards and his opponents; see Wright, *Beginnings of Unitarianism*, pp. 58–114.

41. If there is one subject on which Edwards' tendency towards Anselmian-Cartesian "ontologistic" rationalism makes itself clearer than any other, it is that of the Trinity: Edwards' speculations touch not only its internal structure or "procession" but also its relation to the economy of redemption; and he treats both cases as very largely affairs of deductive reasoning. See his "Observations Concerning the Scripture Oeconomy of the Trinity, and the Covenant of Redemption" and his "Essay on the Trinity," in Paul Helm, ed., *Jonathan Edwards' Treatise on Grace and Other Posthumous Writings* (Cambridge: James Clarke, 1971). I have omitted discussion of this aspect of Edwards' career as Christian Philosopher partly for reasons of space (it would require a long essay in itself) and partly from a sense that Edwards' theology of the Trinity does not touch experience as vitally as many of his other subjects.

42. The word is that of Holbrook (*Original Sin*, p. 34), as he summarizes Edwards' view of the implications of his opponents' position. For a vigorous defense of the truth of that view, see Joseph Haroutunian, *Piety vs. Moralism* (New York: Holt, 1932), esp. pp. 15–42.

43. For the liberal theory of the relation between Scripture and Reason ("supernatural rationalism"), see Wright, *Beginnings of Unitarianism*, pp. 135–60.

44. The "classic" view remains compelling: the covenant idiom is basically rationalist and not voluntarist; see Perry Miller, "The Marrow of Puritan Divinity," in *Errand into the Wilderness* (Cambridge: Harvard University Press, 1956), pp. 48–98. The problematical relation of covenant language to the original style of "Calvinism" remains unchanged, even if Calvin himself turns to covenant explanations; see Everett H. Emerson, "Calvin and the Covenant Theology," *Church History*, 25 (1956), 136–44.

45. Besides Miller (*Edwards*, p. 274), see George P. Fisher, "The Augustinian and the Federal Theories of Original Sin Compared," *New Englander*, 27 (1868), 507–8; and Holbrook, *Original Sin*, p. 50.

46. For the travails of Puritan "Federalism," see Fisher, "Augustinian and Federal Theories"; Miller, "Marrow," and *The New England Mind: The Seventeenth Century* (Cambridge: Harvard University Press, 1939), pp. 365–97; Smith, *Changing Conceptions*, pp. 1–9; and Holbrook, *Original Sin*, pp. 1–16.

47. Wallace Anderson, "Immaterialism in Jonathan Edwards' Early Philosophical Notes," *Journal of the History of Ideas*, 25 (1964), 181–200. Anderson is more critical of Edwards' conflations than is Herbert Schneider, but their interpretations seem to me complementary and convincing.

48. On the one hand see Williston Walker, *Ten New England Leaders* (New York: Silver, Burdette, 1901), p. 257; Smith, *Changing Conceptions*, pp. 35–36; and especially Tomas, "Modernity," pp. 82–84. On the other, Miller, *Edwards*, pp. 278–79—supported by Holbrook, *Original Sin*, p. 101.

49. "The Mind," par. 34, (Townsend, *Philosophy*, p. 39).

50. The explicit application of idealism to the theory of identity is not lacking in "The Mind": "the Most High could, if he saw fit, cause there to be another being who should begin to exist in some distant part of the universe, with the same ideas I now have after the manner of memory." (Ibid., p. 68).

51. Quoted from H.T. Kerr, ed., *A Compend of the Institutes of the Christian Religion* (Philadelphia: Westminster, 1964), p. 132.

52. Elwood vs. Whittemore aside (see note 31), it seems difficult to deny that Edwards' metaphysical anthropology remains problematic and even mysterious. Although the famous passages about substance might be construed so as to refer to material substance only, still it is hard to see that the human soul could ever escape Edwards' pervasive and all-explaining theory of total, instantaneous, powerful, and direct re-creation at every moment. Moreover, the passages about God's being both the *"ens"* and the "sum" of all being (Townsend, *Philosophy*, pp. 17, 87) seem as metaphysically serious as they are unambiguous. And practically speaking, of course, they all support the plain self-denying sense of the *Original Sin*. If Edwards has, outside of that climactic document, some other last work on man as a "soul" or a "created intelligent being," it would seem to be in the "Miscellanies." Edwards is arguing that "the mere exertion of a new thought is a certain proof of a God." Here, he suggests, is a new thing, needing a cause. Where might that cause legitimately be located? "It is not in antecedant thoughts, for they are vanished and gone; they are past, and what is past is not." So much for history. But what of substance? "If we say 'tis the substance of the soul, if we mean that there is some substance besides that thought that brings that thought forth, if it be God, I acknowledge it" (ibid., p. 78). Otherwise, nonsense. Apart from God's all-creative power, the soul of man is not a whit more substantial than the moon.

53. In my view it is Edwards (and not Karl Barth) who completes and epitomizes the Protestant tendency to refer all being and all good in man directly and entirely to God. As Louis Bouyer has argued, both classical Protestantism and some forms of neo-orthodoxy make it seem "as if man could only belong to [God] in ceasing to have a distinct existence" (Bouyer, *Spirit and Forms*, p. 151); the explanation, he argues, lies in Protestant piety's chosen philosophical style—a "radical empiricism, reducing all being to what is perceived, which empties out, with the idea of substance, all possibility of real relations between beings, as well as the stable substance of any of them" (ibid., p. 153). This is, it may be argued, a "sectarian" view. But to me it seems certain that Edwards' eclectic and omnivorous idealism—begun in the style of "ontologism" á la Descartes, and fostered by an immaterialism out of Newton and the empiricism of Locke read in a radical (Berkeleyan) way—constitutes a sort of inevitable *terminus ad quem* and *ne plus ultra* in the (basically Protestant) metaphysics of sovereignty. To this truth Elwood has so far come closest: "Edwards sought to place the whole system of Calvin on more of an ontological foundation, conceiving of God most fundamentally not as absolute will but as unconditional Being" (Elwood, *Philosophical Theology*, p. 58). My not altogether friendly amendment reads as follows: Pro-

testant voluntarism and nominalism receive their perfect redefinition and defense in Edwards' utterly rationalistic proof that no contingent reality can ever be considered as anything but God's will and idea. And it may not be unfair to point out that Elwood and Whittemore, antagonists on everything else, seem to agree that "What Aquinas is to Neothomism, Edwards ought to be to neo-orthodoxy" (Whittemore, "Edwards and the Sixth Way," pp. 73 75; cp. Elwood, *Philosophical Theology*, pp. 3, 7, 9-11, 155).

54. "Of the Prejudices of the Imagination" (Townsend, *Philosophy*, p. 2).

55. Others may argue whether it is proper to speak, as did many early commentators, of Edwards' "mysticism." But surely something real was being discussed when one pointed to Edwards' "wonderful sense of the immediateness of the divine presence and agency" and suggested that "in addition to his youthful ecstasy he had a philosophical basis for his convictions"; see I. Woodbridge Riley, *American Thought: From Puritanism to Pragmatism* (New York: Holt, 1915), p. 29.

56. Without actually disputing the meaningfulness of the intellectual connection between Edwards and Emerson (in terms of either "spiritism" or "typology"), I should yet like to suggest that Edgar Poe may be Edwards' truer intellectual child. On the one hand, negatively, the link with Emerson will always create as many difficulties as clarifications: Edwards and Emerson both suppose—Berkeley fashion—that "idealism sees the world in God," and both show a "pantheistic" tendency to live in the ALL; and yet where one infers that the practical import of such a view is Puritan self-surrender, the other is sure it guarantees a Transcendental self-trust. This would be scanned. On the other hand, positively, Poe's *Eureka* plainly reveals not only a scientific inspiration for his idealism similar to that which Edwards took from Newton; but also a highly similar sense of God's cosmic "plot." Both essentially invoke gravity as a figure of cosmic unity or "consent," and both seem to have seen that, given "atoms" as the building blocks of matter, matter and spirit are really indistinguishable as "power." Nor are they "thematically" all that different: both evince a strong "neoplatonic" drive toward the mathematical One as source, end, and explanation of all reality; and both deal, Platonically, with images based on the memory of a Ligeian experience rather than with Aristotelian reality or the Thomistic analogy of being. To me it seems plausible to regard the man who survives his "Descent into the Maelstrom" as a convert to the "Edwardsean" sense of the "powerful" unity of an all-divine reality. One might even wonder—with the Sereno Dwight edition available as of 1829—whether Poe might somehow have read and responded to Edwards' own true sight of sin: "as [the sinner] is conscious of a dissent from universal being and of that being's dissent from him, wherever he is he sees what excites *horror*" (Edwards, "The Mind," *Works*, I, 701).

If this reading of Poe is sound (and it seems to me consistent with the views of Allan Tate, E. H. Davidson, and Richard Wilbur), then it will also follow that Poe is a more authentic disciple of Edwards than is the superficially much more "Puritan" Hawthorne, who worries the problem of every man's "brotherhood even with the guiltiest" pretty much without benefit of metaphysics; and more authentic even than Melville, who may spend his whole mature career studying "something somehow like Original Sin," but does so in a naturalistic universe whose distinguishing mark is to be just as problematically cut off from God's word and will as Edwards' idealistic universe is utterly dependent upon them for its very "constitution."

57. "Were it needful, it were possible to multiply citations from the later works testifying to Edwards' complete commitment to the category of Being. As for Becoming, that category has no part whatsoever in the Edwardsean ontology" (Whittemore, "Edwards and the Sixth Way," p. 70). Amen. But is that really the last (neoplatonic) word on Edwards? Is it really sufficient to conclude that Edwards is (all simply) "medieval" because his ontology yields a God who is "Pure Act"? Is it even accurate to say that Edwards and Anselm and Aquinas all share exactly the same ontology—without regard to the fact that Anselm is an "ontologist" and Aquinas is not? Or that Aquinas' appropriation of the Aristotelian doctrine of matter and form, act and potency was motivated by a desire to avoid the idealistic panentheism towards which the whole neoplatonic tradition tends? Or that the Thomistic doctrine of the analogy of being provides a precise guarantee of the possibility and the meaningfulness of the Christian doctrine of the God-Man, with which Edwards can do so little? Were it needful, it were possible to multiply citations so to suggest.

FIVE

The Puritan Roots
of American Whig Rhetoric

EMORY ELLIOTT

While most students of American literature and culture now
concede that Puritan influences are still present in the society in
nineteenth-century America and are therefore reflected in American books, the question which continues to worry critics is how
were the values and ideas of Puritan New England transmitted to
the later generations of Americans? After the heroic but failed
effort of Edwards, the strict Calvinism associated with the Puritanism of the seventeenth century is maintained by only a small
minority of religionists during the decades after the Revolution.
The liberal wing of Protestantism which may be traced from
Charles Chauncy to the Unitarians and received eloquent expression in the writings of Charles Channing is far different from the
covenant theology of the seventeenth century. At the same time,
the pietism and fundamentalism of Charles Finney and the great
evangelists of the Second Great Awakening combined the emotional power of Edwards and Whitefield with the liberal church
polity of Solomon Stoddard in ways that would have left Cotton
Mather and his illustrious father nearly speechless. It is quite
valid then to ask when have we stopped talking about American
Puritanism as a theology and set of recognizable beliefs and begun
to mean "puritanical" tendencies in American attitudes toward
economics and morals, which H. L. Mencken was later to mis-
represent as the original Puritan spirit?

When the question is posed in precisely that form, the answer
that the social and literary historian must give is that the Puritanism which the Fathers brought from England in the 1620s and '30s
ceased to exist as a major organized religion with the decline of
the first Great Awakening and the death of Jonathan Edwards.
But to ask the question in this way is not to solve the problem

which we face when we come upon the residue of Puritan metaphors and ideas and the persistent Puritan vision of America's
place in God's design which became part of the American ideology
at the very time that the old Calvinism was passing from the scene.
Quite separate from the moral attitudes which we call "puritanical," there remained in the public idiom an elaborate set of assertions about the role of the individual in the community and the
role of America in the world which were inherited directly from
the sermons and histories of three generations of New England
Puritans. Even though the theology had become diluted in the
eighteenth century, these ideas and images were transmitted
throughout the colonies by the itinerant preachers who struck out
from Princeton and the other Presbyterian colleges to carry this
vision to the back country of the South and the West. Even those
who embraced the theological tenets of Methodism and Angli-
canism learned to think in terms of America as a chosen New
Israel and to dwell upon the need for individual self-sacrifice to
the common ordained goal. The Puritan ideas of elect and nonelect, the calling, and the covenant became key metaphors through
which Americans understood and expressed their social situation.

What is more remarkable is the manner in which Puritan methods of child-rearing, religious education, and preaching conspired
to create certain patterns of psychological response in those who
were exposed to its message and in their descendants. For over a
hundred years the people who lived in America learned the effec-
tiveness of using guilt, shame, and rejection as tools of moral and
social control either in the home or in the community. The identification of saints and sinners and the separation of members of
in-groups and out-groups (be they Quakers, Catholics, Red Men,
or eventually Redcoats) combined with the notion of conversion-
success-salvation in such a way as to encourage obsessive self-
examination to insure that the mission of the individual and
the community were in complete harmony. Those psychosocial
attitudes were fostered throughout the colonies in the seventeenth
and eighteenth centuries through an intricate religious language
which fused biblical images and types to natural imagery and
symbols to form a recurrent narrative of peril and redemption in
Puritan sermons and other writings that could evoke particular
emotional responses in the colonial audiences.

By the middle of the eighteenth century, the intelligent and educated clergymen of the various denominations and, more important, the young secular leaders who would direct the American Revolution were quite conscious of the process of intellectual transmission which had left the marks of Puritan psychological predispositions on Americans. It was only for shrewd manipulators of language such as Benjamin Franklin and Thomas Paine to combine their efforts with the clergy to bring to the surface once more the emotions over which the old religion had once had sole control. Viewed in this way the American Revolution may be seen as a political Great Awakening in which the people were reconverted to their national mission, expressed in an amalgam of religious and political terms. In so recasting the Puritan vision, the leaders of the Revolution played an important part in the process of transmission in which we may discover the continuity of American Puritanism and nineteenth-century American thought and writing. They preserved the Puritan vision of the city on the hill and the garden in the wilderness and refined the Puritan idiom for use by later orators and politicians. It is to this recognizable transmission of Puritan habits of thought and psychological response that such writers as Hawthorne, Melville, Twain, and James reacted and which continues to fascinate American writers in our own century.

Franklin's essay of 1757, *The Way to Wealth,* provides interesting insights into this process of transmission because it demonstrates how colonial economic policies of self-sufficiency and belt-tightening were presented to the common people in the familiar Puritan language.[2] It also reveals attitudes toward economic difficulties which by 1750 were already deeply rooted in the American cultural tradition. While it may first appear that Franklin's argument stressing material gain would run counter to the old Puritan emphasis upon worldly sacrifice to earn heavenly reward, in fact Franklin's reasoning is merely the logical extension of tendencies which were characteristic of Puritan theology.[3] The Puritans emphasized self-denial in the present in order to achieve prosperity in the future, presumably in the afterlife. Franklin secularized this accepted maxim. But more important, on a deeper level Franklin's essay reveals his conscious manipulation of subtle social and psychological tendencies in his society.

When faced with adversity, like worsening times and royal intervention, the Puritans had been taught to search for the enemy within rather than to attack the intruding evil directly. The logic ran this way. If there is trouble from without, it must be because the community's weaknesses have invited difficulties; instead of wasting energy and time ranting against the external threat, be it Satan or the wrathful God, the King or hard times, it is far wiser to expose and purge the inner evils, and eventually triumph over adversity through private labors. This formula of action was more efficient because as soon as God was satisfied with the internal reform of his people, he would act to destroy the external causes of their suffering.[4] Such was the theme of John Cotton's sermon of 1641 which he titled *The Way to Life*. Such was the message of Cotton Mather's sermon of 1690, *The Way to Prosperity*. And in a more readable form, such was the doctrine of Franklin's *The Way to Wealth*.[5]

In the 1750s and '60s when shrewd rhetoricians like Franklin sought to turn the people toward a policy of tight control of private spending in order to increase exportation and American economic independence, they invoked the spirit of frugality and self-sacrifice of the Puritan founders and promised that, as in former times, God would surely help those who helped themselves.[6] In his election sermon of 1754, Reverend Jonathan Mayhew found the parable of the talents provided a fitting text for an inventive elaboration of austere economic policy: "Whatever powers and advantages of any kind men severally enjoy are committed to them in trust by the great Lord and Proprieter of all, to whom they are accountable for the use they make of them; and from whom they shall in the close of the present scene, receive either a glorious recompense of their fidelity or the punishment due to their sloth and wickedness." [7]

After dutifully explicating the religious implications of this doctrine, Mayhew moved logically to the more practical concerns. It is plain that the Lord has given the American colonists great natural resources and therefore, he reasoned, the people are under divine obligation to develop their lands fully. Furthermore, the only government to which they are truly accountable for their lands and labor is the "righteous administration of God." More specifically, Mayhew advised the people and the newly elected magistrates to support efforts for becoming self-sufficient

in their fishing industry and in the granting of public moneys
for defense and to step up production of that other essential
American commodity: Mayhew saw the value in earthly, as
well as heavenly, spirits. He observed: "It is not improbable
. . . that we might have a valuable staple by means of that fruit
which delights so much in our soil as well as greatly lessen the
importation of foreign liquors."[8] Mayhew was certain that God
would not want the colonists to waste their talent for making
good corn whiskey. By returning to the tried and proven common-
sense doctrines of the Puritan ancestors, whose prolific writings
lined the bookshelves of eighteenth-century American divines and
professional men, Mayhew and his colleagues found ready-made
arguments to fit new social and economic problems.

Yet the message which we find in the writings of the 1750s,
which recommend frugality and patience in response to higher
taxes and economic troubles, is a mild doctrine compared to the
cries for total reform and independence that mark the inflam-
matory writings of the 1760s and '70s; and the policy of belt-
tightening and economic self-sufficiency is a long way from
violent revolution. The issue which has most concerned historians
of the Revolution in the last decade is how might we account for
that dramatic change, for the sudden upsurge of human emotion
which triggered the insurrection. Some have come to agree with
the English Tories, who believed that the Americans were not
really an oppressed people and that conditions in the colonies
hardly warranted what one loyalist called "so virulent a Rebellion
which seemed to originate from such trivial causes."[9] Certainly
the questions remain of what it was about the language of the
Whig leaders that sparked such a violent reaction in the people and
what it was about the rhetoric of preachers and pamphleteers
that evoked the fervor necessary for people to risk life and possessions in a bloody conflict with the mother country.

It is my contention that the most effective force in focusing
the generalized complaints and uneasiness of the colonists into
singleness of purpose and action in the years preceding the Revolution was the imaginative use of religious language fused with
expressions of contemporary economic concerns. Although the
ideas of intellectuals like Jefferson and John Adams derived
largely from philosophical sources other than Calvinism, these

leaders looked to the ministers and writers to translate their ideology into a language that would have profound appeal for the people. Faced with the task of uniting a vaguely dissatisfied and internally contentious people, the preachers, poets, and pamphleteers sought a verbal common denominator that would minimize differences of opinion and touch the deepest psychological bonds of a diversified people. They turned naturally to the rhetorical conventions and symbolic language of the established form of public discourse, the sermon.[10]

Writers like John Hancock, Philip Freneau, and Sam Adams, many of whom had been trained for the ministry, discovered that the traditional verbal patterns—the imagery, religious metaphors, and biblical types—continued to hold vital meaning for the Americans. When Jefferson revived the ritual of the fast day in 1774 and copied the exact language of that old Puritan form, he observed that "the effect of the day thro' the whole colony was like a shock of electricity, arousing everyman and placing him erect."[11] A man of reason and natural religion himself, Jefferson was so impressed by this emotional reaction that he immediately sent itinerant patriot preachers into the countryside of the middle and southern colonies to stir the people to action. Tories like Peter Oliver and Thomas Hutchinson were inclined to lay much of the blame for the public agitation upon these servants of God and country, whom they called the Black Regiment.[12]

As fervently as had their Puritan ancestors, these shapers of the rhetoric of the Revolution expounded upon the sinister connection between economic trials and the collapse of moral standards. If they could convince the people that a base preoccupation with money and property and the decay of moral and spiritual life were rampant among all classes, so that the very identity of the American colonies was threatened by these internal evils, they could touch off a process that would lead logically and emotionally toward total reform. Skillfully appealing at once to the indignation of the poor and to the pride and thirst for fame of the elite, these writers managed to instill the old patterns of expression in their speeches and pamphlets with a force and energy that gave them great enlivening power. In searching for a unifying language that would bring together people of different classes and interests behind a common cause, the writers fell back upon long-established formulas. These public spokesmen and interpreters of events played a key role in arousing a sense of unity of purpose in the people, stirring men and women to risk life and possessions for abstract principles and vague promises of reward.

There are two key elements of the general emotional makeup of the Revolutionary War generation which help to account for the stunning success of such public expression. First, the writers discovered what Ezra Stiles observed in 1761—that the reverberations of the powerful religious revival known as the First Great Awakening persisted in America well into the 1760s.[13] The spirit of piety which swept the colonies in the 1730s and '40s made a deep and lasting impact on those who were reaching adulthood in the two decades before the Revolution. After years of moderation in religious education, this generation experienced a sudden resurgence of stern discipline in religious training and a return of strict authority in households. Ministers like Jonathan Edwards called for a firmer control in the home to assure lasting effects of the revivals. The high proportion of adult males converted during the Awakening indicates that families witnessed a reassertion of paternal authority over moral and spiritual life.[14] Since three-fourths of the population of the colonies in 1770 was under the age of thirty,[15] great numbers of those born between 1740 and 1775 shared the common early experience of growing up in homes in which the main authorities were the father, the minister, and the Bible. Thus, while the Great Awakening revealed divisions in doctrine among the clergy, it served on an emotional level to unite vast numbers of the colonists of different regions.

Culturally, the most important feature of this shared experience was the exposure to certain repeated themes and images and to the typological habit of mind which the revivalist preachers absorbed from the Calvinist sermon tradition. The vision of America's millennial role; the emphasis upon guilt and corruption, purgation, and perfectionism; the stress upon contending and irreconcilable opposites such as God versus Satan, saint versus sinner, freedom versus slavery: when used to define America's relationship to English authority, these themes charged the colonists' dissatisfactions with new meaning.[16]

A second point to be noted is that at the same time that the writers found the traditional language so enlivening, they also perceived an intimate relationship between religious feeling and economic concerns. At the deepest level of the American psyche there existed a profound inner conflict between the drives of ambition and self-interest as opposed to the impulse toward self-denial and sacrifice for a higher good, whether earthly or divine. Although Calvinism had been a religion that seemed to stimulate productivity and economic achievement, it established rigorous social and psychological controls over preoccupation with the things of this world. Men reared in Calvinist doctrine were at once inclined to seek worldly success and to suffer pangs of guilt for having done so. The wealthy seventeenth-century Puritan merchant Robert Keayne has left us a poignant statement of this inner torment in his will and diary. A devout church member, Keayne suffered public humiliation and private anguish when church officials publicly reprimanded him for overcharging for his goods.[17]

In addition, the problem of profit and God's Providence was always especially acute in relation to the critical issue of community leadership. The question was this: By bestowing worldly gain on some and not others, did God, in effect, indicate his nominees for political office? How may the people recognize the true "Character of a Good Ruler"? Although the ministers always insisted that the right to rule rested on moral character and not property, it became obvious quite early that political power depended on the leader's economic status and his ability to defend the right of private property in the colonies. While the ministers continued to insist that the common good and the sacred American mission should overcome any tendency toward self-interest in rulers, the question of the relationship between private wealth and public authority remained a nagging concern and took on particular importance during the decade before the Revolution.[18]

In order to draw upon and control the emotional forces springing from these inner conflicts and doubts, the early Puritan ministers and the great revivalist preachers of the eighteenth century developed effective psychological methods. They recognized that the most successful technique for affecting the hearts of those who had been reared in American Calvinism was to arouse their deep sense of guilt while at the same time offering a clear path of action for relieving the burden of inner suffering and achieving a new basis of assurance and hope. The most common cause of such guilt was an awareness that one's life was primarily motivated by a secret craving for wealth, luxury, and idleness.

The best cure for such inner corruption was the purgation of those elements of one's life which lead to this vile self-interest, followed by a renewed dedication to labor for the higher purposes of the common good of God's chosen and the greater glory of God's kingdom. In the individual such reform was often accompanied by the violent release of pent-up doubts and fears; in the community a general reform was accompanied by a period of fasting and humiliation, followed by a renewal of covenant and a surge of public spiritual energy, evidenced in conversions and full churches. Thus, the structure and language of the sermons, the elaborate public rituals of fast days and covenant renewals, and the complex examinations of the sinner's heart were all devised as social and psychological safety valves for releasing tensions caused by the conflict between self-interest and the common good.

Essentially, the method followed a standard pattern from exposure of guilt, to reconversion, to recommitment. In the first stage, the guilty person (or congregation) discovered and admitted that he himself was to blame for whatever troubles had been plaguing him; nearly always the cause was a secret idolatry of profit, luxury, and pleasure. During this act of confession the people would be convinced that they had grown so corrupt that forgiveness and redemption were unattainable. Because the ministers in the late seventeenth century discovered that it was dangerous to leave people in this stage of self-torture for too long, they would move the penitent quickly through this process to redirect the aroused guilt from within toward some external evil which had subtly intruded into the community of true believers.[19]

At this point, all of the pent-up guilt and anguish could be projected upon this scapegoat, be it Satan or his wicked emissaries, or, as it often was in Puritan New England, upon invading outsiders like Papists, Quakers, or royal representatives like Governor Edmund Andros. The minister would picture the evil intruder as a wicked master who had enslaved the people of God and forced them to worship his vile idols. Breaking free of his hold, the people would symbolically, or as in the case of Andros and the other unfortunate victims of righteousness, physically expel the evil from the community and restore their commitment to self-sacrifice for God and the common good.[20] It seems that from the very start of the New England settlement there emerged a pattern in the society that whenever worldly affairs were going especially well or ill, fears of approaching calamity would set this process of inner searching and communal purgation in motion.

In reviving this religious rhetoric and the ritualistic forms, the writers of the Revolution had such startling success because they touched similar emotions in the members of their own generations and set into operation the same psychological processes which Jonathan Edwards and George Whitefield would have recognized as an awakening of the spirit. At heart, many of the colonists feared that their economic troubles were the result of their own personal failures—they had indulged themselves in the pursuit of wealth and luxury. The members of the revolutionary generation were especially inclined to think in such terms about their distress because so many of them had been reared under the influence of the mid-century revivals. They had witnessed scenes in which penitent wealthy people had unburdened themselves of guilt by publicly burning their personal possessions to symbolize their denial of the world and their commitment to higher principles. Men like Hugh Henry Brackenridge and Joel Barlow trained for the ministry because religion had been a vital force in their early lives. In those crucial decades before the Revolution, the society was ready for another revival of fervor. When the ministers and writers revivified those proven techniques, they were able to chan- nel the turbulent psychosocial energies of the people into a political awakening which could only end in the complete pur- gation of the intruding evil through a total reformation of the society.

The social developments which laid the emotional groundwork for the rhetoric of reform actually began after the Great Awaken- ing of the 1740s. The religious enthusiasts and liberal rationalists had made peace with themselves and God, and there followed a period of economic growth which concentrated all affairs upon the pursuit of gain. In the name of the Almighty and the common good, diligence in business became the economic policy of the upper classes and the common sense of the lower. But it was also a time of opportunity for greed and deception in financial affairs. Rapid expansion brought the attendant evils of flooded markets, greater competition, and that most heinous specter, declining profits. By the late 1750s and early '60s, the people were beginning to recognize that things were taking a turn for the worse.[21]

As had become the usual response to economic troubles, the people and their spokesmen began to search within themselves and their society for the causes of their difficulties. Writers declared that rising taxes were not to blame so much as inner corruption. American cities were becoming Babylons, and leaders were hotly pursuing private gain instead of the public good. As one preacher declared, America "never was, perhaps in a more corrupt and degenerate State than at this Day," while another echoed his lament: "To increase in numbers, in wealth, in elegance and refinements, and at the same time to increase in luxury, profaneness, impiety, and a disesteem of things sacred, is to go backward and not forward."[22] Embracing a policy of austerity and colonial self-sufficiency, the political and financial leaders. turned to the writers and preachers to expound the message of belt-tightening. Franklin's *Way to Wealth* and Mayhew's election sermon are only two examples of a decade of exhortations on the theme of self-sacrifice for the general good.

What the leaders and perhaps even some of the writers themselves did not realize, however, was that once the process of self-castigation and confession had begun, it had to run its natural course to purgation and recommitment. When in the early 1770s the financial picture began to brighten, many economic leaders favored working through parliamentary channels. But they were startled to realize that the reform impulse had created in many a seemingly urgent desire for a radical social upheaval. Indeed, once the process of self-denigration and purgation had been set in motion, many Whig writers and orators such as Sam Adams seemed to welcome additional economic hardships. The heavier the taxes imposed by England upon the colonists, the more the people would be forced to emulate the frugality of the founders and the closer the colonies would be pushed toward a crisis of thorough reform. In this view higher prices and reduced imports would serve to keep the objects of European luxury out of the colonies and thus decrease the people's attachment to what Sam Adams called "British Baubles."[23]

In fusing the messages of religious reform and economic corruption, the ministers and political writers returned frequently to recurring motifs which were designed to lead the people to the logical and emotional position of revolution. The most recurrent theme was that by rebellion the colonists were not moving *toward* a position which would increase their wealth and property, but that they were instead revolting *against* a situation in which their ideals had been corrupted by wicked masters who had enslaved them. The years of prolonged subjection to parliamentary policies had been wrong, they argued, because they involved American self-indulgence in the sins of greed, corruption, bribery, luxury, and lewdness of various kinds. Because the King and his appointees had offered bribes of land and money to those who supported the policies of Parliament, many colonists had betrayed the common good in pursuit of self-aggrandizement. Peter Thacher observed, "Men, We know, have sold their children, their country, and their GOD for a small quantity of painted dirt, *which will perish with the using.*"[24]

The spokesmen of reform asserted that such policies can benefit but a few, and therefore, the only recourse from both a moral and practical standpoint is for all of the people, rich and poor alike, to join together in casting out the wicked oppressors and bribers. Such a plan would involve a great risk of hardship, but a willingness to sacrifice one's personal comfort for the good of all would reap great rewards for rich and poor. Thacher concluded his oration with such a plea: "What is our private interest when opposed to that of three millions of men! Let our bosoms glow with the warmth of patriotism; let us sacrifice our ease, our fortunes, and our lives that we may save our country. That a spirit of public virtue may transcend every private consideration . . . sacrifice what men hold most dear to save this oppressed land."[25] Thacher recognized that the purgation of guilt through such suffering would result in a reward of general self-satisfaction.

In depicting the corruption into which America had fallen and in allocating the blame for the present sorrowful state, the writers repeatedly stressed two themes: the vileness of colonial leaders who had sold out the people for private gain and the moral backsliding of the people themselves who in pursuit of their own ends had passively condoned the election of corrupt leaders or consciously elected them to serve special interests. Nearly always associated with these two related themes was an urgent desire to restore the colonies to their original state of purity and prosperity.

In a popular election sermon of 1775, Samuel Langdon intertwined these themes by choosing his text from Isaiah: "And I will restore thy judges as at the first, and thy counsellors as at the beginning: afterward, thou shalt be called, the city of righteousness, the faithful city."[26] Langdon maintained a careful balance between an attack on corrupt leaders and their British tempters and a chastisement of the people who have brought moral and economic catastrophe upon themselves. Langdon asserted that those who win public appointments are too often "men who are ready to serve any master and execute the most unrighteous decrees for high wages" (p. 358). Their only aim is to "exercise lordship over us and share among themselves the public wealth" (p. 358).

Following the frequent practice of preachers and pamphleteers, including the rationalist Thomas Paine, Langdon turned to the Old Testament for typological parallels of the American situation. The relevancy of his detailed explication of Israel's fall from prosperity into captivity was not to be lost upon his colonial audience. In America as in Zion, vice increased "with the riches and glory of an empire, and thus gradually tends to corrupt the constitution, and in time bring its dissolution" (p. 362). In degenerate Israel as in America also, Langdon observed, "Everyone loved gifts and followed after rewards;... the general aim was at profitable places and pensions; they were influenced in everything by bribery; and their avarice and luxury were never satisfied" (p. 363). In summary he declared that the leaders in such a state "exhaust the national wealth by luxury and bribery, or convert it to their own private benefit" (p. 364).

But Langdon did not let the blame rest upon the leaders alone. He was certain that the major causes of such corruption reside in the people themselves, for God only allows wicked rulers where the people are wallowing in sin. In their lusting after profit and pleasure, the people have invited disaster. Thus he was forced to conclude that only "a general reformation will give good ground to hope that the public happiness can be restored" (p. 361). However, if the people can begin to reform themselves, then "divine providence will interpose to fill every department with wise and good men" (p. 361). Langdon closed his oration with an important demonstration of how deeply religious emotion had infused the political struggle when he assailed the British soldiers stationed in Boston for mocking the religious fervor of the people: "The enemy had reproached us for calling upon his [God's] name and professing trust in him. They have made a mock of our solemn fast and every appearance of serious Christianity in the land. On this account, by way of contempt, they call us 'saints' and that they themselves may keep at a great distance from this character their mouths are full of horrid blasphemies, cursing, bitterness, and vent all the rage, of malice, and barbarity" (p. 372). Looking toward such despicable creatures, Langdon closes with the prayer: "May our land be purged from all its sins!" (p. 373).

The most common image in prewar speeches and writings designed to arouse a sense of urgency to reform was the image of the colonists as slaves of the British. Because the Bible is a rich source of tales of economic exploitation and bondage, writers often reinforced the slavery theme with typological parallels, comparing the sufferings of the colonists to that of the Israelites. In a blistering call to action in 1774, John Hancock urged his audience to "fight, and even die for the prosperity of our Jerusalem. Break in sunder, with noble disdain the bond with which the Philistines have bound you."[27] At the same time that he despised the wicked enslavers from abroad, Hancock also pointed the finger of blame at the colonists themselves for succumbing to self-interest. He exhorted his listeners: "Suffer not yourselves to be betrayed by the soft arts of luxury and effeminacy, into the Pit digged for your destruction. Despise the glare of wealth."[28]

Throughout the eighteenth century in the colonies confusion persisted over the nature of good leadership and the manner by which God designates those worthy to act as leaders. Hancock claimed that the people tended to bestow the right to govern upon the wealthy, and thus again, he reasoned, the people themselves must accept the blame for present corrupt conditions: "That people who pay greater respect to a wealthy villain than to an honest upright man in poverty, almost deserve to be enslaved; they plainly show that wealth, however it may be acquired is in their esteem, to be preferr'd to virtue."[29] In his oration of 1772, Joseph Warren presented a compelling summary of the theme of the people's self-enslavement, and he presented the alternative of a decision to spurn luxury and embrace austerity in terms of an experience of religious conversion. "If you with united zeal and fortitude oppose the torrent of oppression; if you feel the true fire of patriotism burning in your breasts; if you from your souls despise the most gaudy dress that slavery can wear; if you really prefer the lonely cottage (whilest blest with liberty) to the gilded palaces surrounded with the ensigns of slavery; you may have the fullest assurance that tyranny, with her whole accursed train will hide their hideous heads in convulsion, shame, and despair."[30]

In 1774 British troops were stationed in the streets of Boston, and they frequently gathered around the fringes of the crowds at Whig speeches to taunt the speaker and audience. Anticipating such antagonism, Hancock made masterful use of their presence in his oration on the anniversary of the Boston massacre: After chastising the people to the point of shame, he shifted the blame and guilt for America's corruption upon the intruding British soldiers. Not only are they "unmannerly pillagers who impudently thrust their hands into the pockets of every American," but even worse, they are corrupters of the youth of the city. They use "all the arts which idleness and luxury could invent to betray our youth of one sex into extravagance and effeminacy and the other into infamy and ruin."[31] The logic and emotional thrust of Hancock's oration leads to the conclusion that only in expelling this wicked foreign influence will the people restore the land to its former prosperity. He warned that there will be great trials ahead when "the Fig Tree shall not blossom . . . the olive shall fail and the Fields shall yield no Meat"; but if the flock stand together "yet we will rejoice in the LORD, we will joy in the GOD of our Salvation."[32]

Time and again throughout the 1760s and '70s, the Whig orators repeated the theme of the connection between the presence of self-seeking government ministers in the colonies and the folly and wickedness of the people who out of naiveté and avarice help to breed such cancerous corruption. Jonathan Mayhew observed that there are those who get appointed to public offices by declaring their undying loyalty to the people only to betray their promises by turning their backs on the public interest. He saw that loyalty to the land and the people is closely akin to religious faith and thus a breach of a political promise is comparable to the sin of hypocrisy. But he sadly lamented: "There will be hypocrites in politics as well as religion."[33] After a lengthy exhortation to the leaders themselves to avoid the "private personal interest" which had led others into crimes against the people, Mayhew expressed his reservations about the character of those about to assume office. He concluded on a note that borders upon gloomy resignation: "Such things [as corrupt leaders] are almost too infamous and horrid to be supposed possible in a Christian country, But Alas! It is a degenerate world . . . we live in!"[34] Behind Mayhew's argument also lies the assumption that the only way to truly rid the country of such decay in high places is through a total reform of the government which the leaders represent.

Of course, Whig preachers and pamphleteers were always looking to the events of the times for occasions to stir the emotions of the people. When British representatives began to tamper with the question of religious rights in the colonies, the patriot writers found an excellent opportunity for resurrecting the old Puritan theme of the external threat to religious, as well as political and economic, liberties. Rumors of an Anglican episcopacy in America served to heighten concern over a British scheme to exercise religious control over the people. However, because there were already many Anglicans of patriotic leanings in the colonies, especially in the South, the writers quickly shifted their emphasis to the threat of an even more abhorrent evil, a popish plot.[35]

When in 1774 the Quebec Act passed in Parliament, permitting the establishment of Catholicism on the American continent, the Whig preachers turned to the Book of Revelation for the script of that cosmic drama which pits Christ's faithful in America against the Scarlet Whore of Rome and casts the British officials in the role of secret agents of Satan. As Henry Cumings expounded it, the Book of Revelation had indeed foretold that "the Scarlet Whore would soon get mounted on her Horned beast in America, and with the CUP OF ABOMINATION in her hand, ride triumphant over the heads of true Protestants making multitudes DRUNK WITH THE WINE OF HER FORNICATIONS."[36] The fact that the British government would permit the forces of popery to invade America was final proof that nothing short of a total purgation of the corrupters would save the land of the Fathers.

In his sermon "The Church's Flight into the Wilderness: An Address on the Times," Samuel Sherwood vividly restated the theme of America's special place in divine history: In his divine economy God had held the continent of America in reserve for his people. The natural resources, therefore, belonged to the chosen whom he had brought to the new Zion and to their descendants. Bringing together in one image an attack on British economic policies, a lamentation on the sins of the Americans, and the threat of a Roman Catholic invasion, Sherwood envisioned that because "despotism has run high, and a lusting ambition after arbitrary power and lawless domination has prevailed . . . the dragon dare[s] to venture into America and put on his long horns."[37] In an effective fusion of powerful biblical language and political events, Sherwood managed to impart to the dragon of revelation a cunning talent for modern economic warfare. The dragon attacked Christ's church by trying to "starve her into a compliance to his despotic and arbitrary rule, by shutting up her ports and harbours, and interdicting her trade and commerce, and cutting her off from all supplies from her fishery."[38]

Although most calls to action were usually constructed in terms of a rejection of the intolerable present state of affairs, Whig speakers and writers sometimes stressed the benefits to be derived from total reform. When the rhetoricians turned to the question of the advantages of freedom which could follow a successful revolution, their promises were also presented through a complex intertwining of financial, political, and spiritual prophecies.

The most repeated vision of America's future glory present in speeches, and in poetry like "The Rising Glory of America" by Philip Freneau and Hugh Henry Brackenridge, pictured the country as "a new Jerusalem sent down from heaven," "another Canaan,"[39] which will prosper in trade and enjoy a special place in God's divine plan. But to strengthen the image with more specifics of how the blessings of heaven will be realized in America, editors, orators, and poets alike could present a more detailed accounting: "What will be the probable benefits of independence?" asked the editor of the Pennsylvania *Evening Post*. He offered a calculated assessment: "A free and unlimited trade; a great accession of wealth; and a proportional rise in the value of the land, and a gradual improvement and perfection of manufacturers. WE CANNOT PAY TOO GREAT A PRICE FOR LIBERTY, AND POSTERITY WILL THINK INDEPENDENCE A CHEAP PURCHASE AT EIGHTEEN MILLIONS ."[40] Appealing to the thirst for fame in the young Whig leaders and in the wealthy elite, writers depicted the enduring gratitude and worship of future generations: "Children yet unborn will rise and call you blessed, the present generation will be extolled and delegated as the happy instruments of God delivering millions from thraldom and slavery."[41]

The persistence of the theme of the conflict between self-interest and the common good and the emotional power of the traditional verbal formulas and public rituals during the pre-revolutionary years demonstrate the profound importance which religious language had in forming a sense of a separate American identity. The language of the preachers and political writers served to awaken in the people a sense of sharing a special cultural heritage that existed apart from the British. Indeed, they now saw themselves as the Puritan founders had viewed themselves, as preservers of the purity of the English traditions at a time when the mother country was in a state of decay. In announcing a desire to purge America of the last vestiges of European corruption, the colonists returned to a rhetoric which had been born in revolution.

Because the enlivening language of the Puritan sermon had originally sprung up in Reformation England, it had in fact always been a revolutionary rhetoric. Of course, once established in America, the preachers had rarely stressed revolution against civil powers. But the verbal patterns of their sermons still emphasized various forms of rebellion: revolution against the vile tendencies of the self, against the attacks and enslavement of Satan, and against corruption and backsliding. Life was a constant battle of the good against the powers of evil which hold sway on the earth and in the human heart.

Thus, the language of revolution was deeply ingrained in the American idiom and in the hearts of Americans by the mid-eighteenth century. For the members of a generation which had experienced the fervor of the Great Awakening during their most impressionable years, the infusion of political and economic crisis with compelling religious language and themes aroused the people to an emotional pitch which could be relieved only through the total purification of the society in the fires of rebellion.

NOTES

1. Part of this essay was given as a lecture on "Economics, Religion, and Revolutionary War Rhetoric" at the Lawrence Henry Gipson Institute Symposium at Lehigh University in the fall of 1975 and will appear in a volume of those papers.

2. Benjamin Franklin, "The Way to Wealth," *The Works of Benjamin Franklin*, ed. John Bigelow (New York: G. P. Putnam's Sons, 1904), II, 28, 38.

3. The idea that the Puritan's pursuit of spiritual gain was directly related to the spirit of capitalism is expressed in the term, "Protestant ethic." But for an important modification of the Weber-Tawney thesis, see Edmund S. Morgan's essay, "The Puritan Ethic and the Coming of the Revolution," *William and Mary Quarterly*, 24 (Jan. 1967), 3–18, in which he explores some of the complexities of the relationship between Puritan theology and American political ideology. For a full study of this theme, see Richard L. Bushman, *From Puritan to Yankee: Character and the Social Order in Connecticut, 1690–1765* (Cambridge: Harvard University Press, 1967; reprinted by W. W. Norton, 1970). My concern in this essay is with the adaptation of religious language, symbolism, and emotional fervor to the service of political and economic ends.

4. For an example of this tendency, see the statements of the early separatist John Robinson in his *Observations of Knowledge and Virtue* (London, 1625), pp. 149–54.

5. This was an elusive and complex relationship which was at the time and still is readily oversimplified. By the end of the seventeenth century, however, some ministers openly drew the connection between spiritual and material success, as in Samuel Willard's sermon *Heavenly Merchandize: or The Purchasing of TRUTH Recommended and the Selling of It Disswaded* (Boston, 1686).

6. For evidence of economic hardships and belt-tightening, see William S. Sachs and Ari Hoogenboom, *The Enterprising Colonials: Society on the Eve of the Revolution* (Chicago: Argonaut, 1965), esp. pp. 122–35, and Joseph Albert Ernst, *Money and Politics in America: 1755–1775* (Chapel Hill: University of North Carolina Press, 1973), in particular pp. 352–62.

7. Jonathan Mayhew, *A Sermon Preached in the Audience of His Excellency William Shirley . . .* (Boston, 1754); reprinted in *The Wall and the Garden: Selected Massachusetts Election Sermons, 1670–1775*, ed. A. W. Plumstead (Minneapolis: University of Minessota Press, 1968), p. 289.

8. Ibid., p. 305.

9. An earlier examination of the language of Revolutionary War writing which stresses its propagandistic nature is Philip Davidson, *Propaganda and the American Revolution, 1763-1783* (Chapel Hill: University of North Carolina Press, 1941). See also Alice M. Baldwin, *The New England Clergy and the American Revolution* (Durham: Duke University Press, 1928). Still a useful source is Moses Coit Tyler's *The Literary History of the American Revolution, 1763-1783* (New York: G. P. Putnam's Sons, 1897).

10. Compare the arguments of Ernst, *Money and Politics in America*, pp. 353-62, with those of Bernard Bailyn, *The Ideological Origins of the American Revolution* (Cambridge: Harvard University Press, 1967), and Gorden S. Wood, "Rhetoric and Reality in the American Revolution," *William and Mary Quarterly*, 23 (1966), 3-32.

11. *The Writings of Thomas Jefferson*, ed. P.L. Ford (New York, 1892-99), I, II. For comment, see also Davidson, *Propaganda and the American Revolution*, pp. 95 ff.

12. See, for example, Peter Oliver, *Origin & Progress of the American Rebellion* (1781), ed. Douglass Adair and John A. Schutz (San Marino, Calif.: Huntington Library, 1961), pp. 41-45. For commentary on the relationship between religion and politics in the colonies, see Carl Bridenbaugh, *Mitre and Sceptre: Transatlantic Faiths, Ideas, Personalities, and Politics, 1689-1775* (New York: Oxford University Press, 1962), and William G. McLoughlin, "The Role of Religion in the Revolution," in *Essays on the American Revolution*, ed. Stephen G. Kurtz and James H. Hutson (Chapel Hill: University of North Carolina Press, 1973), pp. 197-255.

13. Ezra Stiles, *A Discourse on the Christian Union* (Boston, 1761), as reprinted in *The Great Awakening*, ed. Alan Heimert and Perry Miller (New York: Bobbs-Merrill, 1967), pp. 595-96. For previous suggestions regarding the connections between the Great Awakening and the Revolution, see Alan Heimert, *Religion and the American Mind from the Great Awakening to the Revolution* (Cambridge: Harvard University Press, 1966), which examines the intellectual history, and Perry Miller, "From the Covenant to the Revival," in *The Shaping of American Religion*, ed. James Ward Smith and A. Leland Jamison (Princeton: Princeton University Press, 1961), pp. 322-68.

14. Jonathan Edwards stressed the need for more order in families and delighted in the reassertion of paternal authority. See *The Works of President Edwards in Four Volumes* (New York: Leavitt, 1853), III, 235. For discussion of the important impact of the revival upon male converts, see Cedric B. Cowing, "Sex and Preaching in the Great Awakening," *American Quarterly*, 20 (1968), 624-44.

15. Lawrence H. Leder, "Introduction," to *The Meaning of the American Revolution*, ed. Leder (Chicago: Quadrangle Books, 1969), p. 5.

16. For an examination of the possible psychosocial roots of the emotional responses to some of these themes, see Jack P. Greene, "Search for Identity: An Interpretation of the Meaning of Selected Patterns of Social Response in Eighteenth-Century America," *Journal of Social History*, 3 (1970), 189-220.

17. Keayne's torment is recorded in "The Apologia of Robert Keayne," ed. Bernard Bailyn, *Publications of the Colonial Society of Massachusetts, Transactions*, 42 (1954), 243-341.

18. For useful insights into this issue of authority, see T.H. Breen, *The Character of the Good Ruler: A Study of Puritan Political Ideas in New England, 1630-1730* (New Haven: Yale University Press, 1970), and Douglass

Adair, "Fame and the Founding Father," in *Fame and the Founding Fathers*, ed. H. Trevor Colbourn (New York: Norton, 1974), pp. 27-52.

19. Samuel Willard, Edward Taylor, Cotton Mather, and Solomon Stoddard all recognized the importance of this stage of the conversion process. See Stoddard's discussion in his *A Guide to Christ, or The Way of Directing Souls That Are Under The Work of CONVERSION* (Boston, 1735). Cotton Mather effectively transferred the guilt of the people to the intruder Satan and may have thereby laid the groundwork for the witchcraft delusion.

20. Cotton Mather's sermon justifying the expulsion of Andros in the terms of the intruder in the sacred enclosed garden is a rich example of the function of this metaphor; see *The Way to Prosperity* (Boston, 1689).

21. See Sachs and Hoogenboom, *The Enterprising Colonials*, pp. 122-35.

22. Samuel Buell, *The Best New-Year's Gift for Young People* (New London, 1775), p. 53, and Nathan Fiske, *Remarkable Providences* (Boston, 1776), p. 25.

23. Sam Adams, Boston *Gazette*, Oct. 1, 1764.

24. Peter Thacher, *Boston Massacre Oration*, delivered in Watertown, Mass., on March 5, 1776; printed in *The Colonial Idiom*, ed. David Potter and Gordon L. Thomas (Carbondale: Southern Illinois University Press, 1970), p. 273.

25. Ibid., p. 278.

26. Samuel Langdon, *Government Corrupted by Vice, and Recovered by Righteousness* (Watertown, Mass., 1775); reprinted in Plumstead, *The Wall and the Garden*, p. 357.

27. John Hancock, *Boston Massacre Oration* (Boston, 1774); reprinted in *The Colonial Idiom*, ed. Potter and Thomas, p. 270.

28. Ibid.

29. Ibid.

30. Joseph Warren, *Boston Massacre Oration* (Boston, 1772); reprinted in *The Colonial Idiom*, Potter and Thomas, p. 245.

31. Hancock, *Massacre Oration*, p. 264.

32. Ibid., p. 271.

33. Mayhew, "A Sermon," in *The Wall and the Garden*, ed. Plumstead, p. 295.

34. Ibid., p. 315.

35. See Davidson, *Propaganda and the American Revolution*, pp. 123-28.

36. Henry Cumings, *A Sermon Preached at Billerica*, Nov. 27, 1766 (Boston, 1767), p. 12.

37. Samuel Sherwood, "The Church's Flight into the Wilderness: An Address on the Times" (New York, 1776), p. 30.

38. Ibid., p. 32.

39. "The Rising Glory of America," in *The Poems of Philip Freneau*, ed. Fred Lewis Pattee (Princeton: University Library, 1902), I, 82.

40. Pennsylvania *Evening Post*, Feb. 17, 1776.

41. "Proclamation of the people of Windham Connecticut," in Ellen D. Larned, *History of Windham County, Connecticut* (Worcester, 1874-80), II, 125.

SIX

Resolution in *The Marble Faun*: A Minority View

CLAUDIA D. JOHNSON

Ever since Plato banned art from his ideal republic upon utilitarian and philosophical grounds, thinkers have found a disturbing ambivalence in the position of art in society. This is especially true of Nathaniel Hawthorne, who rarely wrote a short story or a novel without in some way exploring within the work itself how the creative imagination works and what its relationship to man should be. For Hawthorne it was a particularly disquieting question because, in the beginning, he pictured a productive artistic imagination as incompatible with that humanistic morality which constantly shaped the direction of his stories.

Hawthorne's dilemma has been repeatedly studied by perceptive critics.[1] Essentially the problem seems to arise from the belief that to be morally complete, man must descend into the tragic hell of his own heart and emerge once again as an active participant in a world of nature, time, and society. On the other hand, to be an artist, man has to remain apart: he has to be alien, an observer, a person who sees but does not participate.

This study does not attempt to refute the psychological thesis of most of the studies of Hawthorne, that subconsciously he was never able to reconcile morality and art; rather it tries to show that in *The Marble Faun* Hawthorne's persistent exploration resulted, at least in his own mind, in a resolution between art and morality. In "The Custom-House," he attempts, in theory, to reconcile the dilemma of art and morality which he had dramatized in the tales. In the three subsequent novels *The Scarlet Letter, The House of the Seven Gables,* and *The Blithedale Romance,* he tries unsuccessfully to reach a practical affirmation of that altered concept of art, a definition of what he called "romance." Success, however, comes only with the final novel. In *The Marble Faun* the two ends of the dilemma are finally brought together. The redemptive journey of moral man is shown to be one of the same with that of the artist. In evolving this reconciliation, moreover, Hawthorne has arrived at a theory of art which is astonishingly modern in concept and in application: it is plastic, fluid, organic.

In the tales Hawthorne explains morality by dramatizing the journey of the fulfilled man. Such a character went through a contemplative stage in which he discovered the dark and helpless side of his nature as did Robin Molineux. The incomplete man, like Goodman Brown, wandered the maze of his own ego forever, but the renewed and fulfilled characters, like the pair of lovers in "The Canterbury Pilgrims," would, for better or for worse, leave the protective womb of ego in order to join with the growing, imperfect world. The typical journey, therefore, involved a period of inner, contemplative trial during which man learned that those things on which he had previously depended would no longer support him. Accompanying this painful iconoclasm was a diminishing of ego, a mortification of the self. Until he was reborn, man was considered to be outside of time, outside of nature, and outside of society, in an inward state of moral decay.

Hawthorne's curious attitude toward art, which has intrigued many critics, is explained by the fact that Hawthorne gives to his artists those very characteristics which identify the unregenerate moral child caught in inwardness. That the artists of the tales display these characteristics indicates Hawthorne's early uneasiness about the place of the artistic imagination in the lives of moral men. Regenerated men turned outward to join a time-affected society in common cause, but the artist operated from outside that cause, in an interior world of imagination and dedication to art. Thus, the artist of the tales is incapable of moral regeneration because his art, by its very nature, necessarily arises from selfish observation and removal from human concerns.

Owen Warland, the artist of the beautiful, is decidedly outside of time, nature, and society. Although is is a watchmaker, he "cared no more for the measurement of time than if it had been merged into eternity" (p. 508).[2] His separation from society is illustrated by his failure to join it in common toil or to marry Annie. His disgust with the earthiness of her father and his need to idealize her show his separation from nature. Unlike Danforth, he does not become a husband and a father, roles which inevitably characterize Hawthorne's morally complete man. Instead Owen so devotes himself to an ideal removed from earth that the dream of the ideal becomes an obsession. He is inspired by nature but only by the most ethereal manifestation of it in the form of the butterfly, which he idealizes as he does Annie. Moreover, his life-long aim is not to embrace nature but, like Rappaccini and Aylmer, to perfect it; Danforth says of the butterfly, "that does beat all nature" (p. 532).

Hawthorne saw in Owen Warland the inescapable dilemma of the artist whose vision and values were so removed from mankind that whatever he moved to create was destroyed by the world.[3] At the same time that Owen has peace of soul in his artistic accomplishment, he displays all the characteristics which Hawthorne gave to the moral degenerate of the tales: isolation, curiosity, obsession, excessive spirituality, time-defiance, and a rejection of earth and woman. It would seem that the realm of ego and other-worldliness, which one had to transcend in order to be a complete man, was the very realm in which art belonged.

A second view of the artist in the tales is less sympathetic than "The Artist of the Beautiful." The painter in "The Prophetic Pictures" has the supernal visions coupled with self-deception, extraordinary curiosity, obsession, and lack of human feeling characteristic of Hawthorne's protagonists trapped in descent. Everything in this gifted portrait painter's life is subordinated to an insane dedication to art: "Like all other men around whom an engrossing purpose wreathes itself, he was insulated from the mass of humankind. He had no aim—no pleasure—no sympathies—but what were ultimately connected with his art. Though gentle in manner and upright in intent and action, he did not possess kindly feelings; his heart was cold; no living creatures could be brought near enough to keep him warm" (p. 206). Like many other Hawthorne characters in descent, in "reading other bosoms with an acuteness almost preternatural, the painter failed to see the disorder of his own" (p. 207).

"The Custom-House" is a turning point in Hawthorne's vision of morality and art. Not only does he begin to recognize greater complexity within the human situation, but he radically readjusts his views of the artist and the workings of the imagination. The inability of the writer of the tales to reconcile morality with art is illustrated in the opening of the Custom House sketch when the voice of morality, in the form of the narrator's Puritan ancestors, derides him for his artistic vocation. The inner conflict is also probably what causes him to pose as an editor rather than an artist.

The imagination, which had languished among the transcendentalists, was an unfallen one. At the opening of the sketch, the writer still has the romantic notion that the ugly realities of the world can be transformed by the imagination, working like moonlight—a view of creativity which had been fostered in his former exclusive, "impractical" literary world. His past associates believed that artistic creation took place within a longed-for transcendence, and the narrator had come, like them, to connect artistic creation with inwardness.

In "The Custom-House," however, Hawthorne alters his former view of the creative imagination.[4] The view of the artist as a passive recipient of the Muse remained appealing, but the narrator learned that art, as long as it remained removed from the business of life and action, can never have a proper life of its own. The germ of an idea, in this case the symbolic "A," can present itself to the artist in a state of inwardness, but the idea can never blossom until the artist passes from a passive to an active state. Should he remain separated from the world's concerns, he becomes either sterile, as does Coverdale, or immoral, as does the portrait painter in "Prophetic Pictures."

The Salem Custom House is even more isolated than his previous literary existence had been. It is dead: the old wharfside bustle has died down; business, such as it is, is carried on by aged workers who sleep most of the time; the grass is "unthrifty" and the flag "droops." A worker within the Custom House is a child who does not "struggle amid a struggling world"—not until circumstance "sends him forth." As long as the narrator is there, "he does not share in the united effort of mankind" nor does he "live throughout the whole range of his faculties and sensibilities" (pp. 38, 39).

The narrator discovers the sterility of the isolated artist when he wants to bring his fictional characters to life after having been inspired in the attic: "My imagination was a tarnished mirror. It would not reflect, or only with miserable dimness, the figures with which I did my best to people it. The characters of the narrative would not be warmed and rendered malleable, by any heat that I could kindle at my intellectual forge" (p. 34).

Coincident with the death of the imagination is his separation from society in that "he does not share in the united effort of mankind"—a condition characteristic of the morally unregenerated man. Thus, "The Custom-House" is an important turning point in Hawthorne's concept of art. No longer did he believe that art was created in isolated preciousness. Inspiration could occur in the quiet transcendence of the world, but the imagination died down and was only rekindled when the artist, like the moral man, rejoined the everyday world.

Despite his discoveries in "The Custom-House," Hawthorne continued to be troubled by the artist's role in society and the workings of the creative imagination. This is evident in his first attempt after "The Custom-House" to portray an artist. Holgrave initially appears to be the answer to the former problems of the artist in society, for although he is understood to be an artist by reason of his picture-taking and his detached curiosity, he also has many of the attributes of a morally renewed man in that he is very much a man of the world and a social activist. Furthermore, he becomes more sympathetic with the other characters as the story moves on, and, like Hawthorne's morally completed man, he marries at the novel's conclusion. The potential harmony between art and morality fails to develop convincingly, for, whatever regeneration Holgrave has, through Phoebe, comes at the expense of his dedication to his craft. His career as a daguerreotypist is described as just one of a number of vocations which he can drop as easily as he discontinued dentistry. His other artistic occupation as a creative writer is mentioned offhandedly, almost solely to introduce the legend of Alice Pyncheon and Maule. Writing tales is "among the multitude of my marvellous gifts," he says (p. 186). Holgrave's future as an artist is not even worthy of note at the novel's close. In short, the problem of the artist and his morality did not disappear in Hawthorne's portrait of a kindly artist, for Holgrave's dedication to his calling is diminished in direct relation to his moral awareness.

In his third novel, *The Blithedale Romance,* Hawthorne affirms for the first time in a fictional portrait of the artist that which had been his experience in the Custom House: that contrary to his early view in the tales, an isolated and passive man can no more be a true artist than he can be a humane person. Hawthorne gives this developing idea of art a new dimension by putting the reader within a sterile and somewhat distorted imagination which turns progressively inward and away from nature, society, and action as the story unfolds. Artistic failure and moral failure are caused by the same condition of isolation. Coverdale's moral failing (his cold, persistent prying) and his artistic failing (his inability to see clearly or to actually write more than a handful of poems) can both be attributed to his inability to move outside the limits of the self. The "leafy cave" is indicative of his position in relation to society. The fact that love, work, and active involvement with people are no part of his life is in direct correlation to his sterility as an artist.

In this unusual novel Hawthorne speculated about an additional problem of art's relationship to moral regeneration which commands much more of his attention in *The Marble Faun:* the continuing problem of recognizing and conveying the wholeness of man's nature and condition, much of which must inevitably be shrouded in mystery. And this is precisely where Coverdale fails as both human being and artist.[5] Because he has not actively cast his lot with others and because his faculties are not fully engaged, he never really appreciates the complexity, the mystery, or the human emotion, which is so necessary for an artist. Coverdale is almost fanatical about carefully observing "facts" and reporting details, but in so doing, he rends the truth apart. His insistence on analyzing and reporting upon the mysteries of the Veiled Lady, of Old Moodie, and of Zenobia's relationship to Westervelt betrays his limitation as a truth-seer and a truth-conveyer. By contrast, the narrator of *The Marble Faun* will come to recognize and respect the mysterious legends and experiences of his characters—mysteries which he insists elude the analytical powers of the intellect. Thus, Coverdale becomes Hawthorne's negative definition of the true artist, a portrait which is consistent with Hawthorne's concept of the morally incomplete man.

In *The Marble Faun* Hawthorne addressed himself directly to the problem of the correlation between art and morality which had troubled him in all of his previous work. Within this novel he developed what he believed was characteristic of an art of the highest order and of the special imagination which creates it.

Hawthorne had illustrated in his tales and earlier novels that he believed man achieves completion—only after a period of inner trial during which self is diminished. Subsequently the character could take a high moral course by turning outward in love to take his place among other men in a natural world of time. Art and the artist in these early tales had remained in a timeless, isolated territory.

But Hawthorne's conclusions about art in *The Marble Faun* seem to be that the highest form of art (in fiction this would be "romance" as he defines it) can only be created by an imagination which has undergone a similar dark trial in artistic terms. During such a trial, both art itself and the love of art for its own sake are diminished. Afterwards art will no longer be self-serving and stagnant. Its purpose thereafter will be to serve man. Its form, learning from nature, will be free and organic. The resultant "regenerated" art will, therefore, become a living thing somehow, taking its place in the world of time, men, and nature as the regenerated soul must. Thus, Hawthorne incorporated into his new aesthetic concept the same characteristics and the same history which he had long before attributed to man's morality.

In the inner trials of the two American artists in *The Marble Faun,* Hawthorne showed that great art must lose its sanctity in order to imitate nature and to serve man by helping him reach spiritual truths. Art must, like all other parts of a man's life, be subservient to that purpose. As the self must be mortified through trial, so must art. As Hawthorne shows in parallel chapters near the novel's close, art, like the self, knows fulfillment by serving man. In these chapters Hilda and then Kenyon know disillusionment and helplessness as artists. In the first half of the novel, Hilda is a copyist who has devoted her life to the Old Masters. She actually deifies them. In her despair, however, she begins to doubt the wisdom of her former surrender to art. Furthermore, the Old Masters lose their power to move her. Most art, she comes to realize, has grown degenerate in its self-serving tradition and in its separation from nature. She realizes that unqualified love of art accelerates this degeneracy because the guiding love of anyone's life must be directed only toward man and God, not toward art: "The love of Art, therefore, differs widely in its influence from the love of Nature; whereas, if Art had not strayed away from its legitimate paths and aims, it ought to soften and sweeten the lives of its worshippers, in even a more exquisite degree than the contemplation of natural objects. But, of its own potency, it has no such effect; and it fails, likewise, in that other test of its moral value which poor Hilda was not involuntarily trying upon it" (p. 340).

The Demon of Weariness even provokes Hilda's disillusionment with the Old Masters: "The mighty Italian Masters, as you deem them, were not human, nor addressed their works to human sympathies, but to a false intellectual taste, which they themselves were the first to create. Well might they call their doings, 'Art,' for they substituted art instead of Nature. Their fashion is past, and ought, indeed, to have died and been buried along with them!" (p. 336).

The love of art, "of its own potency," or in and of itself, belongs in the underworld, removed from nature and human concerns. Neither Hilda nor the narrator can continue to admire painters, solely in the service of art, who "put genius and imagination in the place of spiritual insight" (p. 375), and who fail to be taught by nature. The once-devoted disciple of the Old Masters now finds herself testing the works she sees for truth rather than for beauty of form. We find that many works of art in the novel would probably pass Hilda's test, for they comfort man or convey to him the "deeper mysteries of revelation" (p. 340). Such examples are Sodoma's fresco at Siena, the Laocoön group, and Kenyon's own Donatello. Even though Hilda doubts the value of her early gods, even though she can no longer accept art for art's sake, she does not "give up all art as worthless, only, it had lost its consecration" (p. 341).

Kenyon has a similar experience with art that parallels Hilda's and comes almost immediately after hers in the novel. Like Hilda, he comes to know the mortification of an old idol when, after Hilda's disappearance, he suspects "that it was a very cold art to which he had devoted himself" (p. 391). In the depths of his trial, he tells Miriam that "Imagination and the love of art have both died out of me" (p. 427). Even the re-creation of a Campagna Venus, which would rival all other Venuses, leaves

him feeling empty. But like Hilda, Kenyon loses not his regard
for all art, but only his old reverence for it "as something ethereal
and godlike" (p. 391).

The mortification of art does not result in the death of all
art, but rather in art's regeneration. Hilda's artistic imagination
is raised rather than obliterated following her acceptance of art's
high humanistic purpose. After the confessional, she is inventive,
her imagination quickened by the statue of Saint Michael and the
concept of the seven-branched candlestick. Her mind, in fact,
makes "its plaything of every object" (p. 370); and although
she finds that she can no longer be a copier of the Old Masters,
she now sees more deeply and more profoundly into the heart
of things. "She had known such a reality, that it taught her to
distinguish inevitably the large portion that is unreal, in every
work of art" (p. 375). Her subsequent insight into the wedding
of a new art form with a grand idea in Kenyon's bust of Donatello
is a graphic illustration of her new artistic insight.

Two things suggest that Kenyon's art, like Hilda's artistic
sensibility, will be invigorated as a result of his loss of reverence
for art: his return home—that is, his return to time, to nature,
and to society as it is represented by his union with Hilda—
and his completion near the end of the novel of a piece of sculpture which conveys a living truth. Kenyon will now be removed
from the artistic atmosphere of Rome, with its deification of
the Old Masters, old forms, and old subjects, a place where, the
narrator has told us, the expatriates find originality fast dying
out of them. The vocational trials of these two artists reveal that
true art and morality do come together in common purpose.
Regenerated art, like the regenerated soul, must turn outward,
not back upon itself. It must provide men with truth, not serve
itself in beatific isolation.

Hawthorne's attention in this novel is drawn not only to the
purpose of true art but to its form.[6] Kenyon, in viewing the
painted window, states that the living purpose of true art must
be conveyed by a living form. Unregenerated art is recognized by
its time-defiance and its slavish adherence to old, unquestioned
artistic forms. Regenerated art, responding to human realities,
strives for a fluidity of form which recognizes time and studies
nature. This view is illustrated in the novel by comparing forms

which are static with those which study nature. The antithesis of the vital artistic form is found in time-frozen pieces of sculpture—rigid, cold moments held indefinitely in time like the Dying Gladiator, which is, Kenyon says, "like flinging a block of marble up into the air, and, by some trick or enchantment, causing it to stick there. You feel that it ought to come down, and are dissatisfied that it does not obey the natural law" (p. 16). Sculpture, as Miriam reminds him, is often a "fossilizing" process; its inability to incorporate new subject matter gives it "no longer a right to claim any place among the living arts" (p. 124). Opposite of the cold marble is the living grass which sprouts from ruins. Grass is not "art," of course, but it has the growth and variety which Hawthorne thought true art should learn from nature.

In contrast to rigid artistic forms is the painted window in a village church which Kenyon studies during Donatello's pilgrimage. Light can only fall on the outside of most paintings, but in this window painting, light is "interfused throughout." It "illuminates the design, and invests it with a living radiance, and in requital the unfading colors transmute the common daylight into a miracle of richness and glory" (p. 304). Kenyon sees that the message of the transforming celestial light is perfectly wed to the form which uses changing natural light. Like the many fountains which embellish the novel, the painted window is ever new, ever changing, reflective of depths and shadows, symbolic of life.

Concomitant with Donatello's spiritual growth is Kenyon's artistic growth in finally producing the bust of Donatello, a statue whose rough form captures the sense of development which is its message. It is "not nearly finished" and is "lacking sharpness" (p. 379), but because of these very features, it has an organic quality which is almost always missing in marble. Hilda attests to this when she says, "it has an effect as if I could see this countenance gradually brightening while I look at it. It gives the impression of a growing intellectual power and moral sense . . . here a soul is being breathed into him" (p. 380).

That which weds form to meaning in the Donatello statue is largely Kenyon's mastery of suggestiveness. It is necessary, first, because shadowy truths can only be conveyed in this fashion.

Heartfelt truths evade the finished form, the explicit explanation, and the too-close observation. For this reason, for example, the reader is told that pictorial art surpasses written art in conveying spiritual truths, "involving as it does, deeper mysteries of revelation, and bringing them closer to man"'s heart, and making him tenderer to be impressed by them, than the most eloquent words of preacher or prophet" (p. 340). A suggestive form is also needed because the participation of the viewer is elicited, giving the work an ever-changing multiplicity, like the fountains of Rome.

Hawthorne carries his artistic exploration to a graphic and intriguing extent by making the novel itself an embodiment of the very aesthetic theory toward which he has been groping through these speculations of his characters. Hawthorne tried to bring the form of his novel into harmony with nature, time, and society in two ways. First, he incorporates linear time and nature by taking static mythical and legendary characters and making them human, subject to development and mystery. Second, by appealing to his reader to be co-creator with him, Hawthorne brings his art into an active, social world.

Hawthorne's raw materials, the legends, statues, and painting of Rome, are static "fossils" caught in timelessness. They do not change or grow. Such are the statue of Cleopatra, the legend of the Faun of Praxiteles, and the portrait of Beatrice Cenci. The writer's imagination struggles with these ruins until it creates living characters which are no longer flat or rigid but which begin to put on complexity, depth, and life. Imaginatively created life is represented in the novel by its four characters, particularly Donatello, who enters as a type—a faun—and emerges as a full-blown, growing human being. In this sense, Donatello's regeneration, his developing soul, is coincidental with the narrator's quickening imagination, which concomitantly ascends from the inanimate to the organic, from timelessness to movement, from marble to flesh, from type to three-dimensional character. Thus, all of Rome is that broad, open symbol of the collective inwardness of humankind, teeming with its gloomy evil, intricacy, and enigmas, upon which Hawthorne's imagination works, the story springing from the ruins like living grass.

Hawthorne also appeared to want the form of *The Marble Faun* to embody nature's mystery. Like Robin Molineux, Hester, and Hilda, he had come to know that nature is marked by a mystery which eludes rational analysis. Subsequently, he sought to embody in the novel the enigmas which he thought were nature's reality. It had long been impossible for him to characterize life with the simple, clear-cut allegories of the tales, having come to affirm that the truth of the human condition was essentially complex and mysterious. Now, however, he attempted to capture this reality in an art form, thereby joining art and nature. The narrator thus refrains from explicitly recounting Miriam's past, the identity of the monk, the occurrences within Cenci palace, and the appearance of Donatello's ears, for these rough outlines in the novel create a suggestive form which is more readily wed to a message of natural complexity.

Finally, *The Marble Faun* illustrates that art can join society. Here Hawthorne insisted that the life with which art must be endowed has to arise from the workings of the *reader's* imagination upon the imperfect work. The Preface is directed to that particular reader who, it seems obvious, Hilda describes later as belonging to "that class of spectators whose sympathy will help them to see the perfect through a mist of imperfection," and "find a great deal more in them [works of art] than the poet or artist has actually expressed" (p. 379). In the same vein, certain unfinished sketches by the Old Masters are admired by the narrator because they set "the imagination at work" rather than leave "the spectator nothing to do" (p. 138). The involvement of the reader in the work of art was one notion which Hilda retained even after her troubling doubts about the Old Masters: "There is always the necessity of helping out the painter's art with your own resources of sensibility and imagination" (p. 335). Hawthorne, who seems to subscribe to Hilda's idea, says in the Preface that he scarcely dares to believe that such a reader exists; however, the novel which follows, with its repeated references to the viewer, attests to the narrator's faith in just such a kindly spectator. But the sad suspicion stated in the Conclusion, as he reviews the characteristics of "romance" and the higher forms of all art, is that the ideal reader does not exist. Speaking in the third person, he writes:

He reluctantly avails himself of the opportunity afforded by a new edition, to explain such incidents and passages as may have been left too much in the dark; reluctantly, he repeats, because the necessity makes him sensible that he can have succeeded but imperfectly, at best, in throwing about this Romance the kind of atmosphere essential to the effect at which he aimed.

He designed the story and the characters to bear, of course, a certain relation to human nature and human life, but still to be so artfully and airily removed from our mundane sphere, that some laws and proprieties of their own should be implicitly and insensibly acknowledged.

The idea of the modern Faun, for example, loses all the poetry and beauty which the Author fancied in it, and becomes nothing better than a grotesque absurdity, if we bring it into the actual light of day. He had hoped to mystify this anomalous creature between the Real and the Fantastic, in such a manner that the reader's sympathies might be excited, to a certain pleasurable degree, without impelling him to ask how Cuvier would have classified poor Donatello, or to insist upon being told, in so many words, whether he had furry ears or no. As respects all who ask such questions, the book is, to that extent, a failure [pp. 463-64].

As Kenyon re-creates the Venus of the Campagna from ruins, as the narrator's imagination gives character to the stone faun, so the reader's imagination must be quickened to give the work of art new life and completion.

The participation of the reader insures that any work will have the variety of life; any work will be re-created each time any reader comes to it with an active imagination. Only dead art is created once; the highest form of art is being created, and variously created, each time a sympathetic, imaginative spectator comes to it.

The imagination of a reader who can respond in the deepest sense to the truths of a work of art must also have undergone a regenerative descent. His renewed imagination will have passed through a dark experience with complexity and will no longer assume that simple, clear morals can explain mystery and gloom. He will also have put passivity behind him—that state in which he expects the artist to carefully delineate minute details for him. Instead, the reader becomes active, willingly responding with a loving heart to join the artist in creation, expecting art to serve man, not to serve art. Thus, art of the highest order—its purpose, its form, and its participants—shares the history and characteristics of morality.

In summary, Hawthorne's chief interests throughout his career were morality and art, but the two concepts had early been antithetical because man's morality was part of the main business of life, whereas his art existed somewhere outside society, time, and nature. With *The Marble Faun* that disparity was dispelled in Hawthorne's own mind in the formulation of an artistic theory which arises directly and logically from his concept of moral regeneration. In this, his last published novel, art imitates nature and affirms the truth of time in its depth and changefulness; furthermore, art becomes a social motion between artist and reader.

NOTES

1. Millicent Bell, *Hawthorne's View of the Artist* (Albany: State University of New York Press, 1962), Frederick C. Crews, *The Sins of the Fathers* (New York: Oxford University Press, 1966), and Rudolph Von Abele, *The Death of the Artist* (The Hague: Nijhoff, 1955) are standard studies of Hawthorne's problem. Nina Baym, *"The Marble Faun:* Hawthorne's Elegy for Art," *New England Quarterly*, 44 (Sept. 1971), 355-76, states the problem in terms of the choice between Hilda's morality and an opposing concept of art which is linked to eroticism and inwardness. Robert Shulman, "Hawthorne's Quiet Conflict," *Philological Quarterly*, 47 (Apr. 1968), 216-36, states the problem in somewhat narrower terms as a conflict between "the demands of his vocation as a Romantic artist and the imperatives of a Protestant ethic . . . ."

2. The page numbers of Hawthorne's novels cited in the text refer to *The Centenary Editions of the Works of Nathaniel Hawthorne*, ed. William Charvat, Roy Harvey Pearce, and Claude Simpson, 4 vols. (Columbus: Ohio State University Press, 1962-68). The page numbers of the tales refer to *The Complete Works of Nathaniel Hawthorne*, ed. G. P. Lathrop, 12 vols. (Boston: Houghton Mifflin, 1883).

3. Bell, *Hawthorne's View of the Artist*, p. 110; Richard Harter Fogle, *Hawthorne's Fiction: the Light and the Dark* (Norman: University of Oklahoma Press, 1952); John C. Stubbs, *The Pursuit of Form* (Urbana: University of Illinois Press, 1970), pp. 58-59; James W. Gargano, "Hawthorne's 'The Artist of the Beautiful,'" *Studies in Short Fiction*, 8 (Fall 1971), 607-16; Sherry Ziveley, "Hawthorne's 'The Artist of the Beautiful' and Spenser's 'Muiopotmos'," Philological Quarterly, 48 (Jan. 1969), 134-37; R. A. Yoder, "Hawthorne and His Artist," *Studies in Romanticism*, 7 (Summer 1968), 193-206. On the question of whether or not Owen Warland is ultimately successful or pathetic, opinion is divided. Bell represents the opinion that Owen is the failure of the artist to fulfill a moral, social function as opposed to the opinion held by such critics as Fogle and Yoder that Owen is triumphant.

4. Charles Feidelson, Jr., *"The Scarlet Letter," Hawthorne Centenary Essays*, pp. 31-77; Dan McCall, "The Design of Hawthorne's 'Custom-

House,'" *American Literature*, 21 (1967), 349–58; and John Paul Eakin, "Hawthorne's Imagination and the Structure of 'The Custom-House,'" *American Literature*, 43 (Nov., 1971), 346–58. While McCall indicates that "art involves, in Hawthorne's mind, a kind of social irresponsibility," Feidelson rightly sees Hawthorne's inability to "accept the barren role of alienated imagination." Eakin, like Feidelson, reads the sketch as a study of the working of Hawthorne's imagination.

5. For similar views of Coverdale, see Joseph C. Pattison, "Point of View in Hawthorne," *PMLA*, 82 (Oct. 1967), 363–69; Nina Baym, "*The Blithedale Romance:* A Radical Reading," *Journal of English and Germanic Philology*, 68 (Oct. 1968), 545–69; Frederick C. Crews, "A New Reading of *The Blithedale Romance,*" *American Literature*, 29 (May 1957), 147–70; George Monteiro, "Hawthorne, James and the Destructive Self," *Texas Studies in Literature and Language*, 4 (Spring 1962), 58–71; Frank Davidson, "Toward a Re-evaluation of *The Blithedale Romance,*" *New England Quarterly*, 25 (Spring 1962), 374–83.

6. Bell, *Hawthorne's View of the Artist;* Charles Feidelson, Jr., *Symbolism in American Literature* (Chicago: University of Chicago Press, 1953); James K. Folsom, *Man's Accidents and God's Purposes* (New Haven: College and University Press, 1963); Terence Martin, *The Instructed Vision* (Bloomington: Indiana University Press, 1961), pp. 145–48; Eakin, "Hawthorne's Imagination"; Richard J. Jacobson, *Hawthorne's Conception of the Creative Process* (Cambridge: Harvard University Press, 1965); Darrell Abel, "'A More Imaginative Pleasure': Hawthorne on the Play of the Imagination," *Emerson Society Quarterly*, 58 (II Quarter 1969), 63-71; R. K. Gupta, "Hawthorne's Theory of Art," *American Literature*, 40 (Nov. 1968), 309–24; Roy Male, *Hawthorne's Tragic Vision* (Austin: University of Texas Press, 1957), p. 166; Darrell Abel, "Giving Lustre to Gray Shadows: Hawthorne's Potent Art," *American Literature*, 41 (Nov. 1969), 373–88. These works are useful in a study of the way in which Hawthorne's imagination worked, or of the way in which he conceived of it as working. Male's comment that "truly creative art, therefore, requires both penetrative insight and sympathetic investment" and Gupta's observation that art "subserves" life, point to the heart of Hawthorne's criticism of art for art's sake. The clearest statements of Hawthorne's positive aesthetic theory in *The Marble Faun* are by Abel, who recognizes Hawthorne's insistence on an "unfinished" form and on the cooperation of the reader, and by Feidelson, who notes that Hawthorne was reaching for organicism in art in this last published novel.

SEVEN

Travelling in Concord: The World of Thoreau's Journal

WILLIAM L. HOWARTH

Henry Thoreau opens *Walden* with an unflattering estimate of his home and birthplace, in terms so negative that some townsmen never forgave the offense: "I have travelled a good deal in Concord; and every where, in shops, and offices, and fields, the inhabitants have appeared to me to be doing penance in a thousand remarkable ways. What I have heard of Brahmins sitting exposed to four fires and looking in the face of the sun; or hanging suspended, with their heads downward, over flames; . . . —even these forms of conscious penance are hardly more incredible and astonishing than the scenes which I daily witness."[2]

If Thoreau had travelled in Concord during the American Bicentennial, he would have found its penitents still hard at their labors, serving thousands of remarkable tourists who passed through each day. Yet if his comment has a sarcastic edge, like many of Thoreau's sentiments, it also is double-edged. "I have travelled a good deal in Concord" flashes a glint of affection, implying that Concord has a good deal to offer a traveller, and that travelling there is "a good deal," a solid Yankee bargain. In the context of *Walden* alone this suggestion may seem unlikely, since other chapters (e.g., "The Village") strongly criticize the town and its citizens. But on the whole Thoreau's writings compliment Concord persistently, and thus his phrase may serve as a text for the following homily.

Most students of Thoreau's life and writings share his affection for Concord; but a few critics, notably Perry Miller and, more recently, Leon Edel, think Concord betrayed Thoreau's genius, tempting him not to travel widely in the world, like his peripatetic contemporaries Emerson, Hawthorne, and Melville. Miller thought Concord offered Thoreau "no Byronic fund of experience, sensa-

tion, love affairs to feast on," while to Edel it seemed odd that
Thoreau's worst case of homesickness occurred on Staten Island—
"that wooded and lovely island, as it was then."[3] Staten Island in
the 1840s might seem Edenic to a modern New Yorker, but even
then it was hardly a match for the quieter beauty of Concord.
These critical jibes are themselves parochial, if not provincial, for
they rest largely on personal impressions rather than solid evidence.

The facts suggest that Thoreau, living in an age when touring was
still hazardous and time-consuming, travelled far more widely than
most nineteenth-century Americans. He never went abroad, to be
sure, but the range of his journeys in North America extended
from Quebec to Pennsylvania and from Cape Cod to Minnesota,
the western frontier of his day. Moreover, as John Christie has
verified, Thoreau became a "world traveller" by reading hundreds
of travel books, a habit that allowed him to remain in Concord
while "great-circle sailing" around the globe.[4] If, despite this
measure of worldly experience, he chose to abide in Concord, insisting he could "travel a good deal" right there, his readers owe it
to him—and themselves—to discover just why he was so content.

Foremost in his sentiments was a deep affection for Concord's
prominent role in American history. Its antiquity was impressive,
he wrote in his Journal, for "Concord is the oldest inland town in
New England, perhaps in the States, and the walker is peculiarly
favored here" (ca. Aug. 1850).[5] All other early settlements were
located either in coastal areas or on tidal rivers; in 1635 Concord's
founders marched some twenty miles west of Boston into the
"wilderness" and chose a place where two rivers joined to form a
third. Indians had long hunted and fished on this site, which they
called *Musketaquid,* or "grass-ground," because the lush bankside
meadows were flooded and nourished each year by the rivers. The
Puritan historian Edward Johnson reports that the colonists struck
a bargain with the Indians, paying an unspecified fee for permanent
tenancy. Attaching no importance to land ownership, their numbers reduced by an epidemic the previous winter, the Indians
obligingly took this fee and departed to the West. In September,
1635, the General Court for the Massachusetts Bay Colony
approved the colonists' petition and passed an order: ". . . that
there shall be a plantation at Musketaquid . . . six miles of land
square . . . And the name of the place is changed and henceforth
to be called Concord."[6]

Thoreau was fond of the old Indian name, *Musketaquid,* which in an early essay he translated as "Prairie river," alluding both to the local meadows and the beds of long, trailing aquatic weeds that grew thickly in shallow places.[7] The slow and stately currents of the rivers, he later wrote in *A Week,* shaped the grass into "an emblem of all progress, following the same law with the system, with time, and all that is made; the weeds at the bottom gently bending down the stream, shaken by the watery wind, still planted where their seeds had sunk, but ere long to die and go down likewise. . . ."[8] The ancient Indian name was therefore doubly appropriate; it described both a local scene and the universal law of mutability, the same current of time that had carried the Indians and their names away forever.

Thoreau admired the English name *Concord* as well, because its early settlers also chose it for symbolic purposes. In seventeenth-century usage *concord* expressed for them several positive notions: it meant a peaceful compact—they had purchased the land, not taken it by force; a legal and formal agreement—the Court had established a title and conveyed it to their hands; and an ecumenical union—they had left behind the religious disputes of Boston. On this quiet inland site they wished to live "in Concord," as Christian separatists had labeled many similar communities since the Reformation. To those New England settlers the name "Concord" therefore symbolized all the attributes of social wellbeing: agreement, accord, harmony, law, order, and, above all, peace.[9] Even their place of settlement echoed these virtues, for the rivers met in a confluence, a physical concord, at a place the Indians and English alike called "Egg Rock" (E6; See the map and index on the following pages).[10] There the narrow, rock-strewn Assabet merged with the wider, marshy Sudbury to form the broad and peaceful Musketaquid, now known as Concord River.

Flowing north from Egg Rock, Concord River soon passed under North Bridge (E7), where, on April 19, 1775, Concordians made a stand for American liberty, sacrificing the peace—but not the unity—of their original accord. Thoreau was immensely proud of his town's role in the "Concord Fight." In later writings he often attributed his own independence to the revolutionary heritage of local history and legends. Other Concord authors repeated this *topos*—Emerson in "Hamatreya" and "Historical Discourse," Hawthorne in his preface to *Mosses from an Old Manse*—but

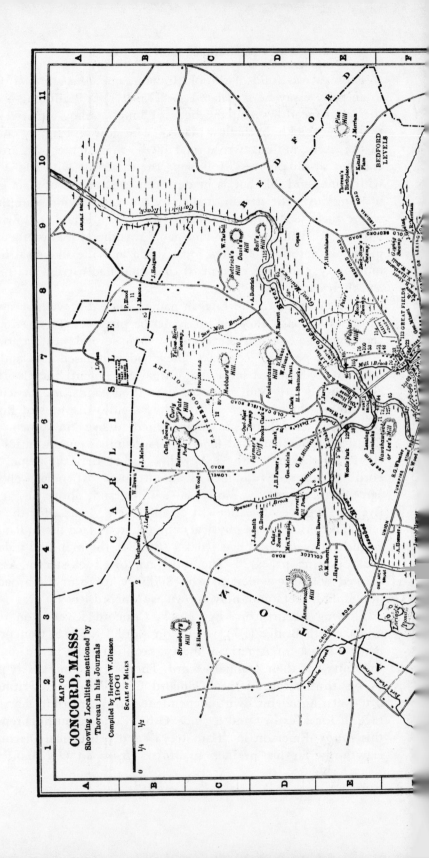

MAP OF
CONCORD, MASS.
Showing Localities mentioned by
Thoreau in his Journals

Compiled by Herbert W. Gleason
1906

SCALE OF MILES

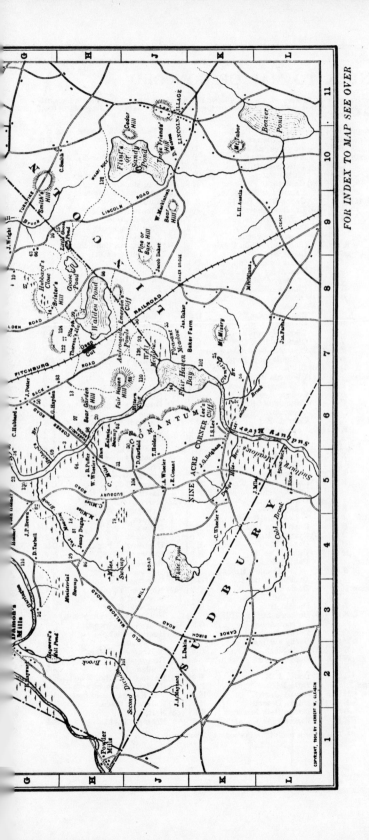

FOR INDEX TO MAP SEE OVER

INDEX TO MAP OF CONCORD

Figures in parentheses correspond with figures on the map. A letter and figure combined indicate the space within which the locality may be found, this space being determined by the intersection of imaginary lines drawn from the corresponding letter and figure in the margin.

[1] This name is spelled "Heywood" by Thoreau.

[2] This name was also given to a bay on the river in Sudbury.
[3] This is the "Saw Mill Brook" most frequently mentioned by Thoreau.

Thoreau's devotion to the theme was more persistent and self-descriptive. At Harvard he wrote a swaggering apology for his small-town origins in the 1837 Class Book: "To what ever quarter of the world I may wander, I shall deem it my good fortune that I hail from Concord North Bridge."[11] True to this promise, his works often depict North Bridge and the Concord Fight as symbols of the highest American virtue, which he defined in *Walden* as "the liberty . . . to do without . . . slavery and war and other superfluous expenses."[12]

Thoreau's affection for historic Concord arose partly from reading and largely from his own elimination of "superfluous expenses." By 1849 he had become a professional land surveyor, striking the best of his good deals with Concord, for this role put him on intimate terms with the natural history of his township. Surveying gave public legitimacy to walking, his daily exercise of private devotion. The new job also earned him honest, regular dollars; it allowed him to name his hours and most of his clients; and, best of all, it kept him outdoors, transacting "private business" with Nature as he ran lot lines and computed acreage for Concord's men of business. In part, surveying also redeemed Thoreau in the eyes of his townsmen, who recalled his role in the burning of Fair Haven Woods in 1844, an accident that destroyed much of the local fuel supply. Yet by the 1850s, this pariah had become a trusted local agent, hired to "perambulate" the town boundaries with its selectmen, in a ritual that affirmed the old charter and Concord's earthly configuration.[13]

These experiences after 1849 made Thoreau the familiar of Concord's landscape, impressing on him a vivid sense of the topography in its twenty-six square miles. The township has irregular political boundaries (see map), but they enclose concentric rings of hills and ponds, left behind by glacial action in the last Ice Age. The Concord landscape thus possesses a naturally symmetrical, basin-like structure, with its three rivers and village converging at the lowest and most central point. That center, appropriately named Egg Rock (E6), lies a half-mile north of Thoreau's home on Main Street. The centrality of his location was a great convenience. Setting out for an afternoon's walk or voyage, he could move in any compass direction and within minutes find a surprising array of topographic features: meadows, forests, swamps, brooks, cliffs, valleys, fields—in short, almost every feature the globe possesses, including some atypical of central Massachusetts. On the western horizon were mountains, especially Wachusett and Monadnock, which he celebrated in a poem, "With frontier strength ye stand your ground."[14] To the southwest lay a desert, an odd sandy knoll where only scattered tufts of grasses grew, named for its principal resident "Jenny Dugan's Desert Place." To the eyes of its principal surveyor, Concord was thus a replica of almost all the sights—and sites—the outside world had to offer. This replica was a miniature drawn to scale, and Thoreau felt singularly blessed to live in such a well-proportioned, Concordant world. "I have never got over my surprise that I should have been born into the most estimable place in all the world, and in the very nick of time, too" (Dec. 5, 1856).

The infinite variety of his surroundings probably accounts for Thoreau's insistent, even belligerent, denunciations of those friends and readers who presume that travel is "extra-vagant," wandering beyond the familiar boundaries of home and country.[15] "It takes a man of genius to travel in his own country, in his native village; to make any progress beyond his door and his gate" (Aug. 6, 1851). In a moral sense he meant that men should cherish what they have, not what they desire and may never attain. But in a literal, personal sense he also meant that for him Concord was world enough and time, for in it he saw a microcosm, or analogue, of larger realms beyond. His thought echoed basic Transcendental doctrine; Emerson, Alcott, and Fuller often asserted that a whole and its parts—the Each and All, Me and Not-Me—are equivalents. Thoreau went beyond their assertions, however, and managed to verify the notion on his own grounds, in his daily life, with a consistency far exceeding the desires or dreams of his philosophic neighbors.

Most of Thoreau's "intra-vagant" travels in Concord are recorded in his Journal, where he transformed his township into a magical kingdom that corresponded with surprising accuracy to the outside world. In youthful days he once proposed to write "a poem to be called 'Concord'," taking for its argument the natural forms lying all about him: river, woods, ponds; morning, noon, and night; winter-spring, summer-fall (Sept. 4, 1842). He never wrote that poem, but in many respects the Journal tells an epic story, governed

by the same rhythms of time and space. According to frequent
Journal entries, he saw a great number of analogies between Concord and the world, all instances of that "radical correspondence"
Emerson defined in *Nature* between subject and object relationships. In deference to the town's symbolic name, Thoreau might
have called his analogies "Concordances," for they persistently
verified a relationship between local places and distant, exotic
locales, as though Concord were a *mappus mundi,* a map of the
world aligned within its own map.

But since he did not live to organize his findings in a completed
fashion, that task remains for readers of the Journal, who may ex-
tract the correspondences he noted and fit them into appropriate
patterns. One pattern could resemble his hypothetical poem,
arranged by geographical features and units of time. A simpler and
perhaps sounder pattern is to use the major quadrants of a compass, the Four Quarters of Concord, to demonstrate how Thoreau
consistently saw within them geographical equivalents for the
globe. Concord was divided into Quarters in the mid-seventeenth
century, each section forming a separate district for property taxa-
tion. With Yankee obdurateness the townspeople defined only
three quarters at first: North, South, and East. The land west of
the river remained unsettled until the eighteenth century, when
the old Quarters had long since been outgrown. But Concordians
in the nineteenth century customarily saw the landscape in quadri-
laterals, like their surveyor, who had to render his measurements
and drawings according to the "true meridians" of local boundaries.[16] Coincidentally, many Indian legends adopt a fourfold
narrative pattern, with the hero departing from a village center and
travelling out to successive quarters of the compass.[17] The same
pattern suggests how Thoreau studied local geography, his mind
always moving away from Concord to the outermost reaches of
global longitude and latitude. His ideas were probably suggested
by travel books as much as by Concord's physiography. The realms
of fact and idea were largely united, of course, by his ingenious
pursuit of analogies between real and imaginary experiences.

This journey must begin in the East Quarter, for Thoreau
always associated that section with beginnings, especially his own.
He was born in the East Quarter of Concord, on the old Virginia

Road (E9), where he lived for the first eight months of his life. Each day in Concord also began in the East Quarter, with the rising sun. Looking in that direction at dawn, he wrote: "I am reminded of more youthful mornings, seeing the dark forms of the trees eastward in the low grounds, partly within and against the shining white fog, the sun just risen over it" (June 7, 1854). The eastward vista also reminded him of "more youthful mornings" because the young shoots on a white pine tree, and indeed, all the young trees in a pine grove, "are bent toward the east. I am very much pleased with this observation, confirming that of the Indians." As the Indians had known, the young shoots thus provide travellers with "a natural compass" (June 23, 1852). Thoreau might have observed this compass anywhere in Concord, but coincidentally or not, his first sighting occurred in Joseph Mason's pasture (B8), lying in the extreme north*east* corner of the township.

There were other coincidences as well: much of East Concord resembled eastern America, thus reminding Thoreau of the "more youthful mornings" in America's past. In Concord, all vestiges of civilization—homes, schools, churches, shops—stretched along the eastern "Mill-dam" (F7), just as the major centers of power and culture in America first stretched along its eastern Atlantic shores. The East Quarter also recalled "more youthful mornings" because the land itself resembled a youth—pleasant enough to behold but not yet marked by any distinctive, well-formed, or prominent features. Away from the Milldam, farther to the east, the land became mostly open, flat meadows and farms, known as the Great Meadows and the Bedford Levels, and these areas often reminded Thoreau of the broad coastal shores and plains where America made its beginnings. In the previously quoted Journal entry, he describes a heavy eastern fog with marine imagery: "All beyond [the trees] a submerged and unknown country, as if they grew on the seashore. . . . The waves of the foggy ocean divide and flow back for us Israelites of a day to march through" (June 17, 1854). Like the New Israelites before him, Thoreau agreed with those Puritan forefathers who thought Cape Cod resembled the "wilderness" through which the Old Israelites passed while escaping captivity. On Peter's Path (E8), which crossed the Great Meadows and joined the Bedford Road farther east, Thoreau found analogous scenery in Concord: "This path through the rolling stubblefields, with the woods rather distant and the horizon distant in front on account of the intervention of the river and the meadow, reminds me a little of the downs of Cape Cod, of the Plains of Nauset. This is the only walk of the kind that we have in Concord" (Apr. 3, 1852).

Other findings in the East Quarter confirmed his analogy: on the shore of "the first little pond east of Fair Haven," probably near the Andromeda Ponds (J7), he found a large cockle shell: "It reminds me that all the earth is seashore,—the sight of these little shells inland. It is a beach I stand on" (Apr. 28, 1852). The impression grew even stronger when he stood atop Nawshawtuct Hill (F6) and looked eastward, into a fog:

> It resembles nothing so much as the ocean. You can get here the impression which the ocean makes, without ever going to the shore. . . . The seashore exhibits nothing more grand or on a larger scale. How grand where it rolls off northeastward (?) over Ball's Hill [D9] like a glorious ocean after a storm, just lit by the rising sun! It is as boundless as the view from the highlands of Cape Cod. They are exaggerated billows, the ocean on a larger scale, the sea after some tremendous and unheard-of storm, for the actual sea never appears so tossed up and universally white with foam and spray as this now far in the northeastern horizon, where mountain billows are breaking on some hidden reef or bank. It is tossed up toward the sun and by it into the most boisterous of seas, which no craft, no ocean streamer, is vast enough to sail on. [June 2, 1853]

As this passage indicates, the Concord scene is an ideal and exaggerated version of Cape Cod, on a scale far larger than its actuality. At the same time, looking eastward toward the Atlantic does not merely suggest imaginary shores and oceans; to Thoreau's mind and eye the East Quarter of Concord actually resembled those distant points.

And indeed, given a day to roam in Concord, he could range even farther eastward, crossing the North Atlantic to Europe and beyond. In the ice-glazed trees and bushes of Hubbard's Grove, east of the Sudbury River (G5), he saw distinctly European forms: "The sky is overcast, and a fine snowy hail and rain is falling, and these ghost-like trees make a scenery which reminds you of Spitzbergen. . . . Finer than the Saxon arch is this path running under the pines, roofed, not with crossing boughs, but drooping ice-covered twigs in irregular confusion" (Jan. 1, 1853). At Colburn Hill, near Annursnack (D3), he admired a wild leek, just about to bloom: "What a surprising and stately plant! . . . It has a peculiarly columnar appearance, like the Leaning Tower of Pisa" (July 22, 1860). On the other hand, wild blueberries gathered at Conantum (J6) were "early ambrosial fruit, delicate-flavored, thin-skinned, and cool, —Olympian fruit" (Aug. 4, 1856).

And he could sail on, to North Africa and the Near East. By Cliff Brook (J6), also east of the Sudbury, he found sandy desert spots used by partridges for dusting places: "Gerard, the lion-killer of Algiers, speaks of seeing similar spots when tracking or patiently waiting the lion there. . . . It is interesting to find that the same phenomena, however simple, occur in different parts of the globe" (July 21, 1856).[18] Looking downstream at sunset, toward the northeast, he saw Edenic qualities in the backlighted water: "The river at such an hour, seen half a mile away, perfectly smooth and lighter than the sky, reflecting the clouds, is a paradisaical scene. What are the rivers around Damascus to this river sleeping around Concord?" (June 22, 1853). The same excitement animates his discovery of a "long narrow, winding, and very retired blueberry swamp" near Beck Stow's (E9), east of the Great Meadows: "as retired and novel as if it were a thousand miles removed from your ordinary walks. . . . It is as far off as Persia from Concord" (July 29, 1853). In these fabulous, exotic eastern places, Thoreau persistently found evidence of *origins:* the origins of his life, his nation, and its parent cultures—Europe, Greece, running back in time to the cradle of Western civilization, near the valley of the Tigris and Euphrates. Concord provided a whole history of man's beginnings, especially in its East Quarter.

In the South Quarter of Concord, where the sun shone longest— and stood highest at noon—Thoreau associated the local scenery with his life's own noontide, his years of young adulthood. Fair Haven Hill and Pond were dominant features in the south, and to Thoreau they recalled cherished memories of his brother John, with whom he taught school, voyaged up the Concord and Merrimac Rivers, and spent many afternoons roaming the township. The top of Fair Haven Hill (H7) was a favorite vantage point; from there the brothers took in a grand view of points farther south, along the Sudbury meadows to Wayland.[19] Walden Pond (H8) also lay in the South Quarter, its distance from town and relative isolation providing the environment Thoreau most needed in the years after John's death, when he matured as a writer. In response to these memories, the scenery of this region is more pronounced and singular in character—dominated by water, especially ponds and brooks, it has several important hills, cliffs, and woods as well. On sunny days the South Quarter is lush and verdant, a riverine landscape that resembles America's southland, which is also dominated by a large river system. When Thoreau first saw a panoramic painting of the Mississippi River, he concluded that the New World had many "rich but as yet unassimilated meadows" (ca. Jan., 1851), an image reminiscent of his own upper Sudbury region. When he saw the real Mississippi ten years later, he studiously examined the flora on its banks for comparison with his Concord findings.[20]

On hot and humid summer days, the South Quarter also seemed to Thoreau a decidedly "tropical" region, like that of Central or South America. In a blueberry swamp on Charles Miles's land (H4), southwest of the Sudbury, he found a glorious jungle of colors and textures: "These are the wildest and richest gardens that we have. Such a depth of verdure into which you sink. They were never cultivated by any" (Aug. 5, 1852). Near the river itself, by John Hosmer's hollow (G5), were legendary troves of buried treasure taken from Caribbean pirate raids "in Captain Kidd's day" (Nov. 5, 1854). If he chose to voyage upstream, going south along the flooded meadows to Sudbury and beyond, he felt that his southbound journey might never end: "What fair isles, what remote coast shall we explore? What San Salvador or Bay of All Saints arrive at? All are tempted forth, like flies, into the sun. All isles seem fortunate and blessed to-day; all capes are of Good Hope. The same sun and calm that tempts the turtles out tempts the voyagers. It is an opportunity to explore their own natures, to float along their own shores" (May 3, 1857).

Everything about the South Quarter suggested tropical adventure, even danger, of the sort a young man would seek—and in later years fondly recall. Standing on Tupelo/Bittern Cliff (J6), he thought, "How rich, like what we love to read of South American primitive forests, is the scenery of this river! What luxuriance of weeds, what depth of mud along its sides! . . . The water, indeed, reflects heaven because my mind does; such is its own serenity, its transparency and stillness" (Aug. 31, 1851). Even the river creatures confirmed this southerly vision; near the island in Fair Haven Bay (J7) he once caught a large snapping turtle that seemed primitive and tropical: "With his great head, as big as an infant's, and his vigilant eyes as he paddled about on the bottom in his attempts to escape, he looked not merely repulsive, but to some extent terrible even as a crocodile" (May 17, 1854). If that monster did not offer adventure enough, his mind could race farther south, beyond the limits of known geography, toward the South Polar Sea. A journey "into the foreign land of Sudbury," he wrote, was a voyage "to undiscovered islands in the sea," where wild berries replaced tropical fruits: "It is not the orange of Cuba, but the checkerberry of the neighboring pasture, that most delights the eye and the palate of the New England child. . . . As I sail the unexplored sea of Concord, many a dell and swamp and wooded hill is my Ceram and Amboyna" (Nov. 22-23, 1860).

To most of his fellow Americans, only the West represented adventure and exploration, but Thoreau's studies of Concord gave him a contrary view. In the West Quarter, where the sun went down each day, he saw lengthening shadows and twilight, all portending that eventual descent. In "Walking" he said that southwest was his favorite direction for walks; and he also noted that his inclination coincided with concurrent movements on the American frontier.[21] The analogy has been misunderstood by later readers, who see it as purely fanciful or a simple statement of fact. One observer believes the assertion is literal, because "in Thoreau's native Concord all the best walking territory is southwest of the town."[22] In fact, Thoreau found excellent walks in all four directions; never did he qualify any one area as the best. Moreover, he explored the West Quarter most consistently in his middle years, the early 1850s, at the height of the westerly migrations, and "Walking" reflects this emphasis because he first composed it then, for delivery as a lecture.

More to the point, however, is the fact that on *his* western travels Thoreau saw a landscape that was strikingly similar to the great American West. After first crossing the Assabet River, or North Branch (E5), which resembles the Missouri River in shape if not in direction of current, he came to country that opened up into broad, prairie-like grasslands occasionally broken by woods or swamps. Crops and livestock thrived there, and the gently rolling ranges with their herds of grazing cattle and horses looked so western that Concordians habitually called this area "Texas." In 1844 Thoreau helped his family build a home just west of Concord near the cattle-show grounds (F6); they lived in this "Texas House" until 1850, when they moved to Main Street.

So Thoreau knew the West Quarter well, well enough to recognize how much it resembled both the landscape and probable fate of western America. For he did not see the West as a land of hope and prosperity; to him it was that bright place on the horizon where the sun inevitably went *down*. Standing on a hill near D. Tarbell's (G4) and looking west toward Acton, the next township, he saw an unsettling vision of America's future: "The still, stagnant, heart-eating, life-ever-lasting and gone-to-seed country," where young wives pined in loneliness, old men waited to die. The young ones restlessly packed up and moved to California; "lands [from] which the Indian was long since dispossessed, and now the farms are run out ... standing there and seeing these things, I cannot realize that this is that famous young America which is famous throughout the world for its activity and enterprise, and this is the most settled and Yankee part of it. What must be the condition of the old world!" (Jan. 27, 1852).

Being a factory town, Acton was partly emptied of its working-class population by the California gold rush of the early 1850s; thus Thoreau tended to associate this town, lying west of Concord, with the general folly of going west, especially to dig gold: "Going to California. It is only three thousand miles nearer to hell" (Feb. 1, 1852). A greater and higher value could be found right in Concord, in the "exquisite fine or delicate gold color" of its yellow birches: "The sight of these trees affects me more than California gold" (Jan. 4, 1853). Acton represented other "western" evils, especially the exploitation of industrial capitalism. When the Action gunpowder mill blew up, killing several workers because the owners were too cheap to place the buildings farther apart, Thoreau saw the grim consequences of so-called free enterprise: "The bodies were naked and black, some limbs and bowels here and there, and a head at a distance from its trunk. The feet were bare; the hair singed to a crisp. I smelt the powder half a mile before I got there. Put the different buildings thirty rods apart, and then but one will blow up at a time" (Jan. 7, 1853).

Beyond Acton, still farther to the west, Thoreau could see the Berkshire Mountains, his New England analogue for the Rockies. Taking in the view from Smith's Hill (G10), he saw these mountains as not merely a physical challenge to travellers, but as "Moral structures. . . . The text for a discourse on real values, and permanent; a sermon on the mount" (May 10, 1853). The real value in going west, he insisted, was not for material goods but for the spiritual good of *wilderness,* the unbounded land where men lived without the trivialities of civilization. That journey began with a single step, since Concord proved that he need not travel far to find signs of the wilderness. On a late afternoon he glimpsed a single white pine just beyond Lee's Hill (F6), its boughs pointed westward to catch the fading sun: "That tree seems the emblem of my life; it stands for the west, the wild. . . . My wealth should be all in pine-tree shillings" (Apr. 21, 1852). By alluding to the earliest form of American currency, Thoreau suggested that the Concord white pine was an emblem for his nation's wealth; for it stood like himself, "on the verge of the clearing, whose boughs point westward . . . which is banished from the village; in whose boughs the crow and the hawk have their nests" (Apr. 21, 1852).

To Thoreau's eyes, the American wilderness was at once his nation's greatest asset and worst liability. Its isolation promised liberty, freedom from old ways and values; but it was also a land of peril, where predators more vicious than crows and hawks tended their nests. In racing westward across their continent, Americans threatened to exhaust the land and themselves, halting at last on their Pacific shores while the heedless sun raced on. With his reverence for the Orient, Thoreau wondered if America might seek some other Manifest Destiny, perhaps journeying serenely beyond California and its gold mines, across the greater Pacific to lands that bespoke the merits of an ancient, wiser, and less material civilization. He predicted this eventuality in *A Week: "Ex oriente lux* may still be the motto of scholars, for the Western world has not yet derived from the East all the light which it is destined to receive thence."[23]

The West Quarter suggested to Thoreau that this "passage to more than India," as Whitman would later define it, was immediately attainable. Between the Concord and Assabet Rivers (E6) he discovered a new variety of willow, common farther north but rare in Concord: "It transports me in imagination to the Saskatchewan.

It grows alike on the bank of the Concord and of the MacKenzie River, proving them a kindred soil. . . . Through this leaf I communicate with the Indians who roam the boundless Northwest" (Sept. 2, 1856). Between these two rivers lay a Northwest Passage for his imagination, driving him on to the deeper West, beyond America's shores. A touch to his nostrils of water horehound, gathered from "westernmost Andromeda Pond" (J7); "That is as near as I come to the Spice Islands. This is my smelling-bottle, my ointment" (Dec. 24, 1856). On the Corner Road (H6) he saw a skunk that ran "even when undisturbed, with a singular teeter or undulation, like the walking of a Chinese lady" (Mar. 10, 1854), as a vestige of that undisturbed and singular civilization. Even more suggestive was a barberry bush he saw on Conantum (J6), the hills standing west of Fair Haven Pond. In full bloom, the bush seemed "orientally beautiful" in form and color: "It suggests the yellow-robed priests of Thibet" (May 25, 1853). In each of these scenes and sightings, the West Quarter verified that America's quest need not end in California. Instead, he had pressed on to the Himalayas, the seat of all early wisdom, home of the ancient Hindu scriptures he revered. Here he found permanent reality; the west fulfilled at last by its opposite, as he had hoped in *A Week* and later confirmed in "Walking": *Ex Oriente lux; ex Occidente Frux.* From the East light; from the West fruit."[24]

Finally, the North Quarter, reserved for the end because it plays no part in the daily solar cycle, and because Thoreau postponed his own systematic studies of this region until his final years, the late 1850s. Appropriately, he associated the North Quarter with waning phases of activity: old age, death, decay, and the oncoming dark night. None of these were morbid ideas for him; he was matter-of-fact about death, especially as his own drew near. The North Quarter was certainly vital enough, for the land consisted of large forests, great rock outcroppings, rushing streams, and high hills. Toward the northeast was a vast and mostly uninhabited tract of wilderness, which Thoreau christened "Easterbrook Country" (June 10, 1853). To his eye, the North Quarter readily suggested northeast New England and Canada; he often noted the strong geophysical parallels. On visits to Saw Mill Brook (C7), which ran out of Yellow Birch Swamp (B7) in the Easterbrook

Country, he noted its similarity to a mountain brook: "For a short distance it reminds me of runs I have seen in New Hampshire. A brawling little stream tumbling through the rocky wood, ever down and down" (Nov. 4, 1851). On another visit he suggested, less plausibly, that the brook's falls seemed equivalent to a larger cataract: "I should not hear Niagara a short distance off" (Apr. 1, 1852).

Both the White Mountains and Niagara Falls suggested Titanic, implacable forces in nature, of the sort Thoreau once glimpsed on another northern peak. Atop Katahdin, the highest point in Maine, he had asked two desolate and despairing questions: "*Who* are we? *Where* are we?" and the mountain gave back no clear or easy answers.[25] In the north of Concord also lay a Nature that exceeded all of man's dreams and designs; it was unchangeable and therefore undeniable, impervious to his puny will and silent to his questions. In describing this force, not at all confined to the imaginations of Poe, Melville, or Dreiser, Thoreau gave an uncompromising view of humanity: an animal blessed with supernal vision but cursed with a frail and all too mortal physique. That was clearly his own fate in those final years as he wasted in the slow and smokeless fire of decay, dying slowly of pulmonary consumption, like his sister and father before him. Increasingly, his mind and body gravitated in those later years away from the other three Quarters and toward the North, as though his imagination were pulled taut along some invisible line of magnetic force.

The Easterbrook Country excited him especially; in it he was pleased to find surviving inhabitants like old Brooks Clark, whom he met one cold day, striding briskly up the Old Carlisle Road (D6), barefoot because he had stuffed his shoes with nuts and wild apples. Thoreau, too, wished for such a merry indifference to fashion and comfort in his old age: "It pleased me to see this cheery old man, with such a feeble hold on life, bent almost double, thus enjoying the evening of his days .... It proves to me old age as tolerable, as happy, as infancy" (Oct. 20, 1857). Everywhere, the Easterbrook Country suggested to him how stoically he must face his own death and dissolution: in the early eighteenth century it had once been settled with farms, roads, and even quarries and small shops; but now the land was wild and deserted. Everywhere lay the relics of previous lives and settlements—the old roads, stone fences, cellar holes—now all abandoned and grown over with large, mature forests. Useless to the village, perhaps, but it provided Thoreau with solid food for thought: "What a wild and rich domain that Easterbrooks Country! Not cultivated, hardly a cultivatible field in it, and yet it delights all natural persons, and feeds more still" (Oct. 20, 1857).

In the North Quarter, as elsewhere, Thoreau's eye could also see realms that lay farther ahead, in the same direction. Above Barrett's Mill (E5) he saw tundra-like areas, reminding him of "northern regions" (Apr. 21, 1852). While cranberrying in a local bog, he felt transported to remote territories: "I feel as if I were in Rupert's Land, and a slight cool but agreeable shudder comes over me, as if equally far away from human society . . . . I shall never find in the wilds of Labrador any greater wildness than in some recess in Concord, *i.e.*, that I import into it" (Aug. 30, 1856). That intimation was later confirmed by the appearance in Concord of a rare Canada lynx, which he studied avidly for several days. He disagreed with the common theory that the animal had strayed south from Canada; like himself, the lynx was "very rare hereabouts. . . . They are nocturnal in their habits, and therefore are the more rarely seen, yet a strange animal is seen in this town by somebody about every year, or its track" (Sept. 13, 1860).

That rare lynx, roaming large areas of local territory but still unknown to most of the populace, was a fair analogue for Thoreau in his final years, when exploration and survival became two of his strongest instincts. In the North Quarter, especially on winter days, his mind could race ahead to still unexplored ground above the Arctic Circle, where survival remained an ultimate question. One of the Arctic explorers whose works he read avidly was Elisha Kane;[26] and Thoreau believed his own life in Concord resembled Kane's account of "the Esquimaux of Smith's Strait in North Greenland. . . . I laugh when you tell me of the danger of impoverishing myself by isolation. It is here that the walrus and the seal, and the white bear, and the eider ducks and auks on which I batten, most abound" (Dec. 28, 1856). Inspired by Kane's account, he could happily explore a small cave dug by Eddy

Emerson into the side of a snowdrift, and conclude: "So you only need make a snow house in your yard and pass an hour in it, to realize a good deal of Esquimau life" (Jan. 20, 1857).

Eddy's father may not have agreed with Thoreau, and many other friends and neighbors thought his affection for Concord was amusingly eccentric. In his funeral eulogy for Thoreau, Emerson reminded the town of this idiosyncrasy: "He returned Kane's 'Arctic Voyage' to a friend of whom he had borrowed it, with the remark, that 'most of the phenomena noted might be observed in Concord.' He seemed a little envious of the Pole, for the coincident sunrise and sunset, or five minutes' day after six months: a splendid fact, which Annursnack had never afforded him."[27]

Some later readers still smile at these stories, but in doing so they overlook Thoreau's honest belief—supported by ample evidence in his Journal—that Concord was a world unto itself. He also believed, as the town's founders had hoped, that the world itself was a "Concord," a compacted agreement between Indian and American, man and God, nature and village. Each person's view of this world is forever wondrous, he wrote, because it is forever new: "for though the world is so old, and so many books have been written, each object appears wholly unexplored. The whole world is an America, a *New World*" (Apr. 2, 1852). How fortunate, then, that he should be born in a representative town of the New World, "nailed down to this my native region so long and steadily, and made to study and love this spot of earth more and more" (Nov. 12, 1853). Concord taught him to travel in depth, not abroad, for its fields, streams, and woods were a virtual "university" in moral education: "I wish so to live ever as to derive my satisfactions and inspirations from the commonest events, everyday phenomena, so that what my senses hourly perceive, my daily walk, the conversation of my neighbors, may inspire me, and I may dream of no heaven but that which lies about me" (Mar. 11, 1856).

For those reasons, Thoreau lived contentedly in Concord, and he would die there, as he told his Aunt Louisa, without ever quarreling with God.[28] He was buried in the Sleepy Hollow Cemetery (F7), resting at last to the north of town. In his final years, he was sustained by the certainty that he had rendered his earthly obligations not unto Caesar but Concord. As he wrote his friend Daniel Ricketson, who often entreated him to visit New Bedford, "I am engaged to Concord & my very private pursuits by 10,000 ties, & it would be suicide to cut them."[29] He kept this promise to Concord, learning the language of its fields all his life, telling its Concordant story as best he could. In one of his last Journal entries he defined the narrative role shaped for him by its pages: "Wherever men have lived there is a story to be told, and it depends chiefly on the story-teller or historian whether that is interesting or not. You are simply a witness on the stand to tell what you know about your neighbors and neighborhood" (Mar. 18, 1861). Those who read his testimony in his Journal can best judge its interest, as they learn from him exactly how one can travel "a good deal in Concord."

NOTES

1. An early version of this paper was delivered at the Thoreau Society annual meeting in Concord, Mass., on July 12, 1975. For kindnesses extended to me while travelling in Concord, I gratefully acknowledge Mary and Mary Gail Fenn, Anne McGrath, Marcia Moss, Roland Robbins, and the late Ruth Wheeler.

2. Henry David Thoreau, *Walden,* ed. J. Lyndon Shanley (Princeton: Princeton University Press, 1971), p. 4.

3. Perry Miller, *Consciousness in Concord* (Boston: Houghton Mifflin, 1958), p. 75; Leon Edel, *"Walden:* The Myth and the Mystery," *American Scholar,* 44 (Spring 1975), 276.

4. John Christie, *Thoreau as a World Traveler* (New York: Columbia University Press, 1965), p. 262. Christie's book is significant yet little appreciated. My present effort was inspired by his chap. XIII, "The Physical Macrocosm," in that I attempt to explore its corollary, the physical microcosm in Concord.

5. Most of Thoreau's manuscript Journal is at the Pierpont Morgan Library, with fragmentary portions at the Huntington, Houghton, and other libraries. All quotations are cited with parenthetical dates; for the convenience of readers, I quote from the incomplete and heavily emended text, *The Journal of Henry David Thoreau,* ed. B. Torrey and F. H. Allen (Boston: Houghton Mifflin, 1906), 14 vols., issued as vols. 7–20 of *The Writings of Henry David Thoreau.* A new text is in progress with the Princeton University Press edition, *The Writings of Henry D. Thoreau.*

6. Ruth Robinson Wheeler, *Concord: Climate for Freedom* (Concord, Mass.: Concord Antiquarian Society, 1967), p. 8. For the pre-Civil War period, this history supersedes Townsend Scudder, *Concord: American Town* (Boston: Little, Brown, 1947). Thoreau's own source for town history was Lemuel Shattuck, *A History of the Town of Concord . . .* (Boston: Russell, Odiorne, 1835).

7. Thoreau, "Natural History of Massachusetts," *The Dial*, 3 (July 1842), 28; see also Thoreau, *Excursions* (Boston: Ticknor & Fields, 1863), p. 51

8. Thoreau, *A Week on the Concord and Merrimack Rivers* (Boston: James Munroe, 1849), p. 14.

9. In *Wonder-Working Providence* (1653), Edward Johnson writes that the town was "named from the occasion of the present time as you shall after hear," but he does not specify that occasion. See Wheeler, *Concord: Climate for Freedom*, "Appendix B," pp. 202-6.

10. Map coordinates refer to the map of Concord compiled by Herbert W. Gleason in 1906; reproduced here with the kind permission of the Houghton Mifflin Company, Boston, Mass. For maps illustrating Thoreau's other writings, see R. Stowell, *A Thoreau Gazetteer*, ed. W. L. Howarth (Princeton: Princeton University Press, 1970).

11. "Class Book Autobiography," *Early Essays and Miscellanies*, ed. J. J. Moldenhauer et al. (Princeton: Princeton University Press, 1975), p. 114.

12. Shanley, *Walden*, p. 205; see also W. L. Howarth, "From Concord North Bridge: Thoreau and the American Revolution," *Thoreau Society Bulletin*, 134 (Winter 1975), 1-2.

13. See Journal entries for ca. June 1850, Sept. 12, 1851, and Sept. 14, 1851.

14. *Collected Poems of Henry Thoreau*, ed. Carl Bode (Baltimore: Johns Hopkins University Press, 1966), pp. 47-50; see also Thoreau, "A Walk to Wachusett," *Excursions*, pp. 73-76; and *A Week*, pp. 168-71.

15. Thoreau punningly discusses "extra-vagance" in Shanley, *Walden*, p. 324.

16. Wheeler, *Concord: Climate for Freedom*, p. 34; see also A. F. McLean, Jr., "Thoreau's True Meridian: Natural Fact and Metaphor," *American Quarterly*, 20 (1968), 567-79.

17. See Robert Sayre, *Thoreau and the American Indians* (Princeton: Princeton University Press, 1977), pp. 70-71. Thoreau does not acknowledge the compass symbolism in his writings or "Indian Books" (Sayre, pp. 101-54).

18. Christie, *Thoreau as a World Traveler*, p. 319, identifies Thoreau's source as C. J. B. Gerard, *The Adventures of Gerard, the Lion Killer*, trans. C. E. Whitehead (New York, 1856).

19. Thoreau's earliest description of visiting the hill with John is in "Musings. April 20th 1835," *Early Essays and Miscellanies*, pp. 14-16.

20. Another early Journal entry seems to describe the Sudbury, "rolling through the fields and meadows of this substantial earth" as resembling "the headwaters of the Mississippi" (Sept. 5, 1838). For his botanical notes on the upper Mississippi River, see "Thoreau's Notes on the Journey West," ed. Walter Harding (Geneseo, N.Y.: Thoreau Society, Booklet no. 16, 1962).

21. Thoreau, "Walking," *Excursions*, pp. 175-77.

22. Attributed to Raymond Adams in Walter Harding, *A Thoreau Handbook* (New York: New York University Press, 1958), p. 71.

23. Thoreau, *A Week*, p. 149.

24. Thoreau, "Walking," *Excursions*, p. 181.

25. "Ktaadn," *The Maine Woods*, ed. J. J. Moldenhauer (Princeton: Princeton University Press, 1972), p. 71.

26. Kane accompanied the two Grinnel Expeditions (1853-55) in search of Sir John Franklin, whose last expedition perished at sea in 1847. See

Christie, *Thoreau as a World Traveler*, pp. 322–23, for Thoreau's sources.

27. A revised version of Emerson's eulogy appeared as the "Biographical Sketch" in Thoreau, *Excursions*, pp. 7–33. This passage is on p. 20.

28. Walter Harding, *The Days of Henry Thoreau* (New York: Alfred A. Knopf, 1965), p. 464.

29. *The Correspondence of Henry D. Thoreau*, ed. C. Bode and W. Harding (New York: New York University Press, 1958), p. 433.

EIGHT

Herman Melville's Wandering Jews

BERNARD ROSENTHAL

To Terminus build fanes!
Columbus ended earth's romance:
No New World to mankind remains!
Clarel, IV, xxi, 167–69

With these words, Herman Melville articulated an idea already old in his day. Any number of Continental, English, and American authors had or would write their variations on the theme of mankind concurrently stripped of secular mysteries and skeptical about religious ones. American writers in particular have chronicled the denial of a promise so confidently given when John Winthrop assured his weary saints that after touching shore they might build their new Jerusalem.[1] Yet, unlike the twentieth-century writers, such as Fitzgerald in *The Great Gatsby* and Barth in *The Sot-Weed Factor,* who assumed the end of "earth's romance," Melville refused to concede that the dream must dissolve. Readily confirming that the New World had failed, he nevertheless looked to remoter places in his continuing spiritual exploration. Probing the recesses of time and history in search of earth's most profound mysteries, Melville in *Clarel* journeyed beyond the immediate "terminus" of Europe where James and Eliot would end their quests. In search of an answer, he took his readers to time before the Crucifixion and there discovered the wandering Jew who lives among us yet.

Melville's encounter with the myth of the Wandering Jew, a motif so attractive to other Romantics of his century,[2] emerged almost ineluctably from his long confrontation with the ambiguities of Christianity. As early as *Typee,* Melville had engaged the matter of Christianity's apparent failure. But the explanations here and in subsequent works were always tentative. For example, the island of Serenia in *Mardi* could not hold Taji, but whether this reflected Christianity's failure or Taji's error in not accepting Babbalanja's way remained uncertain. Continuing the exploration in *Moby-Dick,* Melville sent his hero Ishmael to the metaphysical sea where he witnessed the inability of Christianity's Starbuck to prevent the encounter between Ahab and his Armageddon with the whale. Moby Dick, Melville's extraordinary symbol, with no referent other than ambiguity, obviously triumphed, and Ishmael survived to witness and participate in the circularity symbolized by the image of Ixion in "The Epilogue."[3] Yet the overwhelming question remained. Was the fault with Ahab or with Christianity?

In a final attempt to save Ahab and himself from doom, Starbuck in "The Symhony" chapter invoked the allurements of land and greenery, family and home. Although Ahab rejected the temptation, Melville shifted the location of his next novel, *Pierre,* to the greenery of Starbuck's Christian world. Here Melville repeated his quest for religious understanding, but the message of Ahab's way not taken emerges from the "ambiguities" of *Pierre* with unambiguous clarity. Starbuck's promise had no more substance than Falsegrave's theology.

The short fiction Melville subsequently wrote represented a continuation of his search for religious clarity. Whatever quarrel Melville may have had with his audience and editors, his short fiction went beyond a device for revenge against small-minded readers. Certainly Melville did not squander his artistic talents by writing disguised essays about his friendships or animosities; he had more serious concerns. In the art of this period, he expressed them masterfully and quite consistently in a context of examining the efficacy of Christianity, of probing the possibility of nothingness. In "Bartleby" he re-created the blank walls of Ahab's pasteboard mask; in "Benito Cereno" he wrote his parable of God and man failing to offer any salvation; and in "The Encantadas" he created his vivid analogue for the fallen world in which he feared we might dwell. All the stories emerging from this period address in one way or another the persistent mystery of Christianity.

The culmination of his short fiction, both in its style of subterfuge and in its content of Christian mystery, emerged as *The Confidence-Man.* With an artistic skill possibly never before as fully revealed in his work, he returned to a suggestion from *Pierre,* just as in *Pierre* he had reached back to *Moby-Dick. Pierre* had told the story of a fool of virtue; *The Confidence-Man* defines a world of unvirtuous fools. They fare no better. The controlling force of the universe, symbolized by the avatar in his many guises as Christ, Satan, and oriental deity, or some combination of all these—Melville really could not define his God—cared for man only as the object of his tricks. The cosmic joker conjured by Ishmael in "The Hyena" chapter took human form in *The Confidence-Man* and walked among his victims. Fools all, they succumbed to his pranks, played for the love of the game alone, or so it seemed. In a story where meaning rapidly dissolved to chaos, Melville had taken art as far as he could in his search for a stable, Christian world. His literary journeys across the borders of "reality" to the domain of "romance" had failed to place him in the haven he yearned for. When he appeared in print again with the publication of *Clarel* (1876), he did so in a new context. He began explicitly with the premise that the Christian era was closing. As a literary form and as an intellectual idea, the "romance" had ended.

While everyone understands that religious loss long preyed upon Melville's imagination, he had always experimented with the idea on the other side of "reality," in the region of "romance." Now he would stay within the borders of "reality"; he would look for his meaning from the perspective of a journey that began by assuming the end of an era. At the crossroads of Jerusalem, from which the theologies of his culture emanated, he would confront his hero with the additional alternatives of hedonism, sexuality, and the nihilistic emptiness that always haunts the epic poem *Clarel*. From a Jewish geologist, Margoth, a new and awful creed would be scrawled: *"I, Science, I whose gain's thy loss,/ I slanted thee, thou Slanting Cross."*[4]

Although playing a relatively minor role in the poem, Margoth gives brief representational form to its underlying premise, to the nexus of ideas confronting the key pilgrims. Science had suggested to Melville's era that theological history was false, and the characters who follow the way of the cross and the way of all the shrines travel in the shadow of that knowledge. As characters go in *Clarel*, Margoth may rank as the most unsympathetically treated, for Melville had a long quarrel with science running deeper than any he might have had with God. Religious by temperament, and wounded

by assaults on faith, he had no inclination to substitute as an
object of worship the emptiness he abhorred. Margoth, as Walter
Bezanson states, represents a character "based on Melville's long-
standing quarrel with dogmatic materialism, positivism, and
atheism" (p. 540). In light of this generally recognized truth about
Melville's attitude, a demonstration of contempt for science's
success in upending faith makes sense. Moreover, casting Margoth
as a geologist, a hunter of rocks, adds a richly ironic note to the
whole religious quest for the rock upon which Peter built his
church.[5] But why have the scientist a Jew?

Explaining the matter as anti-Semitism won't do, even if Melville did associate "Jewish prophets" with a "ghastly theology."[6]
Judaism was a dead religion for Melville, and while he shared nu-
merous nineteenth-century stereotypes about Jews, he could hardly
have been more sympathetic to the Jewish women in *Clarel,* specifically Agar and Ruth.[7] Other Jewish characters in the poem are
sufficiently varied in their portrayals to indicate that Melville was
not simply loading all his stereotypes on one villain. Margoth has
to be Jewish because Melville's quest had come to that. In the
wasteland of Jerusalem, symbol for the world we all live in, the
redeeming force of Christianity lay in ruins. Christian history,
when stripped away, leaves the barren wilderness of the unre-
deemed world. The man of knowledge endures, while the man of
faith no longer seems plausible. For those to whom the Messiah
had never come, the wilderness remains. Wanderers before a sect
called Christianity emerged, the Jews wander yet.

In "The Masque" chapter, the legend of the Wandering Jew is
specifically staged. Although, as one might have predicted, Melville
added touches of irony to this widely read myth, for the most part
he adhered to its outlines, to the image of a Jew condemned by
Christ to wander until his return.[8] In accordance with the legend,
the Jew emerges as the bearer of history's accumulated wisdom.
Both the curse and the destiny of knowledge occur almost simul-
taneously:

> "Just let him live, just let him rove"
> (Pronounced the voice estranged from love),
> "Live—live and rove the sea and land;
> Long live, rove far, and understand
> And sum all knowledge for his dower;

> For he forbid is, he is banned;
> His brain shall tingle, but his hand
> Shall palsied be in power:
> Ruthless, he meriteth no ruth,
> On him I imprecate the truth."
>
> p. 351

Mortmain, by no coincidence wearing a skullcap, pronounces a grim epilogue at the end of the masque, while the others stare "through the lurid fume" (p. 354) at the lonely figure who has come to understand the destiny that all mankind shares, Margoth, neither witness to the masque nor pilgrim in the Holy Land, escapes this particular horror. Never having participated in the beatific vision of Christian redemption, the death of a theology he ridicules can scarcely touch him. Yet without Christianity's reality, man remains, like Margoth, a grotesque being who wanders a barren world. The other "Wandering Jews" of Melville's poem are those at "The perilous outpost of the sane" (p. 352) who have been told that Christ would return and who fear that He had never come at all. Playing on the myth of the Wandering Jew without slavishly following its details, Melville has given new meaning to an ancient story. In accordance with the myth of the Wandering Jew, the outcast must periodically return to Jerusalem to see its ruin. From all over the world, Melville's wanderers come to find, in Agath's words, "Wreck, ho! the wreck—Jerusalem!" (p. 408). While Agath's history suggests the calamities of the Wandering Jew, Melville has not resorted to the popular nineteenth-century idea of actually having a character be the literal Wandering Jew. Touching on the myth, he has taken a more profound tack. Rather than glorifying, or romanticizing, or even villifying the Wandering Jew, Melville has employed the myth to suggest a darker curse: that there never was a Christ to condemn us.

He has also tied the myth to an emerging secular view that "salvation" may emerge from human love. Perhaps Eugene Sue offered an essential hint. The most popular nineteenth-century version of the myth Melville found appeared in Sue's *Wandering Jew,* first published in 1844 and 1845, frequently translated, and widely read in America. While the book itself is as much an exploration of Jesuit villainies as it is of a tormented Jew, the prologue offers an arresting backdrop to events occurring in *Clarel.* In

the polar North, two figures look across an icy waste, tormented
and separated: a woman on the American side, representing the
New World, and a man on the Asian side, representing the Old
World. Wandering Jews both, they feel the awful pain of their
destiny and their eternal separation. Whether Melville picked up a
clue from this prologue or not, his poem explores the complex
interrelationships of the New and Old Worlds against the background of two lovers seeking to bridge that which cannot be crossed.

Clarel, a young student, disillusioned in his faith, has come to
Jerusalem from the New World in search of a lost religion. As the
poem progresses, he clearly fails in this quest, but he does turn
more and more to the alternative of secular love. Upon hearing at
Mar Saba that the one countersign is death (p. 373), he fails to
mention, fails even to consider Christ, promiser of salvation from
this particular terror. The courage Clarel can muster finds form
only in the image of secular, temporal love:

> This is cowardice
> To brood on this!—Ah, Ruth, thine eyes
> Abash these base mortalities!
>
> p. 374[9]

However, no reader at this point in the poem could expect Ruth
to offer salvation, even in temporal terms. Melville had already
given enough hints that she was dead.[10] Her question then, uttered
in Clarel's visionary moment in the grotto, *"Dost tarry, tarry yet?"*
(p. 374) emphasizing the key word of Christ's curse upon the Jew,[11]
carries the ironic implication that like the Wandering Jew, Clarel
will walk the earth alone, will never cross the barrier possibly suggested by Sue.

Ruth also has wandered, and her history offers some of the
most significant clues to the poem's ironies. Nathan, her father,
had been an American of Puritan ancestry, a descendant of God's
latest chosen people who, having come to America, found their
dream a failure. His conversion to Judaism and his decision to
marry a Jewess and go to Jerusalem reveal not only him but also
his Puritan forebears as Wandering Jews all. The same impulse that
had brought his ancestors to the New Jerusalem of America brings
Nathan back to the Old Jerusalem of biblical history. Very early in
the poem, in telling us who Nathan is, Melville defines his context
of mankind wandering from shore to shore in search of an elusive

promise. Long ago the Puritans had come to America. God's land had not been there for Nathan, so he returned to his earliest sources, bringing his Jewish wife and the child of that marriage, Ruth, born in America. The Wanderers have come home again to Jerusalem, where Ruth will offer Clarel his last alternative.

Her biblical lineage is striking. Hagar, mother of the outcast Ishmael, offers a name familiar enough to readers of Melville. Yet in this poem, he has chosen to name Ruth's mother with the variant Agar. Since this name appears only in one part of the Bible, and since Melville's choice of it departs so particularly from his past usage, we may do well to see what meaning Paul gives to the word in Gal. 4:22-26:

> For it is written, that Abraham had two sons, the one by a bondmaid, the other by a freewoman.
>
> But he *who was* of the bondwoman was born after the flesh; but he of the freewoman *was* by promise.
>
> Which things are an allegory: for these are the two covenants; the one from the mount Sinai, which gendereth to bondage, which is Agar.
>
> For this Agar is mount Sinai in Arabia, and answereth to Jerusalem which now is, and is in bondage with her children.
>
> But Jerusalem which is above is free, which is the mother of us all.

Agar, not heaven's Jerusalem, is the mother of Melville's Ruth.[12]

The biblical Ruth had followed her mother-in-law to the promised land and had there found deliverance. Marrying Boaz, she bore Obed, who in turn had Jesse, father of David. Thus, Ruth's lineage leads to David and the fulfillment of prophecy, since it extends eventually to Christ. Representing the virtues of faith and the promise of redemption, the biblical Ruth offers prophetic testimony to the emergence of heaven's Jerusalem. Yet Melville has made *his* Ruth the daughter of Agar, Paul's symbol for the ruined city of this world. Melville's Ruth, as does her biblical namesake, comes from a faraway land to Jerusalem. One finds redemption, the other death. If Melville's Ruth had been a Jewess only, her fate would have been less ironic. But she is also the daughter of Nathan, the Jew who has rejected Christ and returned to Jerusalem. Biblical prophecy thus becomes reversed. The "Jews" go to the old Jerusalem to find the new Jerusalem. They die.

Nor does the irony stop there. The biblical Nathan is Nathan the prophet, wise man of his kingdom. Leading David from evil ways, he is instrumental in the succession of Solomon, thus showing the way to God's righteous order and eventually to New Testament history. Melville's Nathan descends from the American Puritans (p. 63), who came to establish their New Jerusalem in America. The experiment having failed, this Nathan years later returns to an earlier faith, brings his Jewish family to the fountainhead of their religion, and precedes them there in death.

Put another way, Melville has named Ruth's family after biblical types whose scriptural history centers in some manner on an identification with Jerusalem. The biblical Nathan helps assure the succession that will lead to the New Jerusalem; Melville's leads his family to the old one. Paul's Agar symbolizes the Jerusalem of the Old Covenant; Melville's follows her husband to a ruin that outlives the Christian era. The biblical Ruth finds salvation in Jerusalem; Melville's finds death. And if one will follow the parallel between Nathan the "Christian" seeking his Jewess and residing in Jerusalem on the one hand, and Clarel on the other hand in the old city likewise seeking his Jewess, then the dreary fate of Melville's hero in the Holy Land has been predictable enough.

These ironic counterpoints occur in the context of Melville's exploration of love as a possible alternative to the failure of faith and the unacceptability of science as theology. Nathan, we recall, found love first and then his new religion. While the abandonment of his Puritan heritage in one sense stemmed simply from his loss of faith, he had also been seduced by the lure of flesh, by Paul's "allegory." Child of a new age, Nathan wants to believe (p. 62) but is unable to find his faith. When the flesh of Agar promises also a return to theology unmoved by the flux of history, Nathan accepts the promise. Again, Melville gives artistic form to a theological postulate. Why not turn Hebrew, Nathan asks himself:

> If backward still the inquirer goes
> To get behind man's present lot
> Of crumbling faith; for rear-wall shows
> Far behind Rome and Luther—what?
> The crag of Sinai. Here then plant
> Thyself secure: 'tis adamant.

> p. 63

Clearly the "crag of Sinai" evokes the Sinai Paul had associated with Agar, as Melville's Nathan merges theology and love into "adamant," the hardest rock of all. Like the rocks studied by Margoth the geologist, like the rock of Christian faith, like the stones that Nehemiah clears from the road in anticipation of Christ's arrival, the hard adamant comes to represent the poem's Holy Grail, stones in the wasteland of Jerusalem.[13]

In the Holy Land Nathan the wanderer fights Arabs in his attempt to recover Jerusalem, just as his "sires in Pequod wilds" (p. 65) fought the Indians. As the biblical Nathan looked to the new dispensation, the new Nathan, child of that dispensation, looks to the old dispensation. History, rather than being cyclical, simply crisscrosses, or moves erratically, randomly re-creating the eternal search for an enduring "adamant." Nathan has become a wandering Jew; yet if the poem hints at anything, it suggests that all of us may be consigned to that fate. And none embodies this fact more than Clarel, who becomes a Nathan, responding to the call of his Agar, the American Jewess in the Holy Land, his Ruth.[14]

Like Nathan, Clarel meets his Jewess at a moment of extreme doubt and dwindling faith. Yet Melville predictably varies his theme, trying another alternative rather than simply repeating a process. Thus, just as each of his novels had turned on a story or idea presented in a previous one, so Clarel's search for Ruth varies the theme of Nathan's attraction to Agar. Nathan's loss of faith leads to love and a re-created religion. The venture fails. Clarel seeks what almost amounts to a new theology, the embodiment of every hope in the love of one woman. On his pilgrimage past the holy sites of Christian history, Clarel has seen weak faith dwindle more with each experience. Finally, he reaches the point where his Agar, Ruth, becomes Paul's embodiment of the flesh. There is no faith, no illusion that Judaism will contain the fixed rock.

When Ruth, in Clarel's vision, chastens him for tarrying (p. 374), the newest wanderer is clearly temporal, hearing the siren song of Paul's Agar. This event occurs fairly late in the poem, a few cantos after the masque of the Wandering Jew. Since the eternal journey should be spiritual rather than erotic, one may wonder whether Clarel has simply gone astray. But Melville very early had addressed the alternative spiritual possibility in the portrayal of Celio, the tormented, disfigured youth who wanders to Jerusalem in search of redemption and finds among the Franciscans no more salvation in Christianity than Clarel would find in earthly love. Quite specifically, Celio had asked the question, "Am *I* the [Wandering] Jew?"

(p. 44).[15] He is, as all the journeyers to salvation in Jerusalem are. But Melville has not given his Wandering Jews immortality. The great horror in the myth of the Wandering Jew had been the sentence of immortality. Concomitantly, however, the myth guaranteed a God. Melville turned the horror to mortality. The Western world had tried one half of Paul's allegory; the other half remained.

Clarel, of course, does not gravitate toward the simplicity of lust alone. In some incomprehensible way, he seeks in Ruth the possibility of a religious faith nowhere else to be found. This is not Judaism. It has no name. " 'Twas Ruth, and oh, much more than Ruth" (p. 392). Clarel's journey toward this ineffable goal begins, appropriately enough, when he encounters a black Jew named Abdon, who has wandered from a distant land to die. This wandering Jew had come to recognize that only the gravestone is "left to such as I" (p. 9)—the grave "in a land how dead!" (p. 10). Having met this Jew brooding in the lamp-lit night, Clarel returns to his "tomb-like chamber" (p. 10), where he accidentally comes across a poem entitled "JUDAEA" (p. 10). Unabashedly allegorical, transparently Spencerian, the poem adumbrates Clarel's pilgrimage by pitting the "World" against the "Palmer." The first asks from the Holy Land things "cheery" (p. 11), what cantos later will become embodied in the Lyonese Jew; the words evoke lushness and hedonism. The Palmer's religious reply, anticipating the asceticism that Salvaterra will alternatively offer Clarel, rejects this vision while ambiguously presenting palms and dust. To these alternatives, Clarel poses his own question: will he journey through the Holy Land finding dust alone and nothing of redemption? For even at the outset, death's dust clings to the theology of Christ.

From the beginning, Melville has established the poem's premise. While the larger glory belongs to religious salvation, the certainty or even the possibility emerges as appallingly dim. The alternative way of hedonism might exist as a possibility, but the reward scarcely warrants the quest. For the way of the flesh must also be the way of death. Not ready to abandon the richer quest, yet at the start aware that another though inferior way exists, Clarel begins his journey through the artifacts of theological history and returns at last to his empty Jerusalem.

However pessimistic, the search has been genuine. Exploring many an obscure theology, Melville's religious analysis most importantly centers on a theological drama casting Protestantism and Catholicism as the central characters acting in a wasteland setting. Concurrently, Judaism offers a ghostly backdrop to the religious dialogue about the virtues of Protestantism and Catholicism—a tragic chorus, as it were, grimly denying both, bleakly asserting that the argument between the two great trunks of the Christian tree grow from a soil that never was fertile. The tragedy of Celio has introduced this play, as each myth tells its own lie, while truth resides in sterile Judea awaiting a Messiah who has never come.

Quite literally, Nehemiah, representing Puritanism's pathetic, unintended offshoot, Protestant fundamentalism, awaits the coming of Christ:

> In Calvin's creed he put his trust;
> Praised heaven, and said that God was good,
> And his calamity but just.
>
> p. 122

Yet Nehemiah suggests more than a Millenarian fool. For a man absolutely certain in his faith he demonstrates a strange disquietude at the site of the Passion while reading the chapter in the Gospel of John that describes the betrayal by Judas. But in that chapter (18:10) there also appears the "Malchus" incident, the ultimate scriptural source for most modern versions of the Wandering Jew myth.[16] Nehemiah himself roams aimlessly (p. 111), hides his past (p. 124), and must await his private encounter with Christ before he can die. More than once he is referred to as the "chief of sinners" (pp. 223, 240), and he has his own wording for the 23rd Psalm (p. 241), where, along with other changes, he deletes the word "death."[17] Nehemiah, of course, is not *the* Wandering Jew, since Melville avoids the fabulous in this poem. His behavior, moreover, is reasonably consistent with the Millenarian on whom his character has been assumed to be based.[18] Indeed, Nehemiah's death by sleepwalking into the Dead Sea might burlesque the Millenarian idea as well as the Wandering Jew notion. Yet, significantly, Melville chooses to treat this strange character sympathetically. If his acts are absurd, they are no less so than the science of Margoth, and at least Nehemiah has an illusion worth having. Firm in his faith, he need not endure life since death promises to relieve whatever burdens it might present. Wandering Jew or not, Nehemiah never suffers from the belief that no Christ exists. But those who suspect otherwise, while adhering to the facade of Christianity, carry a special curse.

Derwent, the modern, educated, enlightened Protestant, reveals this to us. Readers generally choose to see this character as representing the weakness and blindness of modern, intellectual Protestantism. While tempting, such a reading misses too much of Derwent. As the modern reconciler of theology and science, he has had to concede one or the other, and it is finally the faith in scripture that he has lost. It has not slipped away painlessly. Under his blithe explanations and clarifications, he remains the tormented nineteenth-century man, Protestantism's ultimate victim, the individual who by the power of reason has come to believe that his clerical garbs are woven from false thread. Whoever else Derwent fools, he does not delude himself. While Rolfe gives us the cutting lines that ridicule Derwent's eclecticism, "Things all diverse he would unite:/ His idol's an hermaphrodite" (p. 342), the cleric sees more deeply than Rolfe suspects. After the shattering masque of the Wandering Jew, Clarel can no longer refrain from pressing Derwent for some explanation of his ameliorative views. Beginning by playing his role as wise, elder cleric, Derwent soon reveals that the drama has touched him too. Unable to explain man's plight, he almost blurts out a fury as deep as Ahab's:

> Derwent bit the lip;
> Altered again, had fain let slip
> "Throw all this burden upon HIM;"
> But hesitated.

p. 360

Fully aware that his theology cannot withstand the rational assults of scientific inquiry, he draws back from the desperate act of renunciation. Instead, he argues for the transcending myths that allow a religious impulse to remain alive. "Have faith," he affirms, "which, even from the myth,/ Draws something to be useful with:/ In any form some truths will hold;/ Employ the present-sanctioned mold./ Nay, here me out; clean breast I make . . ." (p. 361). And he does. Each culture has turned a common underlying myth into some historical fact. Never mind, he implies, that Christian history is false. Beneath that history a true and transcendent myth endures, one common to mankind and adapting to the culture which generates it. Frazer, Jung, and Lévi-Strauss, to name a few, would codify aspects of this notion. Derwent found his one hope in it. Protestantism might survive if it abandoned Christ, perhaps yielding to something else, as the worship of Apollo had yielded to that of Christ. But faith could endure as man wandered from theology to theology.

Yet losing the miracle of Christianity comes at a heavy price. In the Church of the Star he confronts the Latin text affirming that "THE VIRGIN HERE BROUGHT FORTH THE SON" (p. 450). Derwent responds enigmatically but with the sorrow of disbelief reflected in his knowing look. He knows, as he says later, "Madonna's but a dream" (p. 469). Clinging nevertheless to that underlying myth, he speaks of the reality of insubstantial things, citing the love of Romeo and Juliet (p. 469), though neglecting to comment on their fate. Perhaps this is deliberate. To pursue truth toward its ultimate end may be more than humanity can bear. As Ishmael in the "Brit" chapter had warned against pushing off from the serenity of man's "insular Tahiti," so Derwent at Mar Saba warns Clarel, "Alas, too deep you dive" (p. 364). Yet Melville in his famous comment on Emerson had assured us that he himself loved "all men who *dive*."[19] Those deep divers, whether Ahab or Emerson, held the profoundest of attractions for Melville, but the Derwents and Ishmaels represented a wisdom warning one away from the fruitless, monomaniacal quest that Melville insisted on pursuing. Derwent's Protestantism, his desperate clinging to the continuity of myth, even as he sensed the terror revealed in a masque of the Wandering Jew, thus becomes not an object of ridicule but an expedient, painful compromise between the despair of atheism and the horrifying recognition of a God, if He indeed exists, who could impose such an awful curse. "Midway is best," Derwent says (p. 363), but Clarel, like Melville, must dive to whatever he finds. He cannot stop at the water's edge, and the Protestant way fails not for its foolishness but for its unwillingness to pursue total knowledge. Yet by hovering at its halfway point, it only furthers what it seeks to avoid. The expediency of Protestantism gives birth to the atheism it yearns to escape. Mankind's journey to the New World and Protestant democracy may still appeal to those who view it from Europe, but the Americans in the poem know better, and none articulates the complex relationships among democracy, Protestantism, and atheism better than Rolfe does.

In "The Wilderness" section, while discussing Rome and Catholicism with Derwent, Rolfe refuses to concede that the New World
will never return to the Roman fold. First insisting that "Fate
never gives a guarantee" (p. 233), Rolfe argues that mankind's
latest experiment, American, Protestant democracy, has offered
the world only chaos:

> "Verily,
> Laws scribbled by law-breakers, creeds
> Scrawled by the freethinkers, and deeds
> Shameful and shameless. Men get sick
> Under that curse of Frederic
>   [a benevolent, liberal, despot]
> The cynical: For punishment
> This rebel province [America] I present
> To the philosophers. But, how?
> Whole nations now philosophize,
> And do their own undoing now.—
> Who's gained by all the sacrifice
> Of Europe's revolutions? who?
> The Protestant? the Liberal?
> I do not think it—not at all:
> Rome and the Atheist have gained:
> These two shall fight it out—these two;
> Protestantism being retained
> For base of operations sly
> By Atheism."

pp. 233–234

When Derwent expresses surprise that Rolfe, as a "New-Worlder,"
should speak in such a manner, the American insists that " 'Tis the
New World that mannered me,/ Yes, gave me this vile liberty/ To
reverence naught, not even herself" (p. 234).

Rolfe's comments on the modern experiment that liberal Euro-
peans of the day never seemed to tire of lauding have particular
significance in view of the critical commonplace, often if not
always precisely accurate, that Rolfe tends to present Melville's
own views. At the end of this particular section, the narrator specifically defines Rolfe as "Charged with things manifold and wise"
(p. 235). Rolfe's wisdom carries a view argued by the Catholic
Church from the outset of the Protestant revolution and most
articulately repeated in the nineteenth century by Tocqueville.[20]
Protestantism, the argument went, led to polarities of atheism and

Catholicism. Clarel's answer was not in the New World and hence his backward journey to Jerusalem.

Since atheism horrified Clarel, and since he could accept neither Nehemiah's apparent delusions nor Derwent's compromise with history, the lure of Rome beckoned the student in his search for faith. Against the onslaught of doubt the Catholic Church stood firm. The Dominican and Salvaterra confirm by their examples that a plausible faith may endure. Neither the virulent anti-Catholicism of the Presbyterian Elder, who leaves the pilgrims early in the journey, nor the intellectual arguments of Derwent weaken the poem's flattering case for Catholicism. But the Church's capacity to survive atheism, as Protestantism cannot, offers Clarel merely order. Attractive as this may be, he wants to dive deeper. And in the "Bethlehem" section, Ungar helps isolate the rational basis for Rome's ultimate inadequacy.

This individual, appropriately defined by Walter Bezanson as "the dominant dark figure of Part IV" (p. 547), represents one more exile, another wanderer in Melville's epic. Cursed by democracy rather than Christ, labeled "A wandering Ishmael from the West" (p. 441), and perhaps reminiscent of Hoffman's Cartaphilus "now recently returned from a far Western Land,"[21] Ungar bears witness to Rolfe's analysis of the New World; he offers living testimony to the idea that neither religious background nor geographical location will end man's wandering that began in Eden, long before Christ's curse upon the Jew. Exiled from earth's latest paradise, Ungar yearns for faith, although he too finds it elusive. Sympathetic to Catholicism, because, like Melville, he sympathizes with all genuine religious impulses, Ungar knows that history has failed to confirm Christianity in general as well as Catholicism in particular. Descended from a Catholic family, although not of that faith himself, Ungar perceives that conversion to Christianity represented a change in forms rather than a change in man.

For much of the journey Derwent had argued his position that while Christian history must be suspect in literal terms, its underlying mythology conveyed a vision true to this world. If this offers something less than what Clarel had sought, it at least promises a rational order, an "uneven balance," to use the phrase from "Hawthorne and His Mosses,"[22] that here weighs in the direction of something good. Ungar's theology, however, draws an opposite

conclusion from a similar premise. Earlier, Ungar had responded to
Derwent's claim that while Christianity may be incomprehensible,
the spirit of Christ mediates the world we live in. Granting the
premise that the world had turned to the way of Christ, Ungar
cuttingly remarks:

> "The world but joined the Creed Divine
> With prosperous days and Constantine;
> The world turned Christian, need confess,
> But the world remained the world, no less. . . ."
>
> p. 470

While this view might unnerve Clarel, he could accept it if it
merely posited man's failure to accept his innate goodness, the
light of God (the etymology of his name may even pun on this)
perpetually before him. But Ungar is saying something profoundly
different. Some common myth may bind man together, but the
unifying force is not redemption:

> "Know,
> Whatever happen in the end,
> Be sure 'twill yield to one and all
> New confirmation of the fall
> of Adam."
>
> p. 483

This is why Ungar rejects so emphatically the whole concept of
America and the New World offering anything better than the old
one had presented. When his argument leads to the conclusion that
"Columbus ended earth's romance" (p. 484), his compatriots
understand that the Puritan experiment, the democratic dream,
and all the myriad hopes placed upon the last unexplored continent
would finally reveal man and the world as they always had been
and always would be.[23] Therefore, when Vine asks the overwhelming question, "Is wickedness the word?" (p. 485), he understands
fully that if Ungar is right the words echoing in the Gospel according to John, "In the beginning was the Word, and the Word
was with God, and the Word was God" (1:1), must reverberate
ironically before them all. Ungar has redefined those memorable
lines known to every Christian, affirmed that man is irredeemably
wicked, and suggested that God may be too. There will be no
redemption he has told us, and the very notion of rebirth affirms
man's profound evil, unalleviated by divine intercession:

"This wickedness
(Might it retake true import well)
Means not default, nor vulgar vice,
Nor Adam's lapse in Paradise;
But worse: 'twas this evoked the hell—
Gave in the conscious soul's recess
Credence to Calvin. What's implied
In that deep utterance decried
What Christians labially confess—
Be born anew?"

                    p. 485 (Melville's italics)

Not the fall of man in paradise but the original creation accounts for man's plight.

If Clarel accepts this, then no religious system, no scientific one, no mythic synthesis will dispel a horror more profound than he had yet suspected. Derwent quickly counters Ungar by pointing to the bright beauties of nature which implicitly deny this black vision. But Clarel finds Ungar more persuasive.

Ungar's arguments also treat the same complex point Melville had explored in the Plinlimmon Pamphlet of *Pierre*. Christianity, Ungar argues, inherently denies the possibility of its own reality in this world. His argument with Derwent extends finally to Catholicism and to all of Christianity. "Your methods?" he asks. "These are of the world:/ Now the world cannot save the world;/ And Christ renounces it. His faith,/ Breaking with every mundane path,/ Aims straight at heaven" (p. 477). The Plinlimmon writer had assured his reader that in heaven one "can freely turn the left cheek, because there the right cheek will never be smitten."[24] Flatly and unambiguously Ungar affirms that Christ had "No thought to mend a world amiss" (p. 477). If God created sin before Eden, and if Christ had not come to redeem the world, then Clarel must face a nightmare more frightening than the loss of faith.

In section III, Melville's narrative voice had set the stage for this moment of gnostic terror:

'Twas averred [among the group conversing]
That, in old Gnostic pages blurred,
Jehovah was construed to be
Author of evil, yea, its god;
And Christ divine his contrary:
A god was held against a god,
But Christ revered alone.

                    p. 291

Since "no more/ Those Gnostic heretics prevail/ ... none say Jehovah's evil" (p. 292). None except Ungar. None except the implicit message in the masque of the Wandering Jew, where Christ is associated with the voice "estranged from love" (p. 351). Clarel has come back to the central enigma of Christianity, the divine permission of evil. Ahab's problem has not disappeared in *Clarel.* To *"Be born anew"* one must do more than accept Christ. Only a re-created world would suffice, and no theology offers this. Catholicism, for all its appeal, cannot gloss over the problem. It can only maintain a more intellectually appealing illusion than the Protestant fundamentalism of Nehemiah. Neither the church of Rome, nor the faith of Christodulus, Abbot of Mar Saba, so orthodox that "Rome's Pope he deemed but Protestant—/ A Rationalist, a bigger Paine—" (p. 368), nor the serenely religious Druze can offer Clarel a theology to withstand the gnostic implication of Ungar's vision.

Ungar's lessons come when Clarel's faith has all but vanished in any event. The blows are overwhelming. His journey to the Holy Land has only reaffirmed his doubts at best and added to them at worst. Having sought to rekindle his faith, he has found that the loss might have come even prior to the fall in Eden. If this world is indeed Jehovah's, if Christ is not of this world, and perhaps malign if He is, what remains for Clarel? Maybe, and here Clarel grasps desperately, a theology of human love will suffice.

The idea had appeared early in the poem with Clarel's suggestive attraction to Celio. But the death of this tormented man serves primarily as the harbinger of what humanity can offer Clarel. More directly, Clarel invests in Vine the possibility that a fraternity of masculine love can offer something, however vague. Vine, the curious man with no history and no home (p. 94), exists almost in the realm of pure symbol. Free from sexuality and from history, given only to his inexplicable wanderings and occasional utterances, he seems to offer a way somewhere between heaven's Jerusalem and earth's lust. But the idea is always Clarel's, never Vine's, and the way of fraternal love comes to nothing.[25] The Lyonese Jew offers—or so most readers feel—masculine, sexual love. But Clarel has not come all the way to Jerusalem for this. The last of the Wandering Jews to confront Clarel has a larger role to play. He

will send him at last to the one remaining illusion, the communion
of Ruth.

Clarel understands the perilous road in following the way of the
Jewess. To find that which is "much more than Ruth" one must
first contend with that which *is* Ruth. Since this woman exists
primarily in symbolic terms, her specific attractions are those of
an Everywoman. We see this in "The Recoil" chapter where Clarel
faces the danger of seeking spirituality in a world of flesh. Was the
Blessed Virgin the sister of Ruth? How does one find her spirituality? Melville had posed the problem before in the ambiguities of
Yillah and Hautia, Lucy and Isabel. Clarel is stopped by the
mystery of how one extricates the essence from the woman, trans-
forms the being to a goddess. The question haunts him:

> But if Eve's charm be not supernal,
> Enduring not divine transplanting—
> Love kindled thence, is that eternal?
> Here, here's the hollow—here the haunting!
> Ah, love, ah wherefore thus unsure?
> Linked art thou—locked, with Self impure?
>
> p. 397

Only when Ungar has stripped his faith bare does Clarel contem-
plate the implication and dare the venture.

> If man in truth be what you say,
> And such the prospects for the clay,
> And outlook of the future—cease!
> What's left us but the senses' sway?
> Sinner, sin out life's petty lease:
> We are not worth the saving. Nay,
> For me, if thou speak true—but ah,
> Yet, yet there gleams one beckoning star—
> So near the horizon, judge I right
> That 'tis of heaven?
>
> p. 486

Clarel will turn to Ruth for Paul's "allegory" of Agar and try to
persuade himself that here heaven may yet be found. He is ready
for the final appeal to sensuality from the last of his guides, the
Lyonese Jew. Whether homosexual or not, this hedonist presents
Clarel with the unambiguous attractions of feminine flesh. Upon
discovering Ruth's religion, although he disguises his own, the

Lyonese plays heavily on Clarel's new inclination toward "the senses' sway":

> "There is no tress
> Can thrall one like a Jewess's.
> A Hebrew husband, Hebrew-wed,
> Is wondrous faithful, it is said;
> Which needs be true; for, I suppose,
> As bees are loyal to the rose,
> So men to beauty."
>
> p. 497

In one sense, Melville has succumbed to a cultural myth or perhaps has sought merely to exploit it. That is, the notion of Jewess as temptress and voluptuary was standard fare in nineteenth-century fiction, ranging from the hint of Miriam's Jewish ancestry in *The Marble Faun* to the earlier and more explicit use in *Arthur Mervyn.* Melville was using a cultural cliché, and perhaps he was also extending the image of the two wanderers in Sue's prologue held apart by an inseparable barrier. Whatever the case, certainly the myth of the seductive Jewess offered Melville an extraordinary opportunity. Clarel's last temptation had to be of the flesh, and his journey had to be in the Holy Land among the Jews. Ruth was perfect for the artistic requirement. In getting "behind man's present lot" (p. 63), as Nathan had sought to do, Clarel would embrace the Jewish way, implicitly defined in this poem as hedonistic, lustful: the covenant of Agar. The last voice to speak for a Christian way had been Salvaterra (pp. 499–500), appearing in a dream, contending with the Lyonese for Clarel's soul. But earth's salvation, if any, Clarel concluded, was on earth and not in heaven. He had come to the way of Ruth:

> Yea, now his hand would boldly reach
> And pluck the nodding fruit to him,
> Fruit of the tree of life. If doubt
> Spin spider-like her tissue out,
> And make a snare in reason dim—
> Why hang a fly in flimsy web?
> One thing was clear, one thing in sooth:
> Stays not the prime of June or youth:
> At flood that tide makes haste to ebb.
>
> pp. 507–8

History, slightly twisted, has reoccurred. Like Nathan, Clarel, despairing of Christianity, will seek a Judaic path. Yet not without the private dread heard in the imagined voice of Ruth: "She seemed to fear for him, and say:/ 'Ah, tread not, sweet, my father's way...'" (p. 508). Not without the fearful possibility implied by his own question:

> But what! distrust the trustful eyes?
> Are the sphered breasts full of mysteries
> Which not the maiden's self may know?
>
> p. 508

Melville has brought his hero back to the ambiguity of *Pierre*.[26] While Clarel's decision has become irrevocable, he offers the last irony of appealing to a God in whom he cannot believe for respite against the enduring curse of doubt that Clarel, as well as Melville and his many contemporaries shared: "Ah! God, keep far from me/ Cursed Manes and the Manichee!" (p. 509).[27] And the grotesque pun uttered by "Christ" at the masque of the Wandering Jew has apparently been forgotten: "Ruthless, [the Wandering Jew] meriteth no ruth" (p. 351).

Upon returning to Jerusalem, Clarel discovers the dead. Jerusalem has offered its prize by reaffirming Paul's warning against the covenant of Agar. But the ruined city has not shown the way to the Jerusalem above. On the contrary, it has confirmed for Clarel the despairing cry of Celio in echoing the biblical question:[28]

> "How long wilt make us still to doubt?"
> How long?—'Tis eighteen cycles now—
> Enigma and evasion grow;
> And shall we never find thee out?
>
> p. 43

This was the voice of Clarel's spiritual "mate" (p. 50), the cry of a modern Wandering Jew.

Since Melville, unlike the sea captain he would create for his last work of art, was not a man of "settled convictions,"[29] *Clarel* could not end with the kind of definitive resolution that readers from time to time want to impose upon it. Melville's search for the faith he wanted and could not find would continue. He would try again in *Billy Budd*. For now, he could only leave Clarel with a curious, though profoundly unshakable vision. "Conviction is not gone," he has Clarel say, "Though faith's gone" (p. 513). The world had not conformed to Melville's dream for it—neither the new nor the old one. Nor had either of Paul's covenants shown the way. But the failures had left intact the determination to "endure" (p. 513), to insist on an astonishing proposition: "that which shall not be/ It *ought* to be! [pp. 513-14]"

These words are Clarel's but we make a mistake if we fail to see them as Melville's also. Even if all history and all experience had confirmed what Celio so pointedly implied, that we are all wandering Jews, only the self-pitying would settle for nihilism or a whimpering despair. Oddly enough, only Derwent has given us the touch of hope. This cleric, so maligned by the modern critic intent upon imposing a twentieth-century mythos upon a nineteenth-century writer, early on offered Clarel and Melville, and all of us, the one way. Preposterous perhaps, open to the sneering accusation of rainbow chasing, Derwent's refusal to accept his disbelief offered something better than the simplicity of despair:

> "There's none so far astray,
> Detached, abandoned, as might seem,
> As to exclude the hope, the dream
> Of fair redemption."
>
> p. 158

Unlike Amasa Delano, Derwent, like Melville, knows he chases rainbows. But what else is worth the quest? So in the dreary Epilogue the narrator (Melville, with due apologies to the new critic) offers "the hope" to Clarel that narrowly finds its way between the Scylla of false faith and the Charybdis of despair:

> Then keep thy heart, though yet but ill-resigned—
> Clarel, thy heart, the issues there but mind;
> That like the crocus budding through the snow—
> That like a swimmer rising from the deep—
> That like a burning secret which doth go
> Even from the bosom that would hoard and keep;
> Emerge thou mayst from the last whelming sea,
> And prove that death but routs life in victory.
>
> p. 523

This is not the voice of the monomaniacal characters who haunt the poem, nor the sound of the various theologians, scientists, and mad dreamers. If not precisely Derwent's sensibility, though its insistence on the heart is surely his, it seems to affirm that while the Messiah of the wandering Jews may never have come, since we must wander, we do well to hope.

NOTES

1. John Winthrop's "Citty upon a Hill," in his *Christian Charitie. A Modell Hereof*, offers the best-known rubric for the Puritans' image of their New Jerusalem.

2. The myth of the Wandering Jew has a history too exhaustive for full analysis here. Critics of Melville have generally ignored the idea, although a recent study by Vincent S. Kenny, *Herman Melville's Clarel* (Hamden, Conn.: Shoe String Press, 1973) specifically recognizes the myth and its force in the poem (pp. 98 and 211). The most comprehensive study of the myth itself may be found in George K. Anderson's *The Legend of the Wandering Jew* (Providence: Brown University Press, 1965). Mr. Anderson's section on the romantic employment of the myth should be required reading for students of European and American Romanticism.

Melville's specific acquaintance with the myth, a subject not explored in Anderson's study, could have grown from any number of sources. Shelley was almost obsessed with the theme, and Melville's knowledge of him needs no documentation here. The myth finds expression in *Queen Mab, Hellas, Alastor,* and elsewhere. Mentioned by Melville in *Clarel,* Shelley's works were well known to him.

Other possible sources include Wordsworth and lesser writers, cited subsequently, such as the Reverend George Croly, David Hoffman, and Eugene Sue.

3. For an excellent discussion of the circularity theme in *Moby-Dick,* see Ted N. Weissbuch and Bruce Stillians, "Ishmael the Ironist: The Anti-Salvation Theme in *Moby-Dick,*" *Emerson Society Quarterly,* No. 31 (1963), 71–75.

4. Herman Melville, *Clarel,* ed. Walter E. Bezanson (New York: Hendricks House, 1960), p. 252. All subsequent citations of *Clarel* are from this text.

5. Images of stones and rocks appear frequently in Melville's journal of his visit to the Holy Land. Melville noted their association with New Testament images as well as with Old Testament theology. That geologists should find in stones evidence to attack both was an irony one could scarcely miss. Melville's best-known association of the Holy Land with stones appears on p. 152 of Howard C. Horsford's edition of the journal, *Journal of a Visit to Europe and the Levant* (Princeton: Princeton University Press, 1955). Other allusions appear throughout.

6. Horsford, *Journal of a Visit to Europe and the Levant,* p. 151.

7. For further indication "that no general criticism of Jews is implied," see Bezanson, *Clarel,* p. 540.

8. See note 2 for a discussion of sources. Melville's use of the name "Cartaphilus" in his "Masque" chapter calls attention to the fact that the Wandering

Jew appears throughout history under various names. Melville's particular choice of "Cartaphilus," as opposed to the more popularly used "Ahasuerus" in his day (Shelley's choice, for example), may suggest an ironic association with the variation of the myth in which the Wandering Jew becomes an advocate for Christ. For a discussion of the main trunks of the Wandering Jew myth and their associations with different names, see Anderson, *Legend of the Wandering Jew*, pp. 11 ff., and particularly p. 19.

9. One need not be a great source hunter to recognize Matthew Arnold's similar refrain in "Dover Beach." While I do not insist that Melville was influenced by "Dover Beach," the possibility is strong. Publication of the poem in 1867 makes influence chronologically possible. His possession of the poem and his influence by Arnold in other ways has already been established. For a discussion of that influence, see Walter Bezanson's "Melville's Reading of Arnold's Poetry," *PMLA*, 69 (1954), 365–91. Bezanson, who gives evidence of Melville's possession of "Dover Beach," finds it puzzling that Melville did not mark the poem, since "its central image of the withdrawing sea of faith is germane to the 'wasteland' metaphors of *Clarel*" (p. 390). While one can scarcely explain why Melville or any other author does or does not mark a particular poem, "Dover Beach" remains as one of many likely works that conformed to Melville's shared concern for the receding faith. The poem also has striking affinities with *Clarel* in its suggestive theme of secular love as the possible alternative to religious faith. Without exploring Arnold's own view on this possibility, one may observe that Melville finds more truth in the separation theme of Sue's prologue than in the "redemption" motif evoked in "Dover Beach."

10. The reader's first and most obvious clue occurs as Clarel sets out on his pilgrimage, harboring thoughts of Ruth and encountering the funeral procession of the Armenian bride (pp. 134–35). The image recurs in the poem.

11. Many variations of Christ's language appear in myths of the Wandering Jew. The word "tarry" achieved particular prominence in the Reverend George Croly's *Salathiel* (1827), a novel dealing much more directly with the Wandering Jew theme than Sue's work. The subtitle of the first edition is *"Tarry Thou Till I Come."* Although Melville's frequent use of "tarry" in *Clarel* may certainly have other explanations, its association with Croly's novel cannot be discounted. Highly popular, this book was translated into German and reprinted in English. Interest in it has continued even to the twentieth century. The particular edition I have examined (Cincinnati: J.A. and U.P. James, 1853, 2 vols.) does not carry the subtitle of the first edition. It does present as the opening line of the book, "Tarry thou, till I come" (I, 7). The refrain is repeated toward the end of the novel (II, 223). Probably more than any nineteenth-century work associated with the Wandering Jew myth, *Salathiel* offers heavy emphasis on the association of Jerusalem with sorrow for the wanderer. Its thematic treatment of Jerusalem's sad associations corresponds with Melville's employment of the theme in *Clarel*. One of many examples may be found in Salathiel's (the Wandering Jew) approach to the city: "In sorrow, indeed, had I entered Jerusalem" (II, 71). So also does Melville's *Clarel*.

Another book appearing in 1853 may offer the specific source for Melville's use of the name Cartaphilus to describe his Wandering Jew: David Hoffman, *Chronicles Selected from the Originals of Cartaphilus, the Wandering Jew* (London: Thomas Bosworth). Hoffman died before completing his projected six-volume tome, but the first three volumes appeared and were cited in the *Cyclopaedia of American Literature* by Evert and George Duyckinck. The appearance of the name Cartaphilus in Hoffman's work, one obviously available to Melville, may help explain why he chose the name Cartaphilus rather than the more popular Ahasuerus. As in Croly's book, Hoffman emphasizes the word "tarry" in articulating the curse.

12. The significance of names in Melville's work is well known. See, for example, Hennig Cohen, "Wordplay on Personal Names in the Writings of Herman Melville," *Tennessee Studies in Literature*, 8 (1964), 85–97.

13. See note 5.

14. In *Clarel*, Ruth descends from "Miriam's race" (p. 62). Although the association of Jews with Miriam was not unusual, the name "Miriam" as the choice in this case for representing Judaism calls special attention to Croly's naming of the Wandering Jew's wife Miriam. Hoffman, on the other hand, gives the specific name Mariamne to the mother of Cartaphilus.

15. Clarel sees Celio at "The arch named Ecce Homo" (p. 42). In addition to accepting Bezanson's appropriate gloss of "Ecce Homo" in association with Christ and Pilate (*Clarel*, p. 565), one may do well to note Anderson's association of the Latin phrase with the myth of the Wandering Jew (*The Legend of the Wandering Jew*, p. 10). Melville skillfully merges both aspects of the myth by having Celio as Wandering Jew at the arch which asks us to "Behold the Man": at once Christ and the Wandering Jew. Melville's association of the two is noted in his *Journal of a Visit to Europe and the Levant*, in which he added the penciled words "(Arch of Ecce Homo)" (p. 161) after making a notation about "the preparing of the highway for the Jews."

16. For discussion of the Malchus theme in the myth see Anderson, *The Legend of the Wandering Jew*, pp. 11 ff.

17. Bezanson, *Clarel*, p. 241: "Though through the valley of the shade/ I pass, no evil do I fear;/ His candle shineth on my head:/ Lo, he is with me, even here." The words are repeated after Nehemiah's death (p. 272).

18. See ibid., p. 544, and Melville, *Journal*, pp. 142–43.

19. Jay Leyda, *The Melville Log* (New York: Gordian Press, 1969), I, 292.

20. Alexis de Tocqueville, *Democracy in America*, intro. John Stuart Mill (New York: Schocken Books, 1961), II, 33–34.

21. See Hoffman, "Dedication," *Chronicles Selected from the Originals of Cartaphilus.*

22. *The Shock of Recognition*, ed. Edmund Wilson (New York: Farrar, Straus and Cudahy, 1943), p. 192.

23. For an existential reading of this line, see Dorothee Metlitsky Finkelstein, *Melville's Orienda* (New Haven: Yale University Press, 1961), p. 12.

24. Herman Melville, *Pierre*, ed. Harrison Hayford, Hershel Parker, and G. Thomas Tanselle (Evanston, Ill.: Northwestern University Press, 1971), p. 214.

25. Although critics have routinely seen in the Clarel-Vine relationship parallels with the Melville-Hawthorne friendship, or rather the difficulties of that friendship, these analyses beg the question. Whether Vine has something to do with Hawthorne or not may be left to those who wish to speculate in such matters. Granted that Hawthorne may indeed have been on Melville's mind, the question remains as to what characteristic of Hawthorne Melville sought to explore in his depiction of Vine. A most tempting possibility may be found in Julian Hawthorne's recording of Melville's belief that "Hawthorne had all his life concealed some great secret, which would, were it known, explain all the mysteries of his career" (Jay Leyda, *Log,* II, 782). Whether Vine is Hawthorne or not, like Agath, Nehemiah, and others in the poem, he comes to us shrouded in mystery.

26. Compare *Pierre:* "Is it possible, after all, that spite of bricks and shaven faces, this world we live in is brimmed with wonders, and I and all mankind, beneath our garbs of common-placeness, conceal enigmas that the stars themselves, and perhaps the highest seraphim can not resolve?" (pp. 138-39).

27. Compare Emerson's lament, "Ah, wicked Manichee! . . . A believer in Unity, a seer of Unity, I yet behold two." *Journals of Ralph Waldo Emerson,* ed. Edward Waldo Emerson and Waldo Emerson Forbes (Boston: Houghton Mifflin, 1909-14), IV, 248.

28. See John 10:23.

29. Herman Melville, *Billy Budd,* ed. Harrison Hayford and Merton M. Sealts, Jr. (Chicago: University of Chicago Press, 1962), p. 62.

NINE

God, Father, and Lover in Emily Dickinson's Poetry

NINA BAYM

Criticism often asserts that Emily Dickinson adopted the voice of a child regularly in her poetry, as a means of replicating the sense of direct and simple contact with experience that her era attributed to children. But a reading of her poems shows that she utilized the voice of the child for only a small number of poems overall, and that her purpose was not simplicity but the conveying of complex relationships. Her use of the child's voice is intricately connected to expressions of relations between the child and the male parent, between the sexes, and between the self and God. The child *persona* unites in a puzzling and teasing way a psychological and a religious realm of discourse. Although statistically these poems are not significant, their subject matter makes them among her most interesting works.

Dickinson's poems all transpire in the present, and she speaks almost always in her own voice, though one must never forget her warning to Higginson that "when I state myself, as the Representative of the Verse-it does not mean-me-but a supposed person" (L268).[1] Thus she rarely presents herself as an actual child. In poems utilizing a child *persona*, the situation is such that the adult speaker feels or perceives like a child, or responds in a way the poem defines as childlike, or explains by means of a reference to childhood. A handful of such poems involve experiences in nature, but by far the greater number establish an encounter with a universe assumed to be ruled over by a father-god, or with that father-god himself, or with a human lover approached as though he were a father-god.

God in relation to the self, then, is a father. The self in relation to God is a child. When the universe is perceived as regulated according to the father's rules, the self experiences itself as a child

in the universe. Of course, the phrase "God the father" is a platitude. The platitude becomes vivid in Dickinson's poetry because
she handles it in an experiential or phenomenological way, and
because both child and father in the transaction are not figures of
cliché. The strategy of childhood, we must remember, is by no
means the only way Dickinson approaches certain questions about
life, death, or immortality. In fact, I count no more than sixty
poems that fall into the category, most occurring in the early part
of the canon: thirty-one such poems between poems #400 and
#700, and the rest widely scattered. This small number of poems,
however, embodies Dickinson's chief way of addressing God as a
concept directly. A second way of addressing him is also related;
it is a manner overtly hostile and even cynical, as, for example, in
such poems as "I know that He exists" (#338), "They leave us
with the Infinite" (#350), "Prayer is the little implement" (#437),
or "Of God we ask one favor" (#1601). In other words, Emily
Dickinson regularly associated the concept of God with the concept of father and transferred family relationships to her dealings
with the Deity.

It is not my purpose to argue, as some critics have, that Dickinson's idea of God derived from her own father. I think, on the
contrary, that she used images of the child and the father intended
to be generally applicable; that, insofar as she drew on her own
personal history, she was looking for its universal components.
Nor would I wish to be understood as making the point that,
because in some poems she takes a childlike stance, she was necessarily in her life a childlike woman. Since the stance of the child,
in fact, is relatively infrequent in Dickinson's poetry, we may
assume that when it appears it has a purpose. We should not ask at
the outset what personal experiences the poems imply but rather,
what impressions of personal relations is Dickinson trying to
convey in these child-father poems? To what end does Dickinson
put on the childish mask when approaching God? What kind of
father is implied in the poem? And what kind of child?

Seen through the child's eyes, God's world is full of secrets,
mysteries, events not understood, and explanations as baffling as
the questions they were supposed to answer. As a result the child
lives apprehensively and insecurely, not knowing how to interpret
her experience. This apprehension, moreover, projected out onto

the world, leads to a perception of what might be called fearful rather than joyous mysteries. An emotion compounded of bafflement, insecurity, and distrust is characteristic of the Dickinson child.

Consider, for example, Dickinson's earliest poem about children, #9. In this poem the journey of life appears, as in a Grimm brothers fairy tale, to be a route through a forest full of dangers and threats, including banditti, a wolf, an owl, a serpent, tempests, lightning, and "the hungry Vulture." In the last stanza she writes:

> The satyr's fingers beckoned –
> The valley murmured "Come" –
> *These* were the mates –
> *This* was the road
> These children fluttered home.[2]

Assuming that the satyr's fingers are lightning, and the valley's voice thunder, we see that the poem combines two kinds of childish nightmare, expressing fear of wild animals waiting to devour her and terror of thunderstorms. Much later, in poem #1021, Dickinson used the same metaphors less melodramatically:

> Far from Love the Heavenly Father
> Leads the Chosen Child,
> Oftener through Realm of Briar
> Than the Meadow mild.

> Oftener by the Claw of Dragon
> Than the Hand of Friend
> Guides the Little One predestined
> To the Native Land.

The believer in any faith is regularly enjoined to cease attempting to understand divine mysteries. Recognizing that human understanding simply cannot encompass divine intentions, the soul should rest in an attitude of trust. Although on occasion a Dickinson poem will achieve an attitude of trust—"I never saw a Moor" (#1052) is surely the most famous example—anxiety and worry are much more common. The child is predisposed to believe that explanations are too difficult for her, that her own incapacity makes the world incomprehensible; but she lacks the sense, expressed literally in poem #1021, that she is "in good hands" and responds with anxiety rather than confidence. At other times, she feels that explanations could be given, if the adult would; the father is withholding knowledge. It is not her own fault but the result of a kind of Divine teasing that she is so ignorant. In poems #101 ("Will there really be a 'Morning'?"), #103 ("I have a King, who does not speak"), #114 ("Good night, because we must"), #128 ("Bring me the sunset in a cup"), and especially #576 ("I prayed, at first, a little Girl"), we see this idea expressed.

It is only a short step from the idea of the father who withholds knowledge to the idea of a father who withholds in general: an ungenerous father. The childish response to this is a great sense of unfairness or injustice. We know several of these poems well, for they are often anthologized, and their chief emotion is impotent (i.e., childish) rage against the father who is called "burglar" and "banker" (#49) or swindler, as in poem #476, which concludes with this stanza:

> But I, grown shrewder – scan the Skies
> With a suspicious Air –
> As Children – swindled for the first
> All Swindlers – be – infer –

In poems like #690 ("Victory comes late") and #791 ("God gave a Loaf to every Bird") the speaker makes a heroic attempt to satisfy herself with the "crumb" God has allotted her but covertly makes God's parsimony and unfairness evident. Ultimately, the child's attempts to accommodate herself to her meager portion and even to praise the stingy giver have the effect of glorifying *her* for her large spirit rather than the penurious God. In a poem like #621 ("I asked no other thing"), God the shopkeeper exhibits an indifference to the speaker's wishes that borders on cruelty; and #612 presents an almost Dickensian picture of adult sadism and childish suffering. The adult is God:

> It would have starved a Gnat –
> To live so small as I –
> And yet I was a living Child –
> With Food's necessity
>
> Upon me – like a Claw –
> I could no more remove
> Than I could coax a Leech away –
> Or make a Dragon – move –
>
> Nor like the Gnat – had I –
> The privilege to fly
> And seek a Dinner for myself –
> How mightier He – than I –

> Nor like Himself - the Art
> Upon the Window Pane
> To gad my little Being out -
> And not begin - again -

The child's innate need for sustenance is her desire for life; this, though unsatisfied, also keeps her from escaping into death. Having implanted a need in her that he does not fulfill, and which she cannot escape, God is known as the child's tormenter. The anger rising from this experience spills over into the cynical and hostile poems where the child's mask is dropped and the grown poet asserts directly that life is a vicious joke played on people by a God with a cruel sense of humor: for example, #338 ("I know that He exists") or #724, which begins:

> It's easy to invent a Life -
> God does it - every Day -
> Creation - but the Gambol
> Of His Authority

and ends:

> The Perished Patterns murmur -
> But His Perturbless Plan
> Proceed - inserting Here - a Sun -
> There - leaving out a Man -

One of the most moving of this group, #313 ("I should have been too glad, I see"), makes a bitter statement often repeated elsewhere: that God deprives us of what we love on earth in order to make us willing to go to Heaven. God makes Heaven attractive by making earthly life painful; loss may school the human being into a desire for Heaven, but it cannot possibly create love or trust for the schoolmaster.

The possibility even exists that children get no explanations or puzzling explanations because the truth is really horrible:

> I noticed People disappeared
> When but a little child -
> Supposed they visited remote
> Or settled Regions wild -
> Now know I - They both visited
> And settled Regions wild
> But did because they died
> A Fact withheld the little child -
> #1149[3]

Critics have observed that the poems of deprivation often convey their emotion in metaphors of hunger and thirst; some connect these metaphors to the long tradition of food imagery in mystical thought while others see a psychological disclosure of maternal insufficiency. It is quite true that the mother is absent from most of Dickinson's poetry. The word appears only seven times in the entire canon (along with one "mama"): three times in short poems about the death of Dickinson's own mother, twice in elegiac poems about the death of somebody else's mother, and three times as "mother nature." But in Dickinson's poetry the mother does not have the nurturing function; the father does. The mother who appears in these few instances is a loving, nest-building, protecting figure who merges with all the tired house-wives, the unidentified women whose deaths form the occasion of a significant fraction of Dickinson's poetry. The love and care of women for one another and for children is recognized, but it does not make up for the deprivation blamed on the father.

Moreover, these women are seen as victims, like children, of the father's capricious exercise of power. Many more women than men, taking each elegiac poem as a single death, die in Dickinson's poems. The child sees, that is, that the love of the mother is no buffer. Mothers are as vulnerable as children. The true source of power in the world, the maker and unmaker, the provider and withholder of nutriment, is the father. No Great Mother archetype underlies Dickinson's poetic vision. The structure of the universe, like the family structure, is profoundly patriarchal.

The purpose of the mask of the child in this poetry, then, is partly to demonstrate that a trite metaphor—we are all God's children—is indeed true, and partly to show what that truth really means. Putting on the child's mask, the poet acts out one of the roles routinely assigned the child in romantic ideology, that of telling the truth directly where adults hedge and deny. But this is not a divine child. It is a child speaking out against the Divine, more like Melville's Pip than Stowe's Little Eva. The child will speak in this fashion because, as a child, she is unaware of how dangerous it is to say what she does. Experience has not yet taught her the consequences of such plain speaking.

At the same time, however, the child actually runs a great deal less risk than the adult when she speaks out because her childishness is an excuse. That is, Dickinson uses the mask of a child both to express a truth and as a strategy to avoid the results of speaking that truth. Knowing herself weak, and expressing the emotions rising from that sense of weakness, she also uses her weakness as a shield. This is a trick both childish and feminine, a trick of the powerless. And so we find the child-father poems scattered through with coynesses, references to her physical small-ness, endearing admissions of her naughtiness—devices to ensure that what she says will be discounted, not held against her, even as she speaks. And some poems are quite overtly placating, resort-ing shamelessly to childish or feminine wiles:

> I hope the Father in the skies
> Will lift his little girl –
> Old fashioned – naughty – everything –
> Over the stile of "Pearl."
>
> #70

or:

> Oh some Scholar! Oh some Sailor!
> Oh some Wise Man from the skies!
> Please to tell a little Pilgrim
> Where the place called "Morning" lies!
>
> #101

In these various transactions, or failed transactions, between child and father, love is not an issue. The child is angry because she is treated unfairly, because God does not keep his promises or satisfy the needs with which, as her Creator, he endowed her. On occasion she asks for his forgiveness but never for his love. For her part, the child expresses no love for the father: rather, she loves those on earth whom he takes away from her. God is seen entirely in terms of what he has not given and what he has taken away:

> God is indeed a jealous God –
> He cannot bear to see
> That we had rather not with Him
> But with each other play.
>
> #1719

In the famous poem #49 ("I never lost as much but twice"), God is blamed for taking away, while angels are credited with reimbursing, so that God appears as the taker but not the giver.

Oddly, then, the poet wishes to deny that God has given her any-thing; there are simply no unambiguous poems of thanksgiving to this father. Almost all the poems expressing joy, too, involve an extra-divine experience, either between human beings or in nature where the father-god is absent. In many poems Dickinson describes herself as having found something of value *by chance* and of hav-ing it taken away from her *by design*. Like Robert Frost after her, the only design she can make out is sinister. For the rest—and this is an inconsistency if one wishes to think of Dickinson's world view as primarily religious—she sees a large territory of experience that has somehow escaped design. In this territory are found loving human relationships and joyous experiences in nature; but the existence of this territory must be concealed from the father-god because if he becomes aware of it he will incorporate it into his design by taking it away from the child. It is part of the child's strategy, then, to be secretive; she is doubly justified in this by God's keeping secrets from her and by his invariable habit of expropriation. The catastrophic experiences related in the poems of loss provide the backdrop for those many other poems where, in deliberate disobedience to Puritan command, Dickinson enjoys the earth in and for itself and not as a sign of God's graciousness, or she involves herself in a human love that leaves God quite out of the picture.

It is yet a final strategy of these child poems that, vis-à-vis the reader, they are wonderfully self-serving. The child accepts no obligations toward the father, nor does she accept the inherent rightness of his authority. She acknowledges no more than that he is powerful. She excuses her anger, bitterness, and deceptions toward him by the way he makes use of that power. The poems about the child and father are then, from a parent's point of view, irresponsible and ungenerous. The poet gets away with more than deceit by donning the mask of the child. She gets away with giving God nothing at all even while she makes so many demands on him, and she holds him to account for so many failures:

> Is Heaven a Physician?
> They say that He can heal –
> But Medicine Posthumous
> Is unavailable –
> Is Heaven and Exchequer?

They speak of what we owe –
But that negotiation
I'm not a party to –
#1270

These poems about the child and the father-god reflect the end of the Puritan tradition and also of a certain family situation. As Puritan poems, they record the final dissolution of a bond of love and gratitude between men and God and the perversion of the idea of Covenant into the idea of the confidence game, the swindle. As family poems, they expose a hollow patriarchal structure. On the one hand the children are anxious, apprehensive, secretive, resentful, unloving, and insincere; on the other the father is isolated in his power, unable to share in the family's ongoing domestic routines or their deepest joys, and called upon only to punish, restrain, and deprive. To the extent that a historical father in Dickinson's day was really of a tyrannical and aloof nature, such a role might have given him pleasure; but to the extent that he too was one of the world's children, he would have to be considered a victim of this family structure. The mother, as we have seen, has no role at all; the script calls for a cipher. The mutually supportive Puritan family has disintegrated.

The father poems tell only half the story of Dickinson's encounter with the idea of an anthropomorphic God. Her love poems tell the rest. However, though complementary, the love poems are not parallel to the father poems because the metaphoric process is reversed. In the father poems, Dickinson takes the family situation and projects it onto the Deity so that he assumes the shape of a father. In the love poems she takes the idea of Deity, which she has been unable to realize in God himself, and projects it onto the beloved, creating a lover who is, through the medium of his likeness to the Divine, in fact a perfect father. The evident link between these two poetic categories is their shared *persona* of the child. (There are just under forty of these love poems, distributed much like the father poems in the canon.) Father, lover, and God are all one—in her poems Dickinson responded toward the male as a child to an adult. The child rejects God the father and accepts the lover as her god, giving him what she withholds from God: the devotion, subservience, fidelity, and gratitude that are the just due of a creator from his created beings.

There is no suggestion in the love poems that the speaker is of an equal status with her beloved, and the speaker is absolutely uncritical of her self-abasement. She is aware that she has made a God out of the beloved and in several poems even flaunts this fact at the rejected father-god. The unusually long poem #1260, to the departing lover, reads in part,

> The "Life that is to be," to me,
> A Residence too plain
> Unless in my Redeemer's Face
> I recognize your own –

and concludes:

> If "God is Love" as he admits
> We think that he must be
> Because he is a "jealous God"
> He tells us certainly
>
> If "All is possible with" him
> As he besides concedes
> He will refund us finally
> Our confiscated Gods–

Other poems of this sort include #387 ("The Sweetest Heresy received"), #464 ("The power to be true to You"), #474 ("They put Us far apart"), #636 ("The Way I read a Letter's – this"), and #640 ("I cannot live with You").

Along with the child *persona*, Dickinson uses many metaphors in these love poems to convey the disparity between herself and her lover. In #106 she is a shy daisy, irresistibly turning her face to follow the mighty, radiant sun across the sky. In poem #232 ("The *Sun – just touched* the Morning"), morning takes the daisy's place in this relation:

> The *Morning* – Happy thing –
> Supposed that He had come to *dwell* –
> And Life would all be *Spring!*
>
> She felt herself *supremer* –
> A *Raised – Ethereal Thing!*
> Henceforth – for Her – *What Holiday!*
> Meanwhile – Her wheeling King –
> Trailed – slow – along the Orchards –
> His *haughty – spangled* Hems –
> Leaving a *new necessity!*
> The *want of Diadems!*

> The Morning – *fluttered* – *staggered* –
> *Felt feebly* – for Her *Crown* –
> Her *unanointed forehead* –
> *Henceforth* – Her *only* One!

One cannot miss the traditional religious imagery used here, as well as the Puritan concept of the self's unworthiness unless and only because graced by the arbitrary King, whom one must adore whether or not one is sanctified by him. In poem #162 the relationship is expressed as a river running into the mighty sea and losing its identity there, while in #429 the poet speaks as the sea which is irresistibly controlled by the progress of the moon. In both #162 and #429 the poet is earthbound, the lover in the sky and controlling from a distance. In more than one poem Dickinson images herself as a faithful dog: she writes of "This little Hound within the Heart" in poem #186 and calls herself *"His little Spaniel"* in #236. In #638 she describes herself as a "small Hearth" and the lover as a great fire:

> To my small Hearth His fire came —
> And all my House aglow
> Did fan and rock, with sudden light —
> 'Twas Sunrise — 'twas the Sky —

Repeatedly these poems bring out the insignificance (often in images of physical smallness), unworthiness, passivity, and powerlessness of the speaker compared to the height and might of the lover. These are comparisons that we are familiar with in religious poetry, where we accept them with ease, but feel less comfortable with in love poetry. For some reason, some critics have tried to argue that these poems are written about God and not an earthly lover; but because so many of these poems ostentatiously prefer the lover to God, this view is untenable. More recently, some critics have tried to refer the moment of grace in these poems to Dickinson's awareness of her vocation as a poet, but this reading is undercut by the manifest eroticism of these poems and the clear maleness of the lover.

Perhaps the most totally self-abnegating of these poems is #754 ("My Life had stood - a Loaded Gun"). In *Emily Dickinson's Poetry,* Robert Weisbuch has argued at length that the poem is ironically critical of its own attitudes, that the poet divorces herself

from the "loaded gun" rather than identifying herself with the
image, but this interpretation is wishful thinking.[4] The bias of the
whole group is to glory in the self-abasement of the love she feels,
as exemplified in #587:

> Empty my Heart, of Thee –
> Its single Artery –
> Begin, and leave Thee out –
> Simply Extinction's Date –
> Much Billow hath the Sea –
> One Baltic – They –
> Subtract Thyself, in play,
> And not enough of me
> Is left — to put away —
> "Myself" meant Thee —
>
> Erase the Root —no Tree —
> Thee – then – no me –
> The Heavens stripped –
> Eternity's vast pocket, picked –

In poem #751 she writes, "My Worthiness is all my Doubt – / His
merit – all my fear – / Contrasting which, my quality / Do lowlier –
appear –" while poem #506 is more passionate still:

> He touched me, so I live to know
> That such a day, permitted so,
> I groped upon his breast –
> It was a boundless place to me
> And silenced, as the awful sea
> Puts minor streams to rest.

The poem goes on to use metaphors of religious grace to express
the speaker's sense of new worth, her transformation from gypsy
to queen. Although on occasion Dickinson seems to reserve the
right to give herself where she chooses, as in #303 ("The Soul
selects her own Society") or #664 ("Of all the Souls that stand
create"), more often she implies that the lover was so powerful
that he could not be resisted. Poem #1028 sums up the cluster and
expresses in its commercial metaphor an emotion opposite to that
conveyed in the father-god poems:

> 'Twas my one Glory –
> Let it be
> Remembered
> I was owned of Thee –

Here then are two sets of poems, intricately and confusingly interrelated. On the one hand are poems where the Deity is spoken about in language and approached through emotions deriving from the family situation, so that he becomes a human and badly flawed father. On the other hand are poems where the human lover is deified by applying to him the traditional rhetoric of religious ecstasy. If the central figure in both sets of poems were human, then we could interpret these poems biographically as Dickinson's rejection of her actual father because of his imperfections and her search for a lover who satisfied her ideal of a father. Or, taking a Freudian tack, we might see in the fierceness of her rejection of the father a repressed attraction to him, an attraction that leads to the quest for a surrogate. The fact that the father-lovers are kept at a distance would be evidence that they too are partly covered by the incest taboo.

Or, if we could interpret both figures as essentially divine, then we could see the poems as splitting the religious experience between them into its components of hardhearted resistance to, and irresistible acquiescence in, the will of God—poems in the manner of George Herbert or Edward Taylor. But because God is the tenor in one set of poems and the vehicle in the other, we cannot interpret these poems either as strictly human or strictly divine. We are in a poetic world where the two spheres have interpenetrated, and each has lost its distinct character. Dickinson is in the process of un-deifying God and deifying the human lover instead.

It is most important for our purposes to observe that the rules governing the relationship between the *persona* and the father in his appearances both as God or lover remain constant. The poems taken together can be seen as poems of rebellion against, and accedence in, a basically patriarchal organization of human experience. This expresses a particularly feminine variant of the widespread nineteenth-century trend to seek for a kind of religious gratification in human emotions. This trend in turn is part of the larger retreat from religion that dominated many aspects of nineteenth-century thought. I label it feminine because this trend takes a different form in male writers, where the idea was that through the experience of love the two lovers together would break through to a supernatural experience. Each lover was an enabler for the other, but neither was actually divine; the lovers were of equal status, worshippers together at the altar of the God of Love.

But in Dickinson's version of the secularization of religious emotion, the lover takes on the attributes of the rejected Deity, or more precisely he takes on the attributes the Deity should have had. This variant of secularization is found in writing by and for women particularly and up until very recently could regularly be identified as a powerful element in the conventional mental processes of women and in their upbringing. In his famous essay entitled "Inner and Outer Space," Erik Erikson wrote that "young women often ask, whether they can 'have an identity' before they know whom they will marry and for whom they will make a home."[5] Erickson's essay has been widely criticized for its ready acceptance of feminine inferiority, but there can be no doubt that young women in 1963, when Erikson originally wrote the essay, *did* indeed often ask just the question he attributed to them. The question originates in the same mental set that Dickinson's love poetry illustrates—the idea that the woman is nobody until, and except as, she is graced by the lover.

In the religious framework, this idea marks only a partial secularization, because the idea of man as woman's god is traditional in religious teaching for women, who were enjoined as a matter of course to live for the god in their men while their men lived for God. Although such religious counsel was chiefly pragmatic, concerned with woman's outward deportment and designed to regulate her social behavior, evidently any woman who behaved appropriately and was not a hypocrite would have to feel as though her husband were really a god. This is different from the man's situation since woman was traditionally perceived as more secular than he. To find in woman the means by which he might have a religious experience actually implied an elevation in her status. But the deification of the male in woman's writing and thinking implies the continuation of her traditional perceptions of him and of her traditional status in relation to him. Thus Dickinson's poetry illustrates a residual traditionalism rather than a thoroughgoing rebellion against a set of unacceptable religious beliefs.

From a secular standpoint the poetry reveals the continued acceptance by the speaker of her inferior status; indeed, there is more than acceptance, there is willing participation and joyous self-abasement. Such participation can only rise from a conviction of essential inferiority. The speaker is not accepting her role because, pragmatically speaking, she has no other choice or because she has been persuaded that the smooth functioning of society requires it. She accepts it because she feels it. Her aggrandizement of the lover proceeds from a prior sense of her own insignificance. The continuation of the child *persona* into poems of passionate love represents the existential feeling of her own small self. Love as experienced between the two participants in her poems is not a mutual experience but an episode of radical inequality, which proceeds from the speaker's conviction of her profound unworthiness in comparison to her lover.

It is a truism in all but the most recent studies of feminine psychology that adult women, in comparison to men, are more childlike beings. As a matter of social ethics, too, childishness has been urged on women as a virtue. The child *persona* in Dickinson can be read both as the child within human beings generally or more specifically as the child within the *woman*, the child that woman is alleged to be and, crucially in Dickinson's case, the child that the woman is felt to be. If there were any sign in this poetry of fathers, gods, and lovers that Dickinson was using the *persona* ironically, that Deity was less powerful than pretended and the child more so, that the lover was less exalted and the child more nearly his equal, then we might associate the rebellion in Dickinson's poetry with various movements in her time to alter the condition of women. However, I find no such sign in the poetry, and read it therefore as an expression of a dilemma rather than a search for a solution.

Dickinson's rebellion against the father-god is conducted within the limits of an acceptance of an inferior position based on a felt sense of herself as a child; at least, this is the impression conveyed by the poetry. If the *persona* of the child leads to permissions and allowances, enables her to break some rules, it nevertheless accepts the existence of those rules as governing the supernatural and the secular universe alike. The rules are there. The speaker can hope for nothing more than occasionally to break them with impunity. The freedom to break rules that she gets by assuming the *persona* of a child is more than offset by the freedoms that she relinquishes by refusing to assume, or insist upon, adult status.

The strategy, insofar as it is used to demand a place in the universe for the speaker, is ambiguous because it asks for such a small place.

It is difficult to overlook the likely influence of Dickinson's life on the views expressed in this poetry. The social system in Amherst was profoundly patriarchal, the structure of her family equally so.[6] In the town of Amherst, life revolved around the men's college that her grandfather had helped to found, and Dickinson saw all around her (and experienced) striking inequalities in the treatment and expectations accorded to women and men. Ambitious young men came and went freely, educating themselves for active participation in the national life as well as for professions that would enable them to support families; Dickinson herself got no further from home than the ten miles to Mt. Holyoke, where her father sent her for a year. Whether she chose not to marry or whether nobody chose her, the result was that she remained with her parents under their roof all her life. In all likelihood she continued there as the child of her parents; that is, played the child's part throughout her adulthood. But if this was Dickinson's personal situation, it was also the situation of great numbers of other women in her time, women who did not marry and who remained at home with their parents, products of class and sex restrictions. Dickinson's poetry speaks for all these women as well as for herself; it records a private but by no means uncommon life experience.

In her poetry the child *persona* is used almost exclusively for the purpose of projecting this one complex situation: the relation of the speaker to male figures. For many sorts of abstract speculation, for elegies on the death of beings like herself (women or children), for expressions of mental anguish or physical pain, and for responses to nature, Dickinson used the voice of an adult. The presence of the male as father, god, lover, or some combination, called up the *persona* of the child both as unmediated response and as strategy and protection. The poetry embodies a tension between resistance and acquiescence. Sometimes the poet is fiercely rebellious, sometimes she begs appealingly for authority to be nicer to her, and sometimes she seeks out authority and joyously gives herself up to it. Ultimately, the *persona* of the child is more a constraint than a freedom.

NOTES

1. I follow the text and numbering of the letters in *The Letters of Emily Dickinson,* ed. Thomas H. Johnson (Cambridge: Harvard University Press, 1958).

2. Texts and numbering of Emily Dickinson's poems are taken from the three-volume Variorum edition of her poetry, ed. Thomas H. Johnson (Cambridge: Harvard University Press, 1955).

3. Johnson identifies this as an unfinished poem, but the surviving text makes complete sense.

4. Robert Weisbuch, *Emily Dickinson's Poetry,* (Chicago: University of Chicago Press, 1975).

5. This essay may be found reprinted in *The Woman in America,* ed. Robert Jay Lifton (Boston: Beacon Press, 1967), pp. 1–26.

6. See Richard B. Sewell, *The Life of Emily Dickinson* (New York: Farrar, Straus and Giroux, 1974), pp. 17–27, 44–73, 321–67.

Notes on Contributors

NINA BAYM is Professor of English and Director of the School of Humanities at the University of Illinois. She has published many articles on American literary figures and is the author of *The Shape of Hawthorne's Career,* and *Woman's Fiction: A Guide to Novels by and about Women in America, 1820–1870.*

MICHAEL COLACURCIO is Professor of American Literary and Intellectual History at Cornell University. He has published articles and reviews over the range of classic American literature and has recently completed a book-length manuscript on Hawthorne's historical tales.

EMORY ELLIOTT is Associate Professor of English and Chairman of the American Studies Program at Princeton University. He has published articles on English and American literature, and he is the author of *Power and the Pulpit in Puritan New England.* He is presently writing a book on American religion and literature in the eighteenth century.

WILLIAM L. HOWARTH teaches American literature at Princeton University. He is Editor in Chief of *The Writings of Henry D. Thoreau,* published by Princeton University Press. His works include *The Thoreau Gazetteer, The Literary Manuscripts of Henry David Thoreau, The John McPhee Reader,* and various articles on American writers.

O. GLADE HUNSAKER is Associate Professor of English at Brigham Young University. He has published essays on English and American literature and is presently writing a book on John Milton and Roger Williams.

CLAUDIA D. JOHNSON is Associate Professor of English at the University of Alabama. Her articles have appeared in *American Literature, American Quarterly,* and other major journals. She has published with Henry Jacobs *An Annotated Bibliography of Shakespearean Burlesques, Travesties and Parodies* and is preparing a book on the nineteenth-century American theater.

211

BERNARD ROSENTHAL is Associate Professor of English and Chairman of the English Department at the State University of New York at Binghamton. He has published several articles, has co-edited *Race and the American Romantics,* and edited Margaret Fuller's *Woman in the Nineteenth Century,* and Timothy Flint's *A Condensed Geography and History of the Western States* (1828). His book, *City of Nature: Journeys to Nature in the Age of American Romanticism,* will appear in 1979.

WILLIAM J. SCHEICK is Professor of English at the University of Texas at Austin and Editor of *Texas Studies in Literature and Language.* Among his many publications are *The Will and the Word: The Poetry of Edward Taylor; The Writings of Jonathan Edwards: Theme Motif, and Style; Seventeenth-Century American Poetry: A Reference Guide; The Slender Human Word: Emerson's Artistry in Prose;* and the forthcoming *Half-Blood: The Study of a Cultural Symbol in Nineteenth-Century American Popular Fiction.*

EMILY STIPES WATTS is Professor of English at the University of Illinois. Her publications include *Ernest Hemingway and the Arts* and *The Poetry of American Women from 1632 to 1945.*